RAISING OUR VIBRATION

A GUIDE TO SUBTLE ENERGY MEDITATION

Kevin Schoeninger & Stephen Skelton

ISBN 13: 978-0-578-68078-1

Library of Congress Control Number: 2020907110

Published by Raising Our Vibration, LLC, Lafayette, CO USA

Dedication

This book is dedicated to raising our collective consciousness to resonate with the finer frequencies of Peace, Love, and Light, so we live in a state of elevated Awareness. It is our hope that it contributes to a more conscious, kind, and compassionate world.

Contents

RAISING OUR VIBRATION

Disclaimer

The authors of this book are not medical professionals or providers. Information contained herein is not considered to be medical or psychological advice. The authors recommend consulting licensed professionals for medical, psychological, or other advice. The authors and publisher assume no responsibility for the reader's actions based on the use of any information contained in this book.

Important Notes on Releasing as a Result of Meditation

In meditation, one thing that can happen as your body begins to relax and you focus internally is that your cells release chronic tension and stored stress. This is an important part of a healing process, which is facilitated by meditation in general, and by Subtle Energy Meditation, in particular. While this is generally a gentle and deeply relaxing process, you may experience an emotional release or temporary physical symptoms such as light-headedness, heat flashes, or other symptoms. You may briefly re-experience old memories or injuries as they are releasing.

It's OK to experience these things—it's a sign that your meditation is working. See if you can relate to this mindfully—as a curious observer. Stay present, observe, breathe, rest more if you need to, and allow the natural intelligence of the releasing process to work through you. Trust that there is a higher power guiding this whole process. These feelings and symptoms will release and resolve over time. In fact, this natural healing process is one of the powerful benefits of practicing Subtle Energy Meditation. Through this process, you'll learn to live from a greater sense of calm clarity, peace, joy, inner freedom, and ease.

All this being said, if you have feelings or symptoms that feel beyond your ability to handle them, we suggest you seek the assistance of a counseling professional trained to work with emotional release or a medical professional. By going forward with this course and practicing these meditations, you agree to take full responsibility for their effects and to take good care of yourself.

As long as you are practicing and doing your best to pay attention mindfully, your skill and the positive feelings of these meditations will grow over time. Soon enough, we trust you'll look forward to these meditations as a highlight of your day, and your life will begin to blossom as a result of living in an elevated state of Awareness.

Acknowledgments

Kevin: I would like to acknowledge the love, support, and partnership of my wife, Monica, as well as my sons Greg and Will. Thanks to my father, Douglas, and mother, Joyce, for always listening and supporting the work I feel called to do, especially through the years that I felt pressure to do what I thought I should/had to do, versus what I love to do. Thanks to my sister, Karin, for her quiet supportive presence.

I would like to thank Andrew Heckert and Bataan and Jane Faigao for teaching me T'ai chi, Master Tianyou Hao for instruction in Qigong Meditation, Father Thomas Keating for guidance in Centering Prayer, Roy Eugene Davis for Kriya Yoga initiation and training, William Rand for initiation and training in Holy Fire Reiki, and Dr. Jack Caputo who taught me about the nature of consciousness and gave me deep instruction in mindful inquiry under the heading of "Phenomenology." These experiences are the foundation of this practice of Subtle Energy Meditation. Finally, I would like to thank Stephen Altair for inspiring me with his knowledge, practice, and devotion to helping all beings discover the vast clear space of Pure Awareness.

Stephen: I would like to acknowledge the love, support, and partnership of my wife, Sumire, as well as my daughter Maia and

Orion, Skye, Kiran, Natalya, Andy, Mo, Russy, Livvy, Emily, Thomas, David, Thomas, Derek, Bernard and Suzie. Thanks to my father, Derek for the science and consciousness of energy and my mother, Mary, for faith in miracles, Jesus, Mary, the archangels, angels and saints, as well as her loving selfless compassionate work for all beings from many cultures. Through her I came to know Divine Mother.

I would like to thank: Mother Kathleen Adamson for training me in the Carmelite tradition and the way of St Therese of Lisieux, St Teresa of Avila, St John of the Cross, and St Francis of Assisi. Paramahansa Yogananda, Babaji, Mataji and the line of gurus, Lahiri Mahasaya and Swami Sri Yukteswar, as well as Sri Daya Mata, Swami Kriyananda, Brother Anandamoyi and Brother Satyananda for training me in Kriya Yoga. The Dalai Lama for initiating me in the path of the compassionate heart of Avalokiteshvara and guiding me to the Mother of Compassion Guan Yin, who gifted me with a pearl from her heart. Sogyal Rinpoche and the line of gurus for initiating me into the path of Padmasambhava, Yeshe Tsogyal and Princess Mandarava. St Germain/Master R, Suzie and Tareth for initiating me into the path of Alchemy. Master Wu for training me in T'ai chi, Qigong Meditation, and Praying Mantis Kung Fu. Dr. Ranga Premaratna for initiation and training in Reiki Jin Kei Do. Jack Kornfield, Thich Nhat Hanh, Ajahn Brahm, and Ajahn Chah, who taught me about the nature of anapanasati, mindfulness, samatha, vipassana and jhana consciousness. Brother Roger and Taize who merged me with the Heart of Christ. Swami Shyam for gifting me the experience of spacious awareness and Cosmic Consciousness. And Mooji, Papaji, and Ramana Maharshi who gave me deep instruction in mindful inquiry into "I" and All That Is.

These experiences are the foundation of this practice of Subtle Energy Meditation. Finally, I would like to thank Kevin Schoeninger for inspiring me with his knowledge, practice, and devotion to helping all beings discover the vast clear space of Pure Awareness.

Foreword

A Pressing Need

We live in a time when many of us feel so overwhelmed by the stress and pressures inside and around us that we feel a persistent underlying sense of anxiety. Young and old search for inner resources and skills to handle these challenging times. A growing number of people who identify as spiritual, but not religious, seek inner practices to counter the outer demands that push us to our limits. Those devoted to a religious tradition are increasingly looking for deeper guidance in their inner spiritual life. This book offers hope and guidance for all.

This book is part of an inner curriculum to heal the current emotional crisis of our world. Just as the planet is expressing emotional turmoil in storms, earthquakes, fires, tornadoes, tsunamis, and other dramatic phenomena, these planetary events mirror what we are going through as a global society. Our global culture is shifting, old structures are dissolving, and we are searching for tools and resources to navigate new ways of being.

This book and its related resources arose from an ongoing dialogue between us, Stephen Skelton (aka Altair) and Kevin Schoeninger, beginning in the Fall of 2018. The subject is the personal, spiritual, and planetary transformations possible through Subtle Energy Meditation. After decades of our own research, study, teaching, and practice, we find a pressing need for a thorough, step-by-step guide for this powerful, consciousness-shifting practice.

A Destined Meeting

The journey to this practice started when we were very young. When Stephen was two years old, he had a terrifying recurring dream that sent him on a lifelong spiritual quest into deep states of meditation. Since then, he's had extraordinary visions of dimensions beyond what we perceive with our five senses. At the age of 12, Kevin had a flash of insight that sparked him to train his mind and body. At 22, a transcendent moment while backpacking in the desert forever changed his view of who we are and what is possible for us all.

Introduced via email by a mutual friend, Dr. Ruth Anderson, we met for online video discussions in our late fifties. We discovered that we were born just four months apart, and we were fascinated and amazed by how our paths had followed so many similar practices. We had both studied T'ai Chi, Qigong, Kriya Yoga, Christian contemplative practices, Reiki, mindfulness, Buddhist meditation, and Zazen. We had been guided by a mutual love of Jesus, Guan Yin, Yogananda, and the Dalai Lama. Though we lived thousands of miles apart, with Kevin in Colorado and Stephen in Tokyo, we immediately felt a strong connection, as if we were picking up where we left off in a previous life. As we shared our practices and transcendent states, we knew we had to share what we had learned with a planet in crisis. We knew we had found something with the power to change the world.

As a beginning, we noted several common experiences and steps that facilitated elevated and transcendent experiences in our own practices. Through this dialogue, a process took shape that can be used by anyone, on any path, no path, or those looking for a path. It is a universal process that can be practiced and adapted at any point on your spiritual journey to discover a life of Peace, Love, Light, and elevated Awareness.

Are People Becoming More Aware?

Kevin sees a surge of people becoming aware of their inner world and beginning to dip their toes into meditative practices. As he puts it: "At a recent social gathering, I ran into the husband of a friend of my wife. On previous occasions, I had tried to talk to him about my passion for meditation and mind-body training, relating it to issues he was having. Previously, these discussions died quickly.

However, on this day, something shifted. He told me he had begun taking walks outside, counting his steps, and becoming aware of his breathing. He had never done anything like this before, yet now he felt compelled to do this and was really into it. He described how he felt more energized, centered, relaxed, and connected inside.

He asked me about one of my books, *Clear Quiet Mind*, my blog, and guided meditations. He said he wanted to share these with his co-workers, as he had noticed they were 'privately' looking up this type of information. I was joyfully amazed and grateful for this opening, his interest, and his natural desire for awakening. Something was calling him inward, and he was drawn to it like someone who had been shivering in the cold winter and had suddenly found a warm fire. An inner spark was growing into a flame."

There is a growing need to touch this experience of subtle consciousness—this finer sense of peaceful Awareness found within. Yet, there are two common challenges and related questions asked by those who start on a path of meditation:

1. What do you do when your mind is overwhelmed with stress, and the uncomfortable, rapid-fire, waterfall of thoughts and strong

feelings, like anger, blame, or depression? How do you deal with this? Can meditation help? How do you meditate in this state of mind?

2. Many people say, "I've meditated, and it doesn't do a lot for me. I sit there for a long time, and I get a blank wall. I feel some calmness, and that's about it. No bliss. No Nirvana. I don't know where to go or how to go farther. How do you get to a quiet place in which something more happens, something opens up?" In other words, how do you reach deeper states of joy, inner vision, and profound Peace, Love, Light, Elevated Awareness, and Inner Purpose?

We wrote this book to provide a clear path.

A Vast Inner World Is Largely Unnoticed

Indeed, a vast inner world, an abundant landscape of subtle experiences, experiences that are beyond the five senses and physical reality, await you as you journey deeply into meditation. You can discover the answer to all your questions and everything your soul desires on this path. The path of Subtle Energy Meditation holds the keys to "who you are" and "why you are here" and guidance for every step on your way. It holds the seeds of a new way of being for you, and all of us, here on Earth. Most importantly, there are simple steps to navigate this inner world safely, progressively, and effectively.

Yet, why do so many miss this inner treasure? Why are so many unaware it even exists? Why are so many unfamiliar with the world beyond three dimensions and five senses? Perhaps it's because the sensory world appears so enticing, shiny, and delicious. Many miss the inner world because of distraction and even addiction to outer sensory stimulation. Distraction of attention is a big issue.

The ability to focus attention is at the heart of a whole set of under-cultivated inner skills. These include self-observation, conscious relaxation, inner discernment, decision making, connection to emotions, depth of relationship, sense of life purpose, and the willpower to stick with good intentions instead of being drawn into what is less important, off-track, or harmful.

These days, your attention is pulled in a thousand directions for brief moments of time. Then, it's on to the next thing, and the next, and the next. Your attention can be drawn to the glitter of new and improved high-tech gadgets, tempting info-clicks on all your devices, the lure of social media interaction, and the urge to buy better, easier, more comfortable, and entertaining experiences.

You may devote countless hours to endless task lists and even more hours to work to earn enough money to maintain this insatiable economy. There's a momentum to the outer world of sensory stimulation that compels you—yet, where does it lead? It leads only to the next thing, which requires the next thing, and the next. At some point, it leads to stress, anxiety, worry, frustration, depletion, exhaustion, and perhaps depression. It leads to conflict within you and with others.

It's in these moments of unease that the opportunity arises to turn inward and discover something more. However, like many people, you may be wary of what might lurk inside. Without skillful experience in inner exploration, you may be hesitant to delve deeply into your thoughts, emotions, and memories. Perhaps, you've glimpsed enough inner commotion to know it might not be safe to venture in there.

"What if I discover things I'm not prepared to handle? What if I get overwhelmed by what I think and feel?" If you've ever felt this way, our assurance is simple: there are tried and true steps and inner skills you can learn to safely and gracefully navigate your inner landscape—and the rewards are far beyond what you've imagined.

If you're reading this, you've likely heard the inner world calling you. Perhaps, it's only a whisper in a quiet moment. Maybe, it comes as a wave of relaxation after a deep breath when you take a moment to sit still. Perhaps, it beckons in a moment walking under the clear blue sky or the starry night sky, or gazing at a work of art, listening to a soulful melody, or watching the light in the eyes of a child at play. In this book, you have a guide, a curriculum, to cultivate this "something more," this abundant inner world. You'll be guided to explore and skillfully use resources that previously lay dormant. These skills and subtle states of consciousness are your birthright— invaluable resources that simply require your commitment to consistent, conscious cultivation with a good method.

We have both been inner explorers for years. This practice is our passion and lives' work. We've been through the hard places and helped many others do the same. We also know the immeasurable joy that awaits you on this journey. A new way of being is available to you right now. We feel honored and privileged to be able to offer this path of Subtle Energy Meditation, along with essential tools for your journey.

An Inner Curriculum

So, onto some key notes in this curriculum. Here are some of our initial thoughts inspired by discussions we had on "Seven Experiences of Subtle Consciousness," which is where we began our online meetings in the Fall of 2018. As we shared our experiences with each other, we were excited that each of us could point to seven distinct steps; steps we had both been taking as part of our individual inner practices. These had developed over decades with many different teachers and practices—yet we had arrived at a similar set of steps. This fascinated us. These steps had led us to similar experiences of a transcendent Awareness that now infuses our bodies, hearts, and minds as an ever-present background for all our experiences and interactions—an enduring guiding Light. We had to share this!

To understand what we're talking about, we first contrast it with normal, everyday, sensory awareness. Everyday consciousness is strongly directed by the five senses. It is drawn to experience the world through sight, sound, feeling, taste, and smell. Yet, there is a sixth sense of Awareness, which is an intuitive sense, a subtle inner sense (such as when it dawns on you to meditate, and you do not know where this knowing came from). As this inner sense grows, you begin to experience the world through an emerging and all-encompassing knowingness, rather than just through the five senses. This Awareness surrounds and includes the five senses within a greater consciousness.

So, exactly what do we mean by this more "subtle" Awareness? To better understand, consider the typical progression of sensation and awareness when you practice meditation. In the beginning, meditation focuses on noticing "coarse" sensations. These physiological sensations include the diaphragm's movement in conjunction with breathing or the warm sensation of air leaving the nostrils during exhalation.

As meditation deepens, you begin to notice more subtle sensations. For example, you sense the warmth of energy flowing through your hands, energetic tingling building at the top of your head, or buzzing sensations in various energy centers. These signs of subtle energy flow within the body are still largely physical, but they require a finer sensitivity to notice them.

Over time, meditation takes you to even deeper and more profound states of consciousness. As you become more experienced in meditation, you experience stillness, silence, and spaciousness as distinct subtle sensations. Through these more subtle sensations, you sense a Universal Consciousness that is the Source and Ground of Being. Shifting to these subtle states of awareness takes you beyond your usual sense of self—and the tensions associated with this sense of self—into a place of deep calm. You begin to sense the finer frequencies of Peace, Love, and the inner Light of your essential being. As your inner senses awaken to these extremely subtle yet powerful experiences, you understand that life is so much more than what your physical senses alone reveal.

As long as you are immersed in and distracted by your five outer senses, you cannot begin to access this level of Awareness and the subtle states of consciousness associated with it. You are dazzled by the glitter of the outer world. Yet, at certain moments, this glitter fades and loses its luster, for instance, in moments of anxiety, suffering, or depression. In these moments, you long for something more. You may have sensed this something more for a long time, yet you aren't quite sure what that is. You just know that what you are experiencing through the five senses isn't giving you what you need. It is causing you stress, worry, and conflict. You long to be free!

At these moments, you might be given a taste of "something more" spontaneously. You may have an "Aha" moment of insight or a breakthrough in which you feel your heart burst open. You may relax long enough to experience the gift of deep letting go into an indescribable comforting embrace. As you are drawn deeper, you become aware of a new sense arising, expanding, and calling you forward. It begins as an ability to observe both the inner and the outer world as a "Witnessing Presence." Looking from the perspective of an "Inner Observer" is the trigger for other subtle states of consciousness. As you turn your attention within, a whole new landscape awakens, or you awaken to it. It is, of course, always there—you just weren't aware of it because you were looking elsewhere.

For Kevin, the first flash of insight came as a young boy. In fifth grade, the boys in class were standing in the hall before class, trading biceps flexes. Off to the side, where he hoped they wouldn't notice, Kevin rolled up his shirt sleeve, raised his arm, and made a muscle. Or, at least he tried. Nothing happened; nothing at all. There was no perceptible difference between flexing and not flexing. He simply had no discernable muscle.

At this moment, a light went on. Something activated in his brain. He thought, "I am going to do something about this."

Shortly after that, a friend of his dad's, Dick Snyder, gifted Kevin with a set of weights from his basement. Kevin brought them to his basement and set up shop. He was going to build muscle. In the process, he began to build concentration and confidence. He got strong. He'd be prepared the next time any "flexing" was required.

This first training with weights grew his ability to concentrate and to observe his pain mindfully without being overwhelmed by it. As he grew muscles, he reached a point where the muscle was too much. He needed more stretching, more relaxation, more inner work with his mind and emotions. At 22, on summer break before graduate school, he took a backpacking trip to Colorado, Utah, and Wyoming. Kevin was a city-boy from Philadelphia and had never been west of the Mississippi. After weeks of camping far away from the human world he had known, he experienced a moment in the desert that showed him there was so much more than building muscle.

In the still, silent space of the Canyonlands in Utah, a new awareness awakened. You might compare the landscape of the Canyonlands to being on the moon. It's a stark environment of mushroom-shaped rocks and craters, with few signs of life. Sitting for hours in this landscape worked deeply on Kevin's mind. The stillness calmed his urge to check off activities on his to-do list. The silence quieted his thoughts and cleared his mind. The spacious sky and vast horizon gave an expansive view that opened a state of consciousness unlike any he had known in this life.

Kevin found himself profoundly peaceful and content. He had the thought that if he died right then and there, that would be just fine. He felt an Eternal Awareness. He no longer feared death, because he had a clear sense that there really was no death, simply a transition to other states of consciousness—other states of being. He came away from this experience with a strong desire to know how to repeat, deepen, and sustain this transcendent state of consciousness.

When he returned home, he found himself drawn to learn T'ai Chi, something he had never heard of before this moment in 1984. This led him to Qigong, Reiki, Centering Prayer, Kriya Yoga, and Zazen meditation. Each practice led farther along a path, which led to increasingly more subtle and elevated states of consciousness and ways of being.

For Stephen, the first flash of insight also came as a young boy growing up in New Zealand. His recurring dream of falling off a bridge into a chasm remained as clear as it had been to the two-year-old boy who had woken up every night screaming. For an entire year, until he was three, Stephen dreamed the same dream: he was a monk, crossing a bridge towards his monastery and community. A great conflict threw him off the bridge and into cosmic sound and light. Each time, he woke up to the resounding vibration of OM humming throughout his head.

At the moment the dreams ended, an inner light went on in Stephen, just like it had for Kevin. Stephen suddenly became interested in Asian culture at the age of four. His mother was able to find a Japanese lady named Keiko-san, who taught him the tea ceremony and Japanese culture and language. The stillness of the experience entranced him. He became interested in martial arts and took up judo on his fifth birthday.

The silence of the art and the meditation that accompanied it beckoned him to go deeper. He was drawn to space and the stars, developing an early interest in astronomy at the age of five. He wrote to NASA to ask to be included in the first one-way mission to Alpha Centauri.

The spaciousness of vast Universal Awareness had him hooked. He went on to study astrology, alchemy, Kriya yoga, Zazen, Tibetan Buddhist and Vipassana meditation, Reiki, and martial arts (judo, aikido, karate, Tae Kwon Do, T'ai Chi, and Kung Fu). Each practice led to new, subtle states of consciousness and new ways of being.

Both Kevin and Stephen arrived at an experiential understanding of three significant portals into more subtle states of consciousness.

Three Portals into Subtle States of Consciousness

First, subtle states of consciousness open (like a gate or portal) through the **stillness of the body**. Through stillness, there is an awakening to the inner body, the subtle energy body. A light tingling sense of aliveness is felt in various energy centers, energy pathways, internal organs, and within the whole body at once. This awakening promotes vital energy and health.

For example, when you sit in meditation in a relaxed upright posture, as the body adjusts to its natural alignment, the subtle inner channels which carry the "winds" or subtle energies also adjust, open, and align. These energies activate an inner wisdom as they flow through the Central Channel, which runs through the core of the body, from the perineum up to the crown point of the head, including the spine.

Try it now. As you are reading this, sit a little more upright, straighten your back and feel as if a string is pulling the top of your head from the crown upwards. Notice the slight shift in awareness and energy flow. You feel more alert, intentional, and empowered.

This vital flow through the Central Channel awakens an aliveness in the energy centers and eventually in the whole body, a tingling that transforms into bliss and brings health and vital energy. This is why there are many stories of people seeing the Buddha, or other masters, sitting in a particular way, adopting the posture, and suddenly awakening to a deeper Awareness, like a flash of lightning. When the great spiritual leader His Holiness the Dalai Lama initiates new monks, he emphasizes the importance of an open and upright posture, cupping the hands at the navel with the thumbs touching in a receptive posture and extending the spine upward. The physical form helps facilitate the flow of energy within the body.

This posture also encourages the body to be still, so you can notice more subtle sensations that elude you when you are busy moving around. Stillness is a portal to the inner world, a gateway to subtle states of consciousness. In stillness, you let go of the stress of overdoing. Stillness is a deep surrender to the Grace of Life. You realize how consumed you have been with checking off items on your to-do list and how this has prevented you from attending to anything else. In stillness, your body and mind come to rest, and your attention is free to explore the inner world.

The next portal into subtle states of consciousness is silence— the silence of the voice within. The inner voice constantly chatters throughout the day, reminding us of important duties, cajoling us to like this and dislike that. It inspires us and judges us and others. It feels the need to perpetually narrate, comment on, and label the events of life. There are so many voices as we listen deeply. With practice, we learn to quiet these voices. Eventually, they go silent, first for moments, then as a sustained state of consciousness. So, silence is another portal to subtle states of consciousness. In silence, you let go of the stress of overthinking. There is a nurturing comfort in silence.

A third portal is spaciousness. A sense of open, clear, spacious awareness begins to awaken, first by sensing space inside the body, then expanding to surrounding space, and then extending Infinitely in all directions. This space is boundless and all-inclusive. The sense of spaciousness dissolves attachments, tensions, divisions, and struggles of self-focus.

The open, spacious awareness that arises in stillness and silence is the touch of the Infinite arising within you. In spaciousness, you let go of being attached to your small sense of self, along with all the stress that comes with this attachment. Spaciousness is diffused, inclusive, and energized with the primordial signal that brings forth all of Life.

Next, as the mind settles into stillness, silence, and spaciousness, you come into contact with Pure Awareness without form or content—awareness of Awareness itself—a state of consciousness beyond self, time, and space. This is a primordial Eternal Awareness that is described as the Eternal Truth, Nirvana, Buddha Nature, Kutastha Chaitanya (in Sanskrit), Heaven, or Christ Consciousness in Buddhist, Hindu, and Christian traditions.

It is often said that the heart of all teachings, and the root of all paths, is the undistracted awareness of Awareness itself. This Awareness arises through the portals of stillness, silence, and spaciousness and blossoms as you realize your boundless nature and liberate from the tensions and fears of your limited sense of self.

There is a realization that whatever arises, whether in meditation or not, is the natural radiance of Awareness itself. Life itself is Aware. **Life itself is the thinker of all thoughts, the feeler of all emotions, and the doer of all actions. You are an expression of Life itself, of Pure Awareness coming into form.**

With this realization, you gain a new mission and purpose—to become a clear channel, an open portal, for the Divine Life Force to flow through you into the world. There is One Life, One Light, One Love that flows through each of us in unique ways.

We are each given specific rays of the Primordial Light to cultivate and share through compassionate action. Each of us has a unique mission and purpose. The path of practice is to let go of our self-focused agendas, pay attention to Life's guidance, and become clear channels through which the Universal Life Force flows. This is the path of Subtle Energy Meditation.

In this inner curriculum, this book, and the accompanying meditations, we'll guide you step-by-step into this ongoing practice. We invite you to come along with us. We invite you to participate in raising our collective vibration to resonate with the finer frequencies of Peace, Love, and Light, so we live in a state of elevated Awareness.

Through this process, you'll transform your inner life, your relationships, and the quality of life on our Planet. The time is now. You are here. Let's begin!

1. States of Consciousness

Shifting to a New State of Being

We witness a world sped up to the limits of human capacity. Economic pressures, technological advances, and information overload, fed by the momentum of wanting more and more, along with fears of losing what we have, are driving an epidemic of stress that threatens to overwhelm us. Do you feel this pressure? Do you feel frustration, anger, sadness, fear, anxiety, or confusion from being pushed toward or beyond your limits? Do you feel you just can't keep going the way you're going? Are you caught up in ways of coping, such as over-eating, drinking, or distractions of technology and entertainment that just aren't good for you? Do you do this because the world just seems like it's not such a safe and friendly place to be?

What if you could shift your consciousness from these stressful states to states of peace, love, joy, and purpose—anytime you need? In this book, you'll learn ancient practices, now backed by modern scientific research, that empower you to do this. These techniques can completely transform your experience of stress!

These practices can also make a powerful positive impact on chronic diseases, ADD/ADHD, anxiety, addiction, feelings of low self-esteem, self-criticism, obsessive thinking, negative emotions, isolation, loneliness, depression, and lack of motivation, direction, and purpose.

In the face of these conditions, many are searching for new coping strategies and new ways of being. There has to be another way of living that is more sustainable, purposeful, and enjoyable. Contemporary neuroscience combined with ancient practices such as meditation show a different way. An elevated state of Awareness is possible. Time-honored, proven practices (which, up to now, have been reserved for elite groups of practitioners) can lead you to a qualitatively different experience of life.

You can apply these practices every day, in the normal course of your work, family, and social life, without needing to withdraw from the world and go on retreat to a remote mountain cave for months or years at a time. These practices are available without needing to belong to a specific group, accept any particular beliefs, or engage in extreme or overly demanding disciplines. In fact, they will enhance your ability to relax your body, quiet your mind, follow your heart, and live your unique purposes right here, right now.

In this book, we explore how to consciously shift your state of consciousness to embody the qualities of Peace, Love, and Light, not just as a momentary experience in a meditation session, but as a new way of being. The primary tool we'll use is Subtle Energy Meditation, along with other skills developed in meditation. These include the ability to intentionally relax; focus your attention; let go of negative feelings, distractions, cravings, and self-focus; and receive clear guidance to resolve any problem you're facing. We will also look at what you can do to set up a successful meditation practice in terms of diet, exercise, and sleep practices, as well as what you can do after your practice to develop insight and compassionate action. The goal is to apply the fruits of meditation to every moment of your life.

It all begins by learning to recognize your current state of consciousness.

Understanding Your State of Consciousness

If you're like most people, as you go through life, you have an idea that you see things as they are—that you experience Reality as it is. You are usually not aware that what you experience is a specific perspective on what is happening based on your current state of consciousness.

Your state of consciousness is everything. It determines what you experience, how you feel, and how you relate to others. It shapes how you see yourself and life and what you perceive as real and possible. It influences what you attract and what you give to others. Out of the infinite events happening right now, your state of consciousness selects what comes into your awareness, as well as which characteristics, qualities, and details you focus on and how you relate to them—the story you tell about what you're experiencing.

For example, your state of consciousness determines if you are stressed out or calm, grateful or critical, compassionate or angry, connected or isolated, guided and inspired, or confused and wandering aimlessly. Your state of consciousness can be reactive, judgmental, and hostile, or attentive, discerning, and kind. There are an infinite number of possible ways you can relate to the events of life. Your state of consciousness determines how you relate to what is happening now, as well as what happened in the past, or what might happen in the future.

So, let's start by defining what we mean by "your state of consciousness." For our purposes in this book, we define "your state of consciousness" as your awareness of yourself and your environment, which includes your thoughts, feelings, attitudes, beliefs, memories, perceptions, projections, sensations, and behaviors in relation to internal and external events. Your state of consciousness is fluid and everchanging, as prompted by internal and external cues. In a simpler sense, **your state of consciousness is "where you're coming from at this moment."**

This definition is a practical, experiential, functional solution to the question, "What is consciousness?" that has been called "the hard problem" by philosopher David Chalmers and others.[1] It has been considered unsolvable by some and a simple matter of reducing consciousness to an effect of the physiological functions of the brain by others.

Yet, what if consciousness itself cannot be understood by thinking about it? What if consciousness is prior to language, prior to thinking? What if it exists first in a pre-linguistic realm that can only be understood through direct, non-verbal, non-analytical awareness? In Subtle Energy Meditation, you will come to a palpable, experiential understanding of what consciousness is.

We will guide you there by first helping you to understand different states of consciousness you might be in at any given moment in time and then working our way toward this experiential understanding of consciousness itself. We will do this step-by-step in the process of learning Subtle Energy Meditation. So, while the question of "what consciousness is" and how it relates to the brain are hot-button issues for neuroscientists, philosophers, psychologists, theologians, and others, for the purposes of this book, we accept, as a working definition, that your state of consciousness is "where you're coming from at this moment." For example, feeling peaceful, kind, and loving is one state of consciousness, while feeling combative, adversarial, and angry is another.

OK, so, how do we describe and measure states of consciousness? How do we know if someone is in one state of consciousness or another? Well, how do you know if you're stressed? Angry? Confused? Peaceful? Loving? Or purposeful? One way to discover this is in a dramatic moment of strong feeling. Perhaps, you aren't really aware of how you're feeling until the feeling builds to the point where you explode in frustration and anger or you break down in sadness and tears. A more subtle way is to start to track and make note of your inner experiences. You start to check in with yourself regularly, so you notice when you begin to think or feel something and you learn how to describe it. You turn inward and self-report on what you discover.

This inner sensing and description is the primary basis of the process we will lead you through. You're going to get very good at perceiving and describing your inner state—as well as learning how to shift it. By this means of turning inward, we'll guide you step-by-step to be able to shift your inner experience in a positive direction. After all, isn't that what you are looking for? Isn't that why you'd take the time to read this book and engage in what we're asking you to do? You want to change your experience of life in a qualitative way. You want liberation! You want freedom from the struggles of stress, negative emotions, and confusion about who you are and what you are here to do. This book is about that kind of liberation.

We'll begin this process using five basic questions to help you assess where you are now and where you want to go. Then, we'll lead you through specific practices to transform your current state of consciousness into the experiences you long for, the experiences your soul desires.

So, to recap, we're going to accept your own inner experience as a valid starting point. We'll start by helping you become more aware of the state of consciousness you are in by learning how to check in with your inner state and describe it using mindful attention. Then, we'll help you shift your state of consciousness to the kind of peak experiences you've always dreamed about!

How does that sound? Are you excited about this! We are!

To begin, let's fill in a few more details to get you even more motivated.

Inner States Have Measurable Correlates

One of the most fascinating developments in the study of consciousness is the rise in brainwave-sensing technology. Using electrodes strategically attached to different parts of the head, researchers obtain electroencephalogram (EEG) readings that give a picture of what is happening in your brain when you are in specific states of consciousness. Through the use of this technology, states of consciousness are inferred from self-reports of inner experience while using specific techniques. These are then correlated with EEG measurements of brainwave patterns to determine the brainwave frequency signatures of these states.

We (Kevin and Stephen), have both experimented extensively with this technology and shared results with others who are doing the same. We've gathered EEG data from current neuroscientific research as well as EEG measurements from participants practicing this meditation series and correlated this data with self-reports of inner experiences. We have also spent countless hours following these meditations ourselves and scrutinizing our personal EEG readings using The Muse® Brainwave Sensing Headband.[2] We have confirmed our findings with independent lab testing using professional/medical EEG sensing equipment. This technological feedback has helped tremendously in designing the most effective cues for the series of meditations you'll learn in this book. We are also aware that this technology is in its pioneering days and that new discoveries about brainwaves and updated brainwave sensing technology are constantly updating what we know. This makes the field of neuroscience an exciting and enlightening support for meditation practice.

To inspire you in your practice, in the Appendices we share examples of EEG graphs for different states of consciousness you'll be practicing, along with meditation scripts that describe specific cues for realizing these states of consciousness. For the scientific side of your mind, it's good to see there are measurable shifts in brain function associated with each of these practices. You will substantiate this for yourself by monitoring and assessing personal shifts in consciousness as you go through your own explorations and experiments with these techniques. You don't need to have an EEG sensing headband to do this. We'll point to palpable, felt landmarks by which you can notice and describe these shifts within your own inner experience. If you have access to an EEG sensor, you can use this as a tool to support and refine your practice.

Through this meditative process, you'll learn to live from a whole new state of being—one that is grounded in inner sensations, mindfulness, and the ability to resonate with the felt frequencies of Peace, Love, and Light within an elevated state of Awareness!

If this sounds daunting or not really possible, we suggest it all begins with understanding your current state of consciousness and what is most important to you. So, we'll start by helping you get clear on this. We'll then guide you step-by-step from where you are right now to where you want to be. Along the way, we encourage you to honor your own inner process and accept only what is proven to you within the laboratory of your own experience.

Before we get to this inner work, however, let's lay a deeper foundation in understanding states of consciousness.

What Affects Your State of Consciousness?

Your state of consciousness is affected by what is happening inside and around you. It can be cued by signals from the environment as well as by internal signals within your own body, heart, and mind. In fact, it is cued not just by what is happening now, but by what happened in the past and what may happen in the future. The human mind is such that memory traces from your own past, as well as the past of your ancestors, and even of the whole human race are encoded in the structure of your body, heart, and mind. The human mind is also constantly anticipating future possibilities.

To keep our discussion and practice simple and effective, we'll center on what is happening here and now in your present environment. This present moment implicitly "contains" the past, since it is the result of what has happened up until now. It also "contains" the future, since the seeds of future possibilities are present now. We'll operate on the assumption that what you need to be aware of is presented to you right now, in the circumstances and experiences you are currently dealing with. Life reveals what you need to be aware of each moment.

It's your task to fine-tune your awareness, to become aware of what you are focused on and how you are relating to this, so you can make discerning choices with your attention. This is an effective and practical starting point. It keeps things simple and doable—so you don't get overwhelmed. We'll use "what's happening now" as a primary reference point throughout our process. How you deal with this present moment shapes what you face in the next moment. So, the key is to deal effectively with what is happening right now. As you do this, you may also receive insights about your past and your potential future.

What is happening for you now is the result of an interaction between what is going on "inside" and "outside" of this space you define as "you." This is normally the space inside your skin (though we'll play with this boundary as we go along). For now, let's say that "you" are a space defined by the boundary of your skin.

The Power of Internal and External Cues

Your state of consciousness is shaped by the interaction of what is happening inside you with what is happening around you. For instance, you feel hungry inside and you look to your environment for possible food choices. Or, you feel stress from your environment and you look for relief by doing something internally, like meditating. You feel internally confused and look for guidance out there in the world. There is a constant and complex interplay between what is going on inside and around you.

What you perceive as your available options has a lot to do with your state of consciousness. **Your state of consciousness determines the options you notice and how you relate to them.** For example, when you're stressed, it's hard to think clearly. You're likely to be reactive, critical, and judgmental. You're likely to see what's wrong, to see problems—and be blind to opportunities and creative solutions. You're more likely to think, "That won't work. I'm just screwed."

Albert Einstein is famous as having said, "We can't solve problems by using the same kind of thinking we used when we created them." When you're in a state of stress, you're not likely to think of brilliant, creative solutions. You're more likely to think from your past pain, in a way that perpetuates more of the same and escalates your stress.

When you live in a culture that is amped up on stress, there's a huge momentum that pushes you in the direction of escalating stress. The culture you live in has a massive impact on your state of consciousness, especially before you learn the techniques we're going to teach you to take charge of your inner state. You're going to learn how to cue your state of consciousness from the inside, rather than being a victim of outer circumstances. This is essential if you're going to change your relationship to stress.

Kevin's Story About Stress and the Culture of More!

I was in the supermarket with a full cart heading to the checkout when a voice over the loudspeaker said, "In just two minutes at the back of Aisle 11, we'll be giving away a free gift to everyone who comes to check out these exclusive new items."

My first thought was, "Why would I want more stuff when I don't even know what it is?"

To my surprise, several people with full carts course-corrected from the route they were on and quickly headed to the back of Aisle 11 for that free, exclusive, new stuff.

What was going on here?

There's a cultural momentum on the planet these days that is easy to get sucked into. It begins with economics—defining a healthy economy simply as an expanding one, a healthy business by exponential profit increases, and a healthy consumer as one who is constantly accumulating more money, things, and experiences. We want "more" of everything, which can include more friends, more status, more likes, more points, and more rewards on the latest app we download. We crave repeated hits of "more." Yet, this "more" puts us in an endless cycle of stress. Stress escalates because there is no limit to how much "more" we can crave.

In this craving for "more," we get sucked into over-buying, over-eating, over-thinking, overreacting, and over-working—which is a hard cycle to break. We are constantly thinking about how we can get more of what we want, overreacting to every little thing that interferes with that, over-working to accumulate more money and accomplishments, and over-eating to fill the void that comes from feeling like it's never enough. Strangely, the more we accumulate, the more empty we feel. The minute the euphoria of getting something fades, we are left with the insatiable craving for more.

How do we stop the "Madness of More!"?

Shifting Attention Inward

The solution for stress and living in the culture of "more" begins with a simple inward turn (which is the first skill we're going to practice). This shift in attention is called "interoception."

Interoception is the ability to feel the inner state of your body, to feel inner sensations. This sixth sense is the foundation for experiencing the fullness of the present moment, as well as for cultivating intuitive knowing and experiencing deeper spiritual connections that fill us up on the inside. In a world that so consumes us with outer sensory stimulation of our five senses, this finer inner sense is neglected, atrophies, and fades from consciousness. As we lose touch with interoception, we begin looking outside for what can only be found within. Losing touch is the genesis of the outward craving that can never be satisfied.

Fortunately, interoception can be activated and cultivated, so it becomes a prominent guiding sense. Cultivating interoception is a practice, just like any other skill you might learn. And, it's free and readily available any moment you choose to pause what's grabbing your attention "out there" and shift your attention to what's going on "in here."

At the end of this chapter, we'll begin our dive into interoception. In Chapter 2, you'll learn how to use this skill to shift your state of consciousness in the moments you really need to. You'll learn three inner skills that empower you to consciously and intentionally shift your state of being. We call them the Three Antidotes. If stress, frustration/anger, and confusion are three primary problems, and Peace, Love, and Light are the desired results, interoception, mindfulness, and Subtle Energy Meditation are sure means to get you there. These are time-tested and scientifically proven inner skills.

Three Inner Skills: Interoception, Mindfulness & Subtle Energy Meditation

We talked a bit about interoception, which is basically the ability to sense what is happening inside your body. This is the foundation for the inward shift that enables you to take charge of your inner state. Now, let's introduce the next two skills in our process: Mindfulness and Subtle Energy Meditation.

Mindfulness is a term that's gained much notoriety lately. It's tossed around in business, psychology, education, and spiritual circles. It's sometimes touted as a "panacea," a cure for everything that ails us. Yet, what exactly does it mean? While there are many definitions, here's one adapted from the work of Dr. Jon Kabat-Zinn that we find useful: **"Mindfulness is paying attention, on purpose, in the present moment, non-judgmentally—like a curious observer."**[3]

Mindfulness allows you to witness thoughts, feelings, events, and experiences with calm clarity, instead of being wrapped up in fear, drama, bias, and judgments that slant, cloud, and confuse your perception. Practicing a mindful attention style changes the way your brain operates. It releases lingering stress and welcomes appreciative engagement. A natural result of mindfulness is that, instead of being overly identified with your experiences, you see yourself as "having" experiences. From this vantage point, you don't believe thoughts, feelings, or actions "define you." "Who you are" transcends any experience "you have." This is an essential liberating insight.

Consequently, you feel less need to attach to, hang on to, or ruminate over any experience as if your self-worth depends on it. Instead, you are a curious "witness" who can inhabit an experience and participate in it without being consumed or overwhelmed by it. You appreciate present moment awareness and move on to the next moment without being lost in what's happening. This includes moments you enjoy and moments you wish you could forget.

Why is this important? It's important because mindfulness alters the way your brain encodes experiences. Every experience gains a layer of awareness, freedom, and choice. With mindfulness, you learn you can choose what you focus on and how you relate to it, instead of reacting as a "victim of circumstances." You learn how to cue your experiences from the inside, rather than having how you feel be dictated by your environment.

The third skill in our process is Subtle Energy Meditation. In this style of meditation, we use interoception and mindfulness to cultivate internal energy or subtle life force within. This is where the process leaps to the next level.

So, what is subtle energy? Or qi?

According to Dr. Jerry Alan Johnson, PhD, "More than 5,000 years ago, Chinese physicians came to understand that everything is composed of the same energetic substance called *Qi*" (pronounced "chee"). These ancient masters concluded that " . . . energetically everything is interconnected. . . . all things in the universe are woven together so that we are, quite literally, all symbiotically one with the universe through the system of Qi."[4]

You may be reminded of "The Force" in the Star Wars movies, the Zero Point Energy Field in physics, or the *Tao* in the ancient text *The Way of Life (Tao Te Ching)*. All these sources point to an underlying energetic field that gives birth to and supports all of life. This Field is like "One Body," in which each of us are cells. It is the One Life we all share. As we cultivate awareness of this Field, we come to know subtle energy as the intelligent, peaceful, loving Awareness that brings forth and organizes patterns and forms of life.

Our own bodies are like "microcosms" of this "Macrocosmic" Field. The health of your body is determined by the smooth flow of this life force through it. It is this qi, otherwise known as *ki*, *chi*, Holy Spirit, *prana*, *ruach*, or many other names, that gives us life and sustains us.

We are conduits for many different frequencies of this energy. We operate from and within a multi-dimensional anatomy, which includes physical, mental, emotional, and spiritual bodies. We take in energy in the forms of air, water, food, light, sound, heat, and stimulation from our five senses. Additionally, we receive subtle vibrational input from the natural world and psycho-spiritual energies through other, less obvious channels. As humans, we have the capacity to process these energies because our energetic anatomy includes more than just the physical body.

Subtle energy expresses in many forms and we experience its flow in more physically-based sensations of warmth, tension, pleasure, and pain, and in more subtle sensations such as tingling, lightness, and connection. We experience it after exercise, yoga, or Qigong as a feeling of vitality and we feel it flowing through the hands in Reiki healing. Our intuitive feelings are a form of subtle energy, as are our thoughts.

When we realize that we have more than one body; that we actually have a multi-dimensional energetic anatomy, then the world takes on new dimensions. We see it is possible to relate to our world as subtle energy beyond the physical dimension accessible through our normal five senses. This keystone of energetic healing theory accounts for answers to questions such as, "What part of your physical body processes emotions?" Once you come to realize that you operate from physical, mental, emotional, and spiritual dimensions simultaneously, some of life's mysteries start to make more sense.

When we recognize that all matter is actually energy, we can begin to form a new vision of ourselves and the world around us. Perhaps, reality is more like a network of energetic interactions between different energetic frequencies which are all nested within each other. How we perceive our world and interact with it is a result of how we process the subtle energy signals we receive. For example, if someone walks into a room, some people will just process the physical form, while others may pick up the emotions the person is emanating, and still others may see that person's subtle energy body.

We are all transmitters and receivers of subtle energy, whether we realize it or not. Our thoughts and feelings have a frequency just like a radio wave or a cellphone signal. Once we become aware of subtle energy, we have the opportunity to learn how to work with it to facilitate the health, well-being, and transformation of ourselves, others, and the planet.

Quantum science and quantum energy fields give us the opportunity to learn about and embrace our subtle energy aspects through the scientific mind. People focused on the spiritual worlds have known about subtle energy for eons, cultivating it to enhance their connection to the divine. Healers from all traditions have developed techniques to work with various subtle energies successfully. Many pioneers over the last decade or so have brought forth scientifically-based information, such as Bruce Lipton, Amit Goswami, Fred Alan Wolf, and Lynne McTaggart, as well as organizations such as the Institute of Noetic Sciences (IONS).[5] There are a number of schools that offer accredited programs that include subtle energy studies in their curriculum, such as the California Institute for Human Science and Holos University.[6]

As the teacher Paramahansa Yogananda says, when you start to awaken to the fact of subtle energy, "You realize that all along there was something tremendous within you, and you did not know it."[7] In Subtle Energy Meditation, you learn to access this life force, recognize tensions that interfere with its flow, release these tensions, and cultivate a healthier, more empowered state of being characterized by the infusion of the frequencies of Peace, Love, and Light. Subtle Energy Meditation is not only a highly-effective antidote to stress, frustration, anger, and confusion—it also feels amazing!

In fact, as we shared our mutual experiences of heightened subtle energy states with each other, they were so vivid, transforming, and liberating that we felt absolutely compelled to share them with you! Both of us are convinced that sensing this life force is a real key to changing our world! We can't wait to guide you into this experience!

However, before we step into the process, two more preliminary foundational understandings are important. The first is the basic structure of your internal energy system, and the second is a set of coaching questions to help you assess where you are now and where you want to go in your personal pursuit of expanded consciousness.

A Basic Structure of Your Subtle Energy System

Let's begin with the physiological network within which subtle energy flows—the fascia, or connective tissue system. This network surrounds every organ, muscle, and bone in your body and connects every part of your body as a whole. The fascia system is like a whole-body suit that integrates every part of your anatomy and physiology together as a functional unit. You can think of the connective tissue system as an integrated communications network that relays chemical, biomechanical, electrical, and emotional information signals throughout your whole body.

Connective tissue is made of three components: elastin, collagen, and a ground substance that surrounds and fills the spaces between all cells. This ground substance has a gel-like crystalline structure that makes it like an internal ocean. Exchange between the blood and the cells happens as a process of diffusion through this ground substance. Biomechanical, electrical, and emotional signals are also transmitted through the connective tissue network.

Fascia is highly responsive to emotions and will contract and tighten when you feel stress, anger, or fear. Unresolved emotions are held in the body as tension which interferes with the flow of vital force and inhibits your natural state of relaxed joy and enlightened Awareness. When there's tension in the fascia, its conductivity is dampened and it becomes more rigid and stiff—often storing tension as "knots." These knots restrict the flow of subtle energy and set up the conditions for illness to take root. As you become aware of these knots, they can be released. When focused attention, conscious relaxation, heat, stretching, pressure, or vibration are applied to the fascia and ground substance, tension is released and it becomes highly conductive, flexible, and malleable once again.

Another fascinating point is that the fascia can be considered the home of "consciousness," since it stores your life experiences and is the basis of your sixth-sense ability to feel sensations inside your body and all around you. The fascia system is a primary vehicle for interoception (your ability to feel inner sensations and track the impact of your emotions), as well as your ability to empathically feel what is happening with others and in your environment.

Finally, the connective tissue system houses the meridians through which subtle energy flows between the vital energy centers. As such, it is the physiological foundation of Subtle Energy Meditation. Qigong Meditation is one of the ancient forms of subtle energy practice that is related to Tibetan Yoga, Kriya Yoga, Reiki, and other systems of subtle energy practice. In the understanding of Qigong, the subtle energy system is organized around three primary energy centers and a Central Channel through which they connect: the lower, middle, and upper *dantians* and the Central Channel. These three energy centers are related to the seven chakras of the Yoga systems, but exist in a more primary position, prior to their differentiation into the personality functions of the chakras. You can think of the three dantians and Central Channel as containing the energy of your soul essence.

Interestingly, the three dantians correspond to the three "brains" of the human body. Current scientific research shows that, in addition to the brain in your head, you have a vast neural network that operates like a brain in your gut and also in your heart. In fact, the brains in your gut and heart are so powerful and influential in terms of your state of consciousness that they send vastly more information through the vagus nerve network to the brain in your head than your brain sends to your heart and gut.

So, you have, in effect, three brains that work together to shape your state of consciousness: the enteric nervous system in your gut, the cardiac nervous system in your heart, and the brain in your head. The brain in your head is the primary network associated with thinking.

17

It is the brain that is used most extensively when you process concepts, facts, images, and plans. It is intimately related to your senses of sight and sound, seeing, and hearing.

The enteric nervous system in your gut is the primary brain for health and vital energy. The majority of your immune function happens in your gut, as does the digestion of food and liquid that brings nutrients and energy into your body. The "gut-brain" produces a wealth of neurotransmitters that communicate with the rest of your body and affect mood, energy, and vital function. Focusing on the sensations of calm breathing in your gut, or lower dantian, can facilitate deep relaxation of body and mind and is a powerful stress reliever. The lower dantian is the primary network for "sensing" what is happening inside and around you.

The cardiac nervous system is centered in your heart and is responsible for emotional regulation as well as the delivery of the more subtle energy of life (breath, oxygen) throughout your body via the circulation of blood. Your "heart brain" also produces a wealth of neurotransmitters that affect the functioning of your body and brain and produce feelings of emotional comfort and well-being. The energy field of your heart extends well beyond your body, creating a feeling of having a "personal space," which is a primary medium of subconscious communication with others.

According to research from the HeartMath Institute, the electromagnetic field of the heart is up to 5,000 times stronger than the field emitted by the brain in the head, making it a powerful vehicle for entrainment of the whole subtle energy system.[8] It is also a powerful center for activating feelings of love and connection with others. Focusing on loving feelings in your heart and extending them to others cultivates a sense of compassionate relationship that counters feeling of isolation, loneliness, and low self-esteem. The cardiac nervous system is the primary network for "feeling" your emotions and for cultivating your relationships with others and your environment.

As we said, both the gut-brain and heart-brain communicate with the brain in the head through the vagus nerve. In fact, as we noted, more information travels from your gut and heart to your head than vice-versa, giving your gut and heart even more influence—influence that has been traditionally associated with the brain in your head.

The vagus nerve originates in the medulla oblongata in the brain stem and is responsible for the regulation of wakefulness, alert attention, interoception or perception of inner sensations, sleep cycles, respiration, heart rate, blood pressure, digestion, and levels of tension and relaxation in the body. The vagus nerve is also responsible for the parasympathetic response or relaxation response. It is, therefore, a primary signaling system that supports the shift into meditative states of consciousness.

In meditation, cues for these three brains can be used to initiate meditation in an integrated fashion. You can begin by focusing on posture cues that activate all three: relaxing your feet on the ground (gut-brain, lower dantian), then relaxing your hands cupped in your lap (heart brain, middle dantian), and finally imagining a string attached to the top of your head, drawing your spine gently upright (brain, upper dantian).

This last cue also activates the Central Channel that runs up through the core of your body, including your spine, from the perineum to the crown point of your head. This Central Channel is "The God Cord" that integrates all three primary energy centers within a shaft of light that "connects Heaven and Earth" through the Central Channel of your body.

In our final Subtle Energy Meditation called the "Light, Love, and Peace Meditation," you work with all three dantians by focusing on being elevated, infused, and informed by Light from above through the upper dantian; transformed by Love extending out from the Heart in the middle dantian; and grounded in deep Peace found in stillness in the lower dantian.

Each of these energetic frequencies (Light, Love, and Peace) can become part of your baseline state of consciousness—the predominant state you live from. Familiarity with moving into and between these frequencies gives you flexibility of attention and inner skills you can draw upon as needed. Integrating these three frequencies through the Central Channel is a powerful alchemical process that transforms your state of consciousness so you can live in an elevated state of Awareness. It's our belief that, as you do this personally, you help to raise the vibration of our collective consciousness, because we are all part of One Life, One Body, One Shared Heart, One Vast Spacious Awareness.

We're going to lead you through this process slowly, step-by-step, so it becomes a rich felt experience and a reliable set of inner skills, rather than just concepts in your mind. As a foundation for this, we want to help you get clear on why you might want to put forth the effort to learn Subtle Energy Meditation and what you want to get from it. By getting clear on your "Why," and continually reminding yourself about it, you'll discover the motivation that inspires you to complete the process. When you find the steps along the way uncomfortable or you lose your motivation, remember your "Why" to propel you onward to the next step. It's important that you make a strong commitment to achieving what your soul desires to carry you through moments that feel challenging.

We are so excited for you to get started! We ask you to begin by taking time to answer the following Five Questions sincerely, with the best knowledge you can gather at this moment. These questions are a foundation for moving through this process.

After you answer these Five Questions, take some time to ponder them. Absorb them deeply in your body, heart, and mind. Visualize what your soul desires in full sensory detail and really feel what it would be like to live this experience. Then, make a firm commitment that you will take the steps to overcome any struggles along the way. You'll discover that, when approached mindfully, your struggles become opportunities for greater awareness and gateways to what you truly desire.

Finally, we highly recommend you write your answers in a journal. Writing your answers down makes them more real and substantial. The activity of writing records your responses more deeply in your consciousness. Your journal will also become a record to keep track of your progress, as well as a place to record all of the exercises we'll guide you through in this book.

Now, on to the Five Questions. Kevin first discovered a version of these questions in the coaching classes of Eben Pagan.[9] Since then, Kevin, Stephen, and Kevin's wife, Monica (who is an Intuitive Life Coach), have adapted, added to, and reordered them based on what has worked best with our students and clients.

Before asking yourself these questions, we suggest you take a moment for a Mindful Check-in inside:

- Notice how you feel right now.
- Take a few, slow, deep breaths, feeling the sensations of breathing inside your body, to come into the present moment.
- Then, float these questions to your deeper mind, your heart, your soul essence, and allow this deeper core part of you to respond.

Five Questions to Find Your "Why"

Question 1. What is your biggest need/frustration/issue/challenge right now in your life? This can be a mental-emotional pattern, an unwanted behavior, or a physical symptom.

Question 2. How do you want this to improve? What result do you desire?

Question 3. What is blocking you?

Question 4. What do you fear will happen in the future if you don't resolve this?

Question 5. How will you know you've achieved what your soul desires? What will you feel? Perhaps you have an image in your mind associated with this feeling.

After you write down your response to this fifth question:

- Focus into your heart and connect to your soul's desire and the feeling of it. What would it look like to experience this? What image comes to mind?
- Step into this picture as if you're living in this experience with all your senses. Where are you? What are the visual details? What does it smell like? Taste like? What sounds do you hear? Who are you with? What are you doing? What are you saying?
- Make sure your visualization brings you joy. If it doesn't, make any shifts to the scene until it feels completely joyful—until it really makes you smile.
- Then "record" the image and feeling of this experience deeply in your body, heart, and mind, so you remember it and can return to it at any time.

Reflection & Insight Journaling

We suggest you journal daily. Begin your journal by writing down your answers to the Five Questions above.

- Reflect on your answers to the Five Questions. How do you feel about what you've written?
- Is this information new for you or have you thought about these things before? Have you been aware of this issue in your life? Have you been aware of what your soul desires in this area of your life?
- Are you ready to make a shift?

- Each day, note how the issue you are working with comes up in your life. Notice how you respond to these moments.

Whatever you think and feel is OK. Just make note of it and write it down. Do this as best as you can without self-judgment.

Daily Mindfulness Check-Ins with One Conscious Breath

In addition to journaling, as a way to begin turning inward and accessing your inner world throughout the day, we suggest you set specific times during the day when you pause what you're doing, notice how you feel, and take One Conscious Breath. During this breath, pay attention to the sensations of breathing inside your body. Really feel these sensations. Then, notice how you feel after taking this moment to Check-in.

We suggest you begin every day, the moment you wake up, with one of these Check-ins. We also suggest that you end each day with another Check-in. Then, set a couple of other times during the day when you will Check-in. For example, you could set Check-ins for the moment you go to brush your teeth, have your morning tea/coffee, start your car or sit down on public transit, sit at a stoplight, sit down at your desk, enter a meeting, fold the laundry, do the dishes, sit down for lunch, get in your car or get on public transit to come home, or lie down in bed at night.

Choose four times that might work well for you to pause, notice how you feel, and take One Conscious Breath.

What times will you use?

Check-in 1:

Check-in 2:

Check-in 3

Check-in 4:

--- --- ---

After you've answered the Five Questions, journaled your reflections, and set your Check-ins, we look forward to joining you in our next chapter. You'll learn how to access your inner world in a powerful way you might never have imagined possible—through interoception.

2. Interoception: Turning Inward

The Gateway to Intuition and Higher Consciousness

So, how did it go with answering the Five Questions? Did it help you uncover what's underneath the experiences you're having and what you truly desire? If you aren't sure how to answer all these questions right now, that's OK. At the beginning, it's the asking that's most important. As you go through the chapters of this book, you can expect these answers will become more clear—as well as what to do about them, so that you can move forward!

Let's ask a few more questions to refresh your motivation and intention as you go through this next section:

- What's your overall experience in the world these days? Do you feel safe? Does the world feel like a friendly place?
- Or, do you feel stressed, anxious, and overwhelmed? Frustrated? Angry?
- Do you feel a lack of inner guidance and purpose? Do you know how to find clarity and insight? Have you tried many

things, but nothing seems to take you to that next level you're looking for?

In this chapter, we're going to work with a primary skill that is a gateway to cultivating higher states of consciousness, clear insight, and elevated states of being. In these states, you'll discover the answers you're seeking.

You'll recall from Chapter 1 that your state of consciousness determines what you experience, how you feel, how you relate to others, and how you relate to anything that's happening. Awareness of your state of consciousness means being aware of your needs, feelings, and thoughts as they arise—as well as being aware of how these relate to others and your environment. Meditation is a simple proven technique of getting in touch with your current state of consciousness, while reducing stress and gaining clarity, by focusing attention on specific cues for a period of time.

A first step into meditation is learning how to turn inward to access your inner experience, a process called "interoception."

As we said in Chapter 1, interoception is the ability to tune in to the inner state of your body, to notice and discern inner sensations. It is a way to approach what is happening inside by noticing felt sensations inside your body. Tuning in to this sixth sense is the foundation for experiencing the fullness of the present moment, as well as for cultivating intuitive knowing and experiencing deeper spiritual connections—the kind of connections that fill you up on the inside, so you don't feel the need to keep looking outside yourself for what you need.

In a world that so consumes us with outer sensory stimulation of our five senses, this finer inner sense is often neglected, atrophies, and fades from consciousness. As we lose touch with interoception, we begin looking outside for what can only be found within. This is the genesis of the outward craving that can never be satisfied.

By accessing your inner world through interoception, you begin to tune in to what is going on internally without getting stuck in rumination, self-criticism, or emotional reactivity. This is because interoception works through pure sensory awareness, so it is free from the interpretive layer of thoughts and emotions. In our next chapter, on mindfulness, we'll explore how to defuse the emotionally charged thoughts and feelings that form on top of sensory awareness, so you can engage with them in a way that is liberating and healing.

How to Tune In to Inner Signals

Imagine for a moment, you are like a radio, and you can decide what signal to tune in to. The signal you select determines what information you receive and how you feel. In this analogy, instead of radio waves, possible signals you can focus on include: outer sensations of sights, sounds, smells, tastes, and tactile sensations; inner sensations such as pain or pleasure; and finer frequencies of thoughts, emotions, and other subtle energies from yourself, others, and the whole quantum field in which you exist.

How do you navigate through all these signals? In this chapter, you'll learn how to tune in to this vast sea of information and use interoception to select the signal that gives you the information you need right now. You'll use interoception to access information related to the Five Questions. This will help you release inner tensions and blocks that are holding you back.

Drowning in a Stormy Sea of Noise

Most of us are floating in a stormy sea of information overload, which makes it hard to discern what really matters. It's all **so important** and **time sensitive!** It all shouts, "Come over here, now!" Being subjected to too much noise for too long makes us lose contact with our inner world and the guidance of our inner senses.

As a simple example, stress can make you forget to drink your eight glasses a day of water. When you're calm and tuned in to your body, you can tell that you're thirsty and know to take a drink long before you get dehydrated. When you're stressed, you're less likely to tune in to signals of thirst your body is sending to your brain. You may misinterpret "thirst" as "hunger" and overeat as a result.

The same applies to signals of stress itself. If you are tuned in to your body, it tells you when you're overheating from over-stimulation, external and internal pressures, and not setting appropriate limits on demands. When you don't sense signals of stress early, they become more exaggerated symptoms, such as tension headaches, backaches, stomach aches, rashes, lashing out, or emotionally shutting down.

If you spend the majority of your time and energy trying to consume the wealth of information that is clamoring for your attention and responding to every request for feedback, one thing is for sure— you're going to be stressed out! If you do nothing else but try to keep up, you're on a path to overwhelm. You'll lose your discerning sense of what is really important and what matters to you most. And that's the best case. One day you may wake up and wonder, "What the heck am I doing?" or "What's the point of it all?" and even perhaps, "Why am I here?"

Activating Your Interoceptive Navigation Systems

Fortunately, we each come equipped to handle all this information and sort through the infinite demands. You can do this by activating the interoceptive navigation systems of the vehicle you use to sail through this sea—your body, heart, and mind. You have interoceptive senses which are designed to sort through everything you're facing and select the precise information you need from the sea of information in which you exist.

The problem is you can become so consumed in keeping up with the ongoing processing of information that you have no bandwidth left to activate and use your interoceptive navigational tools. All your time and energy is spent in the vain attempt to keep up. So, you've got to take some concerted intentional steps to take a break and tune in differently. We'd like to suggest a few:

Step 1. Insert a Mental Pause in the Stream of Information

Schedule ongoing time-outs in which you close the doors to the outside world and work on learning the ins and outs of the navigational tools you possess. You'll need to be strict with yourself about these time-outs because the waves of information are going to come pounding against your inner doors. You've got to close them firmly and set a lock with a timer, so you won't go back out until you've learned what you need to know from the inside. Setting a time for daily meditation is one way to do this. Setting a time where you put aside technology for an hour to do some gardening or take a walk out in nature are also good alternatives.

Step 2. Activate Your Inner Senses through Counting Calm Breaths

If you're like many people, you've been focusing on all the information available in your outer environment and neglecting the intuitive information available inside. So, you've got to make a turn inward and see what there is to discover "in here." The first thing to discover (and the foundation of all other inner discoveries) is the world of body sensations available through your sense of interoception.

When was the last time you checked in with your body, besides when you were prompted by pain, hunger, or some big emotion? And, did you really check in with your body then, or did you simply rush to take something to relieve your pain, hunger, or emotion and make you feel better?

A simple, effective, time-honored, and proven way to turn inward is to focus on counting the sensations of breathing. This may sound mundane or boring, but it becomes a magical practice as you practice it intently. Focusing on counting the sensations of breathing counters the habit of being distracted by every little tantalizing bit of information that comes across your path. If you focus on the sensations of breathing and count your out-breaths in cycles of 10, you begin to establish conscious control of your attention and tune in to a different frequency band on your radio—inner frequencies that elude you when you focus on signals from the outside world.

As you practice this, it's good to quiet the noise in your external environment, silence your phone, sit comfortably upright, and close your eyes. We'll guide you into this practice in the exercises below. Before you do this, here are some helpful tips:

- A good place to feel the sensations of breathing is in your lower abdomen, a spot far away from your thinking/analyzing/external-information-processing brain. The thinking mind tends to be consumed by outer information and thoughts about all this information without being able to free itself to do anything else. So, to counter this, you can establish your attention in a place far away from this mental chatter, a place such as your lower abdomen. You can put your hands on your abdomen to reinforce this focal point.

- As you inhale, notice the gentle sensation of expansion in your lower abdomen until you naturally pause; as you exhale, notice the subtle relaxation inward until you naturally pause. Make sure you are *feeling* the sensation and are not just *thinking about* the breath. See if you can become completely absorbed in sensing the cycles of your breathing, as if nothing else matters at this moment. To track your attention and mark if you are really staying focused, count each breath on the exhale, in cycles of 10.

If your mind wanders and you forget the count, begin again at one. If you get to 10, begin again at one.

Step 3. Follow Your Breathing Mindfully

Mindfully means "paying attention, on purpose, in the present moment, non-judgmentally—like a curious observer." This means you "witness" your breathing without commenting on how well or how poorly you're doing. You maintain a gentle, curious attitude of paying attention, like a scientist calmly making observations and taking notes.

When you notice your mind wandering, you recognize what grabbed your attention, release this, and return to counting the sensations of breathing. These are the **3Rs of focused attention**: **Recognize, Release, & Return**. Do this whenever your mind wanders to anything other than the sensations of breathing. Again, see if you can do this without judging your performance. Gently note what happens as you focus on feeling the sensations of breathing and keep practicing the 3Rs when your mind wanders. Your mind will wander. It's OK. Recognizing, releasing, and returning is how you train your attention to focus in a more sustained way.

As you continue to focus on counting your breaths, see if you can tune in to and differentiate the subtleties of sensation:

- Can you sense the moment you begin to inhale? What is the quality of this in-breath? Is it long/short, smooth/rough, quiet/loud, thin/full? How long is the pause? How does it feel during this pause? Can you sense the moment you begin to exhale? What is the quality of this out-breath? Is it long/short, smooth/rough, quiet/loud, thin/full? How long is the pause before you breathe in again? How does this pause feel? Is the inhale longer or shorter than the exhale? Are they even in duration?

- Are you trying to breathe a certain way or just noticing how you *are* breathing, without trying? Does your breathing rate and quality change as you pay attention? If you notice the tension of trying too hard, what happens if you let go and just watch, listen to, and sense your breathing like a curious observer?

- Give this breath counting a try for a couple of minutes now. See if you can really notice the inner sensations of breathing and observe what happens as you follow the instructions below.

Exercise: Simple Interoception of Breathing

Place your hands, one on top of the other, on your abdomen. Feel the sensations of breathing here, inside your body. Notice the subtle expansion as you inhale and the subtle relaxation inward as you exhale. To tune in deeper to the inner sensations, you can close your eyes.

We encourage you to try this now for about 10 breaths. Close your eyes, feel the sensations of breathing inside your body, and count your breaths on the exhale until you get to 10. See if, each time you exhale, you can relax and feel the sensation of "letting go" a little more. When you get to 10 breaths, open your eyes and come back. If you lose count, begin again at one. If you find you can't get to 10, that's OK. It's natural for the mind to wander. As you practice over time, your ability to sustain focus will improve.

Go ahead and give this a try now.

So, how did it go with breath counting? Did you enjoy the sensations of breathing, relaxing, and letting go? Perhaps, it felt like a relief to just breathe for a few moments? Or, did you find it hard to keep your attention on your breathing? Did you get agitated or bored? Did you want to get on with the rest of this chapter or go to something else instead? Whatever you experienced is fine. There is no right or wrong experience. It's the "noticing of your inner experience" that is most important—that's interoception.

What's so Great about Counting Your Breaths?

At first, this breath-counting practice may feel pretty boring and pointless. You may be so accustomed to exciting moments of outer stimulation that you've lost the feel for finer sensations and detailed information available inside. You may need to awaken and cultivate your inner senses. As you do, you'll find the breath is quite beautiful, calming, and fascinating. Sensing your breathing feels like coming home to something primal, essential, and spiritual.

As you can see in the list of questions about the qualities of your breath above, there is a lot you can pay attention to as you breathe. As you tune in to these subtleties, you awaken your inner senses and fine-tune them.

Feeling the sensations of breathing opens you to feeling other subtle sensations, such as shifts of emotion; the connection between thoughts, emotions, body sensations, and cravings; and inner signals that alert you to what is important to pay attention to right now.

As you become absorbed in the sensations of breathing, you'll notice your body relaxes. You feel more centered. Your thoughts quiet down and emotions calm. Your parasympathetic nervous system, your rest and recovery mode, activates, as your sympathetic nervous system, or action mode, takes a break. You feel relief as stress drains. In a short time, you feel rejuvenated. Or you might feel tired. You may notice that you've been revved up in stress mode for so long that you really need a rest.

In a state of relaxed, yet alert attention, you are receptive to what is most important to you. Outer noise has faded to the background and inner chatter has quieted. In this quiet space, you can discern what comes into your awareness and sort it according to relevance. From this inner quiet, you can sense the Whole Field in which you exist and consciously decide what to focus on and what to let go. You've regained an intuitive sense. You discover that you do know what you need to focus on. There is a discerning part of you that knows what to do—a gut sense that is all about right action. You just couldn't hear this inner voice when you were busy responding to the overwhelming din of information clamoring for your attention.

Your gut sense (centered in your lower abdomen or lower dantian) is connected to sensory signals from your environment and interoceptive signals inside your body that are all recorded in a subconscious process called "neuroception." Neuroception calculates all this information together into a "gut feeling." This is prior to the layers of emotion that evaluate your relationship to this information and prior to language and thinking, which interpret information according to your dominant thoughts, beliefs, and life stories.

Your gut sense, based in your enteric nervous system, is your means of access to this neuroceptive information, which communicates through the vagus nerve network to your brain (primarily the insula and brainstem). There is an 80/20 ratio of information sent from your gut to your brain versus information sent from your brain to your gut, which shows just how much information your gut sense provides and how vital this is to the functioning of your body, heart, and mind.

When you're connected to your gut sense, you are able to pick out the information you need to know, both internally and in the sea of information around you. Certain information will "light up" and stand out from all the rest. What you need to know will glow with a certain type of attraction. You'll know this attraction because it will feel just right. You won't feel rushed or anxious. It will feel inspired, yet matter of fact, like "OK, this is it. This is what I need to know, feel, and do." This information can come in gut feelings (sensations), inner seeing (visions, images), inner hearing (guiding sounds or words), and emotional connections.

As you follow these intuitive prompts, they'll lead you to exactly what you need to know, feel, and do now, which will lead you to your next step, and your next in life.

Make paying mindful attention to discerning inner and outer prompts a constant practice. You'll be guided forward in ways you might not have imagined possible. This guidance is always available. However, in the stormy sea of information, it can take a concerted and dedicated effort to access it.

Summary of the Interoceptive Process

Here's a summary of the intuitive process we've just described:

- Pause.
- Close your eyes.
- Turn inward to the subtle sensations in your lower abdomen of breathing.
- Count your out-breaths in cycles of 10 to relax and focus internally.
- Tune in to your gut sense and notice information that "lights up" in the space inside or around you.

Through this process of awakening your inner senses, you become a conscious radio operator, tuning to the frequencies of inner wisdom and letting the outer noise dissolve in the background. We're going to practice interoception and apply it to gather information pertaining to the five introductory questions in a couple of exercises at the end of this chapter.

How Do Both of Us Experience Interoception?

For both of us, intuitive information has a relaxed, matter-of-fact feeling to it. There is no tension or anxiety around it. There is no rush to make something happen. It is just so.

Stephen: One way that information "lights up" for me is that a blue light appears in my awareness whenever it is important for me to connect with a person or a piece of information. I can be speaking to people, listening intently, paying attention to what the person is saying, and self-regulating by checking in with my breathing while listening. When someone says something that is deeply true for them, and it is important that I notice it, a radiant blue light will shine in the space in and around them. I will often share this with the person I am listening to, and they are often led to share even more—as if the confirmation encourages them and helps them to access even more information.

--- --- ---

Kevin: For me, intuitive wisdom and guidance most often come in the form of words or phrases accompanied by a feeling of deep relaxation and inspiration in my body.

Take a moment to acknowledge the way in which *you* access intuition. Is it through inner seeing, hearing, feeling, sensing, writing, drawing, vocalizing, or some other way? There are so many ways you might access intuitive information.

How Interoception Helps You Let Go of Stress and Access Inner Knowledge

Let's take a deeper look at how interoception works to give you more confidence in the process:

1. Interoception accesses neuroceptive information that is subconscious and prior to emotion, language, and thinking. In other words, it works with parts of your body and brain that are not engaged in thought. The more you tune in to interoception and become absorbed in it, the more your non-stop thinking, analyzing, judging, and planning function quiets down, so you can rest from all of that and access deeper resources.

2. Interoception of breathing sensations calms your nervous system. It activates your parasympathetic nervous response and dampens your "fight or flight" stress mode. As your nervous system calms, you can deal with other inner sensations less reactively, such as emotions that may be driving you without your conscious consent. Instead of overreacting, you can tune in to the messages your emotions are trying to give you, which are meant to guide you to appropriate action.

3. Interoception enables you to feel the impulses that are driving your actions before they get a hold of you, rather than being a victim of these impulses. You learn to discern the impulses behind addictive behaviors and cravings, step back and observe them, and make better choices aligned with your well-being. For many people, this is over-eating, over-buying, drinking alcohol, or distraction through entertainment. All these cover deeper feelings that, when addressed, can end the cycle of craving the moment it enters consciousness—which is something you'll notice through interoception.

4. Interoception is a gateway to deeper feelings of connection with "who you are" and "why you are here," as well as deeper connections with others and life itself. As you use interoception of breathing to enter into relaxation, this can lead to deeper states of concentration, in which you experience the life force within you, the life force around you, and your unity with all of life. You also start to feel more at-home and at-ease in your body. You come to experience your body as a safe place to be. This gives a deeper sense of trust in life.

5. Through interoception of more subtle sensations, such as sensing life-force energy, you experience yourself as more than just a body—more than just your thoughts, feelings, and actions. You become aware of yourself as open, clear, spacious Awareness. This is a felt sensation that begins within and extends beyond you. You become aware of being part of One Life and One Consciousness that we all share. Is this perhaps the connection you were craving in the first place?

Is all of this real? Is it true? You can find out for yourself. These experiences are discovered by turning inward, activating your own powers of interoception, and exploring deeply. You've experienced the results of not doing this—the stress, anxiety, depression, anger, sadness, reactivity, hostility, and addiction. Pick your poison. If you don't do something different, you'll continue repeating these same experiences.

What might happen if you consciously, deliberately, intentionally, and purposefully decided to turn your focus inward and cultivate your inner senses? Let's find out.

What Is Your Current Level of Interoception?

How do we measure interoception? The University of California San Francisco Osher Center for Integrative Medicine has developed a simple assessment tool called the "Multidimensional Assessment of Interoceptive Awareness." It can give you a sense of how tuned-in you tend to be to your interoceptive senses. Below is a simplified presentation of the MAIA Questions.

MAIA Questionnaire Instructions[10]

Ask yourself the following questions and respond with a scaled rating from 1=Never to 6=Always. Use the questions to notice if and how much you pay attention to different aspects of your interoceptive sense. Answer with the first response that comes to mind by surveying present or recent experiences that apply to each question. Don't worry about getting the "right answer." The point of the questions is to spark inquiry and notice where you are at this time. By asking yourself these questions, you may notice yourself becoming more aware of your inner tendencies moving forward. Consider answering these questions now in your journal, adding up your total score, and then coming back to them at the end of this book and see if there is any change in your score.

The MAIA Questions: Using a Six-point Likert Scale

1. Noticing ("I notice where in my body I am comfortable.")
2. Not Distracting ("I distract myself from sensations of discomfort" – reverse scored: 1=always, 6=never.)
3. Not Worrying ("I can notice an unpleasant body sensation without worrying about it.")
4. Attention Regulation ("I can return awareness to my body if I am distracted.")
5. Emotional Awareness ("I notice how my body changes when I am angry.")
6. Self-Regulation ("When I bring awareness to my body, I feel a sense of calm.")
7. Body Listening ("I listen to my body to inform me about what to do.")
8. Trusting ("I feel my body is a safe place.")

What do these questions tell you about your relationship with interoception? Do you feel at home in your body through interoception? Is this something foreign to you or something you access often? If you're like many people in our current culture of overstimulation, which emphasizes mental processing of external sensory information, you may not be in the habit of tuning in to inner sensations much at all. There is just too much going on out there in the world! It's stressful enough dealing with everything you have to do and respond to, without having to deal with everything you feel inside!

In contrast, Stephen has a daughter named Maia. She is particularly in tune with her body and her inner experiences and can recall them vividly. She says she can remember what it felt like being in her mother's tummy before being born and just after being born. She said she remembers looking back at her mother and saying to herself, "Are you the mother who just gave birth to me?" Many of us have natural inner knowing like this when we are young. Due to stress and overwhelming external stimuli, as well as being told to pay attention to the outer world and suppress our feelings, we lose touch with this deep sensitivity.

So, if connecting with your inner world feels foreign or too much to consider in the midst of all the rest you have to deal with, don't worry. We're going to lead you into this slowly, step-by-step, in a way you can work with a little at a time.

We highly encourage you to take time to practice each of the following exercises and our first meditation before moving on to Chapter 3, because they are the foundation for all that follows.

Exercise: Inner Body Scan Meditation

The benefits of this body scan include increased inner body awareness (interoception), recognition of stored tension and stress, a conscious release of tension, and a felt sense of deep relaxation, inner peace, and well-being. It is also great for strengthening concentration, sustaining attention, and relaxing, and it's a wonderful way to awaken your interoceptive senses! We suggest you read through the sequence below, then lie down and give it a try:

- To begin, lie on your back on your bed, couch, or a yoga or exercise mat, with your legs apart and your arms to the side, palms up in a receptive gesture. Cover yourself with a blanket if you tend to get cold, so you are not distracted midway through the body scan. First, simply lie there and notice what it feels like to be connected to the ground. Feel the sensations of contact with the surface underneath you.

- Start with your left toes. Check in and sense how they feel. Are they cold? Are they holding tension? Focus your breathing in on the area of your attention, directing your breath deep into your toes. Can you feel the sensations of breathing in your toes? Whatever you feel or don't feel is fine.

- Release awareness of your toes and move your attention to your heel, focusing your breathing into your left heel.

- Move upward to your arch, your ankle, your calf, your knee, and your thigh. Then, repeat the process with your right leg, starting with your right toes.

- Once you have scanned your legs, concentrate your awareness and breathing into your pelvis, traveling to your lower back, abdomen, chest, shoulders, arms, hands, neck, and head.

- Once you've scanned your individual body parts, unite them, focusing on how the fingers connect to the hands, which connect to the arms and so on. Be aware of sensations—the feel of the blanket or the chill of the air on your skin. The objective of a body scan is to sense your body as a whole, united by the breath flowing in and out of it.

Now that you have some practice awakening your inner senses, you can apply this ability to work with the issue you identified in the Five Questions in Chapter 1.

Exercise: Discovering the Message in Your Body

Call to mind the issue you are working with in this book—the issue you identified in the Five Questions from Chapter 1. Call to mind what is blocking the experience your soul desires. As we saw, this can be a mental-emotional pattern, an unwanted behavior, or a physical symptom. We will access the energy block associated with this issue by locating it in your energy field and asking questions about its shape, size, color, texture, weight, temperature, and sound frequency.

As we go through these questions, see if it's possible to go with whatever comes up, without worrying if it is right or wrong. Just go with whatever comes into your awareness and work with that. Some questions may give you clear answers right away and others may not. Proceed with whatever information you receive. It's not necessary to get an answer to every question.

You can close your eyes after each question if it helps you to tune in inside. Then open them to read the next step in the process. Another option is to record this and play it back while you follow the process internally. Or, you could read through the whole process and memorize the basic outline of it, then go through it internally with your eyes closed.

To begin, sit comfortably upright with your feet firmly on the ground and your hands resting comfortably on your legs. Take a moment to check in inside and notice how you feel. Take a few, slow, deep breaths focusing in on the sensations of breathing.

- Again, call to mind the issue you are working with. As you hold this issue in your mind, ask yourself:
    - If the block associated with this issue was located anywhere in my body, where would it be?
    - If it had a shape, what shape would it have?
    - What size would that shape be?
    - If the shape had a color, what color would it be?
    - If it had a texture, what texture would it be?
    - If it had a weight, what would that be?
    - If it had a temperature, what would that be?
    - If it were to make a sound, what sound would it make?

- o If it had a message for me, what would this be?
  - o Let your attention rest in this area and notice anything that arises.
- Now that you have gathered this information, simply allow your awareness to lightly rest in this area and breathe through it. As you breathe in, imagine and feel your breath infusing the area. As you breathe out, imagine and feel any tension releasing in your out breath.
  - o Ask yourself, "Am I willing to let this go?"
  - o If you are, nod and say, "Yes, I am willing to let this go now."
  - o Continue to breathe through the area until you feel a shift in the energy here or until you feel the process is complete for the moment.
- Slowly open your eyes and take in the space around you.
- Take a few moments to write down anything that is important for you to remember from this meditative experience, any insight you've gained, and how this relates to what you want to grow in your life and your relationship with others.

Daily Subtle Meditation Practice: 1. Relaxing Down Three Lines

Now, we'd like to introduce you to the first meditation in the Subtle Energy Meditation Series: "**Relaxing Down Three Lines**."

In this meditation, you cultivate your skills of interoception and conscious relaxation by imagining and feeling warm, soothing, liquid light traveling down through three pathways in your body.

You can find the **meditation script** in the Appendices. You can memorize it, record it in your own voice, or follow along with the recording we've created, which can be found in the ROV Meditation App, available for Apple and Android devices in those app stores. [11]

As you practice, you may notice certain areas where you easily sense this warm soothing flow of energy and others that feel tense or where you feel nothing at all. Whatever you feel or don't feel is fine. What's most important is paying attention and noticing whatever happens. Practice mindfulness to notice what happens non-judgmentally. Use the 3Rs whenever your attention wanders.

We suggest you practice this meditation first thing each morning to set the foundation for making meditation a part of your daily routine. If you want to deepen your experience, you can repeat the meditation during the day and/or before going to bed at night.

Make special note of the moment when you compare the right side of your body with the left and notice any difference. Most people are surprised to notice the difference. This will show you the power of paying attention, focusing on specific inner sensations, and consciously relaxing. Inner sensing and focusing have a subtle, yet palpable, effect in your body (much of which is underneath your conscious awareness until you take time to notice). Tune in to any areas that feel warm, tingling, energized, especially relaxed, and comfortable, as well as areas that feel tense, painful, or numb.

You may find that some areas are difficult to focus on. In these areas, your mind may wander almost immediately. Through consistent practice over time, you'll be able to sustain your attention for longer periods of time, stronger inner sensations will awaken, and you will be able to consciously relax and feel calm and comfortable in your body whenever you feel the need.

Practice Relaxing Down Three Lines at least once before going on to the next chapter. Then, practice it once or twice a day until you feel confident with it before moving on to the next meditation in the series.

Reflection & Insight Journaling

What did you discover through these interoception experiences? What was comfortable? What was uncomfortable? What was your dominant sense, for example, shape, texture, color, or sound? What insights did you receive about the issue you're working with, and what is blocking you from experiencing what your soul desires?

Continue Your Daily Practice with Mindfulness Check-Ins

As we suggested in Chapter 1, set specific "Check-ins" in your day as moments to pause, check in with how you feel, and take One Conscious Breath. As you focus in on the sensations of this one breath, ask yourself: "Where do I feel this breath? What is the quality of this breath? How does it feel to check in with my breathing?"

Tracking Your Practice

We suggest you log your practice using the **Meditation Log**, found in the Appendices. You can also use the log as a template to make notes on your meditation experiences in your Reflection & Insight Journal.

- For each session, log the day, time, and name of the meditation you did.
- Give a brief description of the inner cues you found significant. (An example of this could be, "Imagine a string attached to the top of your head, drawing your spine gently upright.")
- Add a brief description of your inner felt experience of these significant cues. (An example of this could be, "I felt more alert, intentional, and empowered.")
- Finally, give yourself a rating of from zero to 10 for your Energy, Mood, and Mental Clarity.

Our suggestion is to use these as personal scales to compare day by day. The purpose is to fine-tune your awareness and your practice. Part of this is differentiating between Energy, Mood, and Mental Clarity and then noticing the effect of your practice on each of these.

Energy is your physical vitality—your "go power." Mood is a scale of positive, uplifted, or inspired feeling, such as calm happiness. Mental clarity is clear focus, and a clear, quiet mind (10), versus brain fog, mental clutter, and monkey mind (zero).

Perhaps the easiest way to score them is to ask your subconscious mind for a number for each and go with whatever number comes to you.

See if you can approach this self-report as objectively as possible, as a curious observer, with an attitude of mindfulness—simply making note of your experiences as objectively as possible. Taking the time to meditate is a good thing and all meditation sessions are valuable. Every day will be different. See if you can report whatever happens in the spirit of discovery and without self-judgment. It's all about learning and growing in awareness.

--- --- ---

In the next chapter, we will explore mindfulness in a deeper way and show you how to develop the skills of being a curious observer.

3. Mindfulness: Being a Curious Observer

Cultivating a Calm Baseline State of Awareness

At times, we all get stuck in stress and locked into negative thoughts, feelings, behaviors, and beliefs we can't seem to shake off. Something in your environment triggers associations (a work demand, a family emergency, a hurtful comment on social media, bad news from a doctor, a story about a tragic event, or criticism from a colleague) and a mood comes over you that feels thick, heavy, dark, and sticky. You get stressed, defensive, anxious, or depressed. Life loses its luster, and you lose your power.

In this chapter, we explore what you can do in these moments to break free and get back on track. This information also applies to those more chronic patterns of thinking, feeling, belief, and behavior that keep you stuck repeating frustrating patterns in your life, rather than expanding into your unlimited potential. One simple skill can liberate you. This skill is mindfulness—**paying attention, on purpose, in the present moment, non-judgmentally—like a curious observer**. As you cultivate mindfulness, you develop a calm baseline state of awareness that you can live from and return to whenever you get pulled away.

Hijacked by Stress and Negativity

One thing that tends to happen in stuck moments is they feel substantial and permanent—as if that's just "the way things are." Even though you know that moods change, when you're in the midst of them, you probably worry that they'll last forever. In these moments, you doubt if things will get better. In the heat of the moment, you tend to experience a mood as a permanent "fact of life." It feels pervasive and tends to permeate everything around you. You see everything and everyone through the lens of your mood. Moods change the feeling tone and color of your world.

When a mood is pervasive, it's hard to step outside it. It's hard to shake it off. You'd have to change your whole perception of reality. That's a tall order—especially when you're feeling bad.

The mood also feels like it is "yours," a part of "who you are." You will tend to identify "who you are" with the thoughts, feelings, and experiences "you have." In this way, you may become very attached to these thoughts, feelings, and experiences, not only because they are known and familiar, but because they feel like they define you. They are part of your story about who you are.

Habitual ways of experiencing life become neurologically and chemically wired into your body and brain. You have neural circuits associated with each mood and these fire in response to environmental cues. These cues are triggers that set in motion a whole cascade of inner events, including chemical reactions that reinforce thinking, feeling, and acting as you always have in these circumstances. Not only are you reacting to what's happening in your environment, you are also being pushed to have a specific reaction based on the way you've reacted to these events in the past.

If you're going to get free, you've got to find a way to respond differently to the same triggers. You need to learn to respond independently from how you've responded in the past. You must find a way to step back and let go of identifying with these specific ways of thinking, feeling, and acting and stop seeing them as permanent fixtures of your life. This involves changing the way you view yourself, others, and the world around you.

Getting over Yourself

When you feel stressed, angry, joyful, peaceful, appreciative, sad, or afraid, *who* feels this? When you get up in the morning, *who* decides what you are going to do? The obvious unquestioned answer is "me." This goes without saying. Isn't your whole life built around a sense that there is someone called "me" doing, thinking, and having experiences? Isn't your whole day built around the idea that *you* have things to do, places to go, people to meet with, and resources to gather to continue the survival and well-being of "me?" Of course, it is!

Isn't this "me" motivated to know what you want, so that you can get it? Aren't you afraid of this "me" dying, because you want "me" to continue, because you cherish this life of "me?" This "me" isn't some vague, philosophical, theoretical conundrum; it is a seemingly very real being that gets up every morning and navigates through life. It is the very basis of the acts of doing, thinking, and having experiences that constitutes what you think of as being alive.

Yet, what if you aren't really who you think you are? What if the way you think of yourself is the source of your stress and suffering? Let's explore the possibility that this "me" might not exist at all, at least not in the way you normally think of it. While this may sound scary, this realization can liberate you! It can end the cycle of tension, stress, and fear!

49

The Illusive Nature of You

So, who is this "I" you identify as "me?" What is the nature of this "I"? Can you define who you are? I mean, really, can you do it? Is it possible there is no "I" in here at all? Now, before you put down this book and turn to something seemingly more interesting, practical, useful, or graspable, consider this:

"According to the teaching of the Buddha, the idea of self is an imaginary, false belief which has no corresponding reality, and it produces harmful thoughts of 'me' and 'mine,' selfish desire, craving, attachment, hatred, ill-will, conceit, pride, egoism, and other defilements, impurities, and problems. It is the source of all the troubles in the world, from personal conflicts to wars between nations. In short, to this false view can be traced to all the evil in the world."

What the Buddha Taught[12]

Wow, is that possible? Is this idea of "me" an illusion? If it is, this realization could really change the world! What if the source of all your problems, worries, fears, and frustrations *is* an illusion? What if who you think you are, the very felt sense of being "me," is just an idea without substance? What if your "self" is a fleeting moment of arising and fading away, like a wave in the ocean? What if being free of this idea of being your "self" is not only possible, but the greatest liberation possible?

This is not just a Buddhist idea, it's fairly universal in the great spiritual traditions of the world. Isn't this liberation from self-identification the very meaning of the cross in Christianity?

Before we get tangled up in theological or philosophical debate, let's take a more experiential approach—one you can readily test and verify for yourself.

What Maintains and Grows the Self Function?

For a moment, consider that the self might be something like a function, a collection of inputs that combine to create a specific experience. In this sense, your "self" is the result of the coming together of the genes of your mother and father (along with a host of other unseen forces) into a particular body, at a particular time and place, in a particular culture or mix of cultures, on this planet, within this solar system, within this galaxy, and so on, ad infinitum. There is a whole ocean of forces that come together to create this wave called "you," which is at some point on the journey from forming, to rising into a crest, and dissolving into the ocean again.

You might even consider that the "self" functions as a result of particular areas of your brain activating and that "self" transcendence happens when these areas deactivate. The self is experienced when these brain structures are actively firing and when they quiet down the "self" drops away.

Now, you might not normally think of yourself as being so ephemeral and transient. You have this sense that who you are is more permanent, substantial, and enduring. At least you'd like to think you are. You, like all of us, have a strong attachment to this sense of self, to who you think you are. Most of your life revolves around gaining and growing a more substantial and enduring sense of self. You want to become more, not less. (At least, as long as you see this "self" as "who you are.")

There are three dominant ways you grow your sense of self: doing, thinking, and having (in which we'll include collecting relationships, possessions, feelings, and experiences). So, you identify who you are:

1. With the things you do. The more you do and the better you do things, the better and more substantial you feel about this self you think you are, the doer.
2. With the thoughts you think. The better thoughts you think, the better you feel about this self, the thinker. One famous philosopher, René Descartes, went so far as to define the self solely by thinking in his famous phrase, "I think,

therefore, I am." Most of us identify who we are by the thoughts in our minds, this "narrative self" constantly comments on and tells a story about what is going on inside and around you.

3. By what you "have." These include the feelings and experiences you have and the memories you have of these experiences, the relationships you have, and the things you have. You like to accumulate more and more of these experiences, relationships, and things, because they make your sense of "self" feel more substantial. The inner narrator then takes these things you have and tells stories about them—and you identify with these stories of who you are. You have a story about "you."

According to the Buddha, the problem with the sense of self you grow by doing, thinking, and having is that all of these are impermanent. No matter how substantial your achievements, thoughts, or collections of things, experiences, and relationships, in time, they all fade away. No matter how much you want these things you identify as "me" to endure, they don't. They, like your body, are born, stay for a while, and die. They are all impermanent, like waves in the Ocean of Life.

So, if nothing you are in the habit of calling "me" endures, isn't this scary? According to the Buddha, it's only scary if you remain attached to this idea of "self." When you let this go, it's Nirvana—liberation! It's possible to suspend the "self-function" and realize a peace beyond measure.

In meditation, inner sensations, subtle energy, and still, silent, spacious Awareness, stimulate a transcendent experience beyond self that comes to the fore with such focus, intensity, depth, and breadth that it is undeniably more beautiful and compelling than the activity of the world of the narrative self. When this happens, the self-function loses its luster, deactivates, and dissolves.

The self-function is transmuted, so it is no longer strongly identified with and attached to; it is no longer the motivating and driving force of activity. Instead, it is like a costume, a set of clothes you put on to play in the world of forms. Life itself is the actor, the doer of all actions, the thinker of all thoughts, the feeler of all emotions, the One who has experiences. This liberation from identification with the "self" changes everything.

The First Step toward Liberation Is to Adopt Mindfulness

This brings us back to the subject of this chapter. An antidote to free you from the illusions of attachment, identification, and permanence of "me" is mindfulness. Mindfulness is a term that's gained much notoriety lately. It's tossed around in business, psychology, education, and spiritual circles. It's sometimes touted as a "panacea," a cure for all that ails us. Yet, what exactly does it mean? You may recall one of the definitions of mindfulness, based on the work of Dr. Jon Kabat-Zinn: "Mindfulness is awareness, cultivated by paying attention in a sustained and particular way: on purpose, in the present moment, and non-judgmentally." [13] We sum this up in the easy to remember phrase, "being a curious observer."

You can contrast mindfulness with self-referential mind wandering (SRMW), which is mind wandering related to thoughts about yourself, your experiences, and your relationships with others. Notice the term "*self*-referential" in the definition. This state of consciousness is all about "me." It is an ongoing inner voice that constantly narrates the events of life and has a comment, a like or dislike, a judgment, or a label for everything that happens. When we identify *who we are* with the thoughts in our minds, this inner narrator consumes the majority of our mental energy and space. This mind chatter can be pervasive, stressful, and exhausting.

SRMW activates what is called the default mode network (DMN), which is a neural network associated with the posterior cingulate cortex in your brain. The DMN activates when your mind wanders in meditation, or when you daydream or ruminate. As the name implies, the DMN activates by default when you are not intentionally focused.

This contrasts with mindfulness, which is paying attention, on purpose, in the present moment, non-judgmentally. Mindfulness activates the anterior cingulate cortex (often called the "executive control center," because it relates to intentional focus and choice). When meditating, there is the switching between mindfulness and the DMN until attention becomes fully absorbed in focus.

Practicing a mindful attention style changes the way your brain operates. It releases lingering stress and welcomes appreciative engagement. Mindfulness allows you to witness thoughts, feelings, events, and experiences with calm clarity, instead of being wrapped up in and identified with fear, drama, bias, and judgments that slant, color, and cloud your perception. It frees you from the pains of the past and worries about the future and enables you to witness "what is" without the need to comment on, narrate, evaluate, and judge yourself, others, and the events of life. Mindfulness frees you from the "narrative self" who has something to say about everything.

A natural result of mindfulness is that, instead of being overly identified with your experiences, you see yourself as "having" experiences. From this vantage point, you don't believe thoughts, feelings, or actions "define you." "Who you are" transcends any experience "you have," as well as the stories you tell about your experiences.

Consequently, you feel less need to attach, hang onto, or ruminate over any experience as if your existence and self-worth depends on it. Instead, you are a curious "witness" who can inhabit an experience and participate in it without being consumed by it. You appreciate present moment awareness and move on to the next moment without being lost in what's happening. This includes moments you try to hang on to because you enjoy them, moments you wish you could forget, and moments you anticipate happening in the future.

Why is this important? It's important because mindfulness alters the way your brain encodes experiences. Every experience gains a layer of awareness, freedom, and choice. With mindfulness, you learn you can choose what you focus on and how you relate to it, instead of reacting as a "victim of circumstances," as a victim of cues from your environment. You can learn to witness what is happening without judging yourself or others, without feeling compelled to take sides, and without needing to comment on and have an opinion about everything. These activities of the narrative self quiet down and you rest in a state of calm clarity.

Learning to Relate to Your Experiences Differently

Mindfulness research shows that consistent practice leads to less emotional suppression and a greater ability to reappraise how you relate to any thought, feeling, or event so you feel less fear, anger, anxiety, and depression. Your ability to focus your attention and regulate your emotions is enhanced, so you are more aware and more able to choose how you relate to whatever happens. As a result, the skill of mindfulness makes you more stress-resistant and stress-resilient. It centers you in the present moment and empowers you to release attachments, identifications, and associations of permanence that keep you trapped in stress and negative thoughts, feelings, and behaviors.

The best way to understand what mindfulness means is to practice using it. So, let's start with a simple exercise related to why you are reading this book.

Exercise: Personalize Mindfulness with Your "Why"

Take a moment to recall your answers to the Five Questions from Chapter 1. You may want to refer to your journal for your previous answers.

Now, take a look specifically at your answer to Question 3: What is blocking you?

With this answer in mind, let's look a little more closely at the nature of inner blocks. Consider the possibility that your whole life history is stored in the cells of your body. Blocks are stored tensions from past painful or unresolved experiences. Any experience that created anxiety, trauma, pain, or fear is stored as tension in your body until it is released. This stored tension can be triggered by any event or interaction that in any way resembles those past painful moments.

Blocks are protections against experiencing those same things again. They are patterns of thinking, feeling, and behavior that attempt to protect you from the sort of pain you have experienced in the past. Inner blocks are closely tied to the narrative self, since most of the narrative self's life is oriented around protecting itself, based on the stories it tells about past experiences.

Kevin's Block Around Public Speaking

I had a block around public speaking based on my experience of giving a speech at my elementary school graduation ceremony. Walking up the hall to the stage, I was terrified. I felt unprepared and was worried I'd forget what to say. I wanted to get out of there and run away. As I walked up to the mic and looked out to the crowd, I noticed a couple of kids snickering. Panic shot through my body. For a moment, I froze and said nothing. Though I got through the speech, part of me said, "I never want to go through that again." This experience created a tension deep in my body around public speaking. I told himself, "That's just not for me. I'm not good at it."

And this tension stayed with me for decades until I learned how to release it.

As Carl Jung is famous for saying, "Until you make the unconscious conscious, it will direct your life and you will call it fate." Now, it can be tricky to see what's blocking you because it is a *subconscious* protection mechanism. It's so familiar and known that you may just think, "That's the way things are." You may not realize it's just a story you're telling. It's a perspective that tries to protect you, but in the process, it creates tension, stress, and limitation.

Another reason you may not see your inner blocks is that you project them out onto the world, noticing what is wrong out there or with others, rather than acknowledging that this way of seeing is the result of a tension that exists within you. To dig deeper and discover what is blocking you, you have to tune in to what's underneath your discomforts and fears. As you do this, your moments of tension, discomfort, frustration, and irritation become your greatest opportunities to become aware of your blocks and consciously release them.

Let's do this as a mindful journaling exercise. In other words, write down your answers to the following. Let's do this with an attitude of mindfulness, as a curious observer.

Again, recall your answer to Question 3 or, maybe, you have new insight into what is blocking you now. What is blocking you from resolving your biggest need, frustration, issue, or challenge and experiencing what you truly desire?

Take a moment to contemplate this block and see if you can do so mindfully, by paying attention to what comes into your awareness right now, non-judgmentally—just noticing anything that arises as a curious observer.

Now, see if you can acknowledge any ways that you are attached to this block. What does *having* this block give you? There's a reason why you maintain this block. What function does it serve? What might this be? In what way does it protect you from something you fear?

Does it take the pressure off, so you don't have to change, try harder, or face your fears? For example, if you are afraid of public speaking, you may tell yourself that you are not good at it, that no one is interested in what you have to say, or that it's something others can do, but you can't. Maintaining this block keeps you safe in a small comfort zone of what you view as possible for you. Being attached to this block makes you feel safer.

The more you build up this block in your mind, the more you will justify it and find evidence for it. As you gather evidence that it is real, it becomes more substantial—and you feel safer. If you identify this block as part of "who you are," it becomes a permanent part of being you. If that's the case, you are very unlikely to overcome it.

So, take a few minutes to look at your block through the eyes of mindfulness and see how you have built it up into a "big thing" that is hard to overcome. You may even feel that you *need it* to feel safe!

Go ahead and take a few minutes to contemplate your block mindfully and ask yourself what function it serves. Write your responses to the questions above in your journal.

How Mindfulness Frees Us

If you were able to maintain mindfulness as you did the brief exercise above, you may have noticed something—you are able to stand back and observe your block without being caught up in it and completely consumed by it. You can observe your inner narrative without believing it, without buying into it. You can begin to see that these words in your mind are just ways of relating to life, they are not "*the*

58

way life is." There are other ways to look at things. This is the beginning of inner freedom.

Mindfulness changes how your brain operates by putting you into different brainwave states. It increases those associated with relaxed focus (alpha) and those associated with contemplation and intuitive insight (theta). Research shows that the " . . . co-presence of elevated alpha and theta may signify a state of relaxed alertness which is conducive to mental health."[14]

Theta and alpha brainwaves appear to " . . . correlate with the appearance of previously unconscious feelings, images, and memories."[15] Mindfulness helps you observe your experiences, and dampens reactions of anxiety, fear, and anger in the middle of your brain—your limbic or feeling brain. "Mindfulness can upgrade your internal operating system by helping to make the unconscious conscious and create the space for reasoned and skillful responses, even in the face of highly-charged feelings."[16] It enables you to relate to challenging thoughts, feelings, and behaviors by facing them directly, without "freaking out" and being hard on yourself. It enables you to approach your subconscious blocks intentionally and purposefully, with an eye to how you can gain insight that allows you to let them go. Using mindfulness, you can learn to defuse the charge of negative thoughts, feelings, behaviors, and events so they don't control you. Instead, you are able to notice them as they arise and dissolve. They are not permanent or substantial. They arise as a result of triggering circumstances and dissolve as you take action to address them, choose to let them go, or direct attention to another focal point.

The action of mindfully "witnessing" defuses the emotional charge of past experiences and recodes their memory without the emotional charge. This is why the twin skills of interoception and mindfulness are crucial. You'll recall from Chapter 2 that interoception helps you approach the subconscious, first as a sensation (rather than through our embedded stories, thoughts, emotions, and memories). Adding mindfulness to the equation defuses the emotional charge of the layered stories and the emotional escalation that comes with attachment, permanence, and identification.

Studies confirm what yogis have experienced over thousands of years, that the brainwave states associated with interoception and mindfulness initiate a cleansing or purification process in which unconscious blocks are released. This release means that you can relate to present events less reactively, in a more conscious intentional and proactive way.[17]

You'll learn more about what different brainwaves mean as we explore meditative states in later chapters. For now, understand that alpha states of relaxation and theta states of intuitive insight are opened up through mindfulness. These states support the processing of subconscious material, so it is cleared and released.

How Do You Practice Mindfulness?

OK, so mindfulness changes how your brain processes experiences, so you can relate to them differently. This can be extraordinarily helpful, especially when you come up against inner blocks. Above, you had a brief practice using mindfulness observing an inner block. Now, let's explore how to use it in the heat of a stressful or emotionally charged moment. This is when mindfulness reveals its full power. Let's try another short exercise together.

Exercise: Tracking Triggers as a Witnessing Observer

In this exercise, you'll cultivate your ability to be a Witnessing Observer by noticing and differentiating layers of sensation, emotion, thinking, behavior, and events. In other words, you'll learn to separate raw sensations from emotional reactions and mental interpretations. You'll see how emotional reactions and interpretations of sensations lead to specific behaviors and results.

Let's see how to apply Tracking Triggers when your issue or block arises. There are four steps:

Step 1. Call "Time-out" and Put on Your "Mindfulness Cap"

As a start, in highly charged moments, see if you can insert a mental pause. Consciously tell yourself, "Time-out." This stops the momentum of your mood before it can take you any farther down a dark road.

Step 2. Track Back to the Moment You Were Triggered

See if you can track down the moment you began to feel the way you do. As you do this, adopt a mindful stance, step back, and observe your inner experience. Notice the relationship between what you are thinking and feeling and outer circumstances and events.

Go back in time, noting how you felt and what was going on, until you discover the moment you were triggered. You'll know this moment because it is when you started to have a shift in feeling.

You can ask: How did I feel five minutes ago? This morning? Last night? Each time you go back, note what was happening and how you felt at that time.

As you do this, you can go back until you find a moment in which you felt good or at least a lot better or different than you do now. Then, track moments forward from that time until the moment you were triggered. This moment may stand out, or it may not have felt like much at that time. However, from that moment forward, a mood began to build. You started to see yourself and your life differently, and this feeling stuck with you until now.

When you arrive at that moment when your feeling shifted:

- Check in with your body. Focus in on what you are feeling.
- Invite the feeling to be here now. Invite the feeling to the surface.

- Feel it. Allow yourself to stay with it. Notice it. Feel it. Stay with it longer.
- You may feel yourself wanting to avoid it or judging it. Simply acknowledge when you are doing this. You may want to label it, such as "avoiding" or "judging." Keep returning to the feeling.

You may need to repeat this step if a variety of related feelings may arise.

Step 3. Reframe the Situation through the Eyes of Compassion

See if you can view yourself and others at that moment you were triggered through the eyes of compassion.

- Notice what triggered you and how this made you feel.
- Remember similar times in your life and what you learned to do to feel safe.
- Apply the same lens of compassion to others involved in the situation. How might they have been triggered? Can you see ways they were just trying to feel safe?
- Now relax.
  - Feel your feet on the floor. Sit back. Feel comfortable. Close your eyes.
  - Bring your awareness to the breath. Relax.
  - Remember a time when all your needs were met. This could be a simple time in your life when you felt peace, love, or an abundance of energy and joy.
  - Relive this experience by seeing, hearing, and feeling where you were, who was there, and what was happening. Remember exactly what it was like, slow it down, and replay it over and over again in your mind and heart.
  - Let the feeling of this experience reawaken and come alive in your body.

- o Relax into the feeling like a warm bath. Bathe in the feeling until you feel full and complete.

- Allow this witnessing presence of fullness and completeness to view the moment you were triggered through the eyes of compassion. Notice what triggered you and how this made you feel. What did you really need in that moment? What was your need? Now look at the others involved in the situation through the same eyes of compassion. How might they have been triggered? How might they have been feeling? What did they need in that moment?

Step 4. Take Appropriate Action to Resolve the Situation Skillfully

Once you've reframed how you view yourself and others, what needs to be done, if anything, to resolve this situation compassionately and skillfully? What do you feel inspired to do? Perhaps, it was enough to be able to observe the situation mindfully and let it go?

Tracking Triggers and Kevin's Dreaded Social Media Comment

A while back, I posted a comment on a Facebook community page about a meditation experience I had that day, and the technique I used when I had it. Someone replied, saying, "Some people have such big egos that they lie about experiences, making themselves seem like they are some kind of Enlightened Master."

"Wow. I didn't see that coming," I thought to myself. I was taken aback because sharing this experience was in the context of a group where we all share experiences and try to describe them to each other while sharing EEG graphs of these experiences. I felt shocked and deflated.

I went back and reread what I had written. I didn't see that I was coming across arrogantly. I had described my experience and posted an EEG graph that supported this experience, but the comment still bugged me. It baffled me, and I found myself caught up in wanting to justify to myself and to others that I really had this experience and that I had shared it appropriately.

"Ahh, don't give it so much energy and attention," I said to myself. I decided to go on with my day. I consciously set the comment aside and let it go. Yet, underneath my awareness, the comment still stuck with me. It bled over into other things that happened in the day. I had a slight edge. I continued to feel deflated, and my energy sunk lower and lower. In conversations with others, I didn't feel as open, warm, and compassionate as I like to be.

When I reached the end of the day, this subtle underlying edginess and deflated energy were still with me. I now realized that comment had, in fact, influenced how I felt all day without really being aware of it.

Just before bed that night, I called a mental time-out for myself (Step 1). I put my "Mindfulness Cap" on and mindfully tracked the feeling back to earlier that day (Step 2). Before reading that comment, I had felt great. I had just come out of a wonderful meditation session and wanted to share my experience.

As I mindfully stepped back to observe myself reading that comment, I noticed the shift in my mood. I had felt shocked and had a visceral sense of being attacked. My intention had been to share what I experienced, but I had been told that my intention was to boast—and to do so by lying.

From my vantage point later in the day, I was now witnessing that moment as an Observer. I saw myself being offended and hurt. I wanted to protect myself. I wanted to prove that I had good intentions.

As I continued to observe that moment without reacting, just noticing it, I became aware of my intentions at that time. I had been excited to share. This brought to mind other moments in my life when I had been excited to share but was either made fun of, criticized, or people just didn't get what I was saying. It was an "Aha" moment. (This is Step 3—reframing with compassion.)

The feelings of edginess and deflation had stuck with me because it had triggered past moments when I felt isolated, alone, and unaccepted. At those moments, I had identified myself as different—someone who just didn't fit in. This had become a block—thinking that I was *different* and others didn't "get me." When I saw this, I was able to feel compassion for my younger self. I realized that my younger self had learned two strategies. First, to keep to myself, not share my inner experiences, and keep my inner world protected. Second, to come across strongly about things I experienced, because I felt I had to stick up for myself.

Perhaps this came across to others as arrogance. Certainly, it was arrogance at moments when I said what I had to say in a way that made my experience the "best" or the "right" experience.

So, I looked back at how I had shared my experience that morning. As I read it back, I felt good about the intention and the way I had expressed it. In this case, I didn't feel the need to edit or apologize for coming across too strongly.

I realized that I can't be responsible for how others take what I say, only for saying it as clearly, openly, and compassionately as I can. And, when I don't, I can go back and try to do better.

As I mindfully observed all of this, the charge of the event dissolved. I saw it as a brief moment in time. It was simply an interaction that triggered associations and feelings that made this event into a "big thing" tied into a way of thinking about my "self."

The same kind of thing probably happened for the person who had commented on my post. He might have been triggered by something

I said, regardless of my intention. "I can let him off the hook, too," I decided.

Within the wide space of mindful awareness, I was no longer identified with my small sense of self who needed to be defended. I no longer felt a need to defend. As I let go of defending myself and rested in wider awareness, the emotional charge dissipated.

I was no longer stuck or reactive. I saw more clearly and felt free to express from a place of love and compassion. I felt compassion for myself and the other person.

The purpose of mindfulness is to return us to this space—this vast space of awareness, which is naturally compassionate. From here, we can more clearly choose an appropriate response.

In this case, my response was to decide to let it go. (This is Step 4-- appropriate action). In previous interactions with this person, I had found that trying to explain my side, to apologize, or ask to understand the other person better had only led to escalation. I had repeatedly noticed the same thing in Stephen's interactions with the same person. So, I resolved to let go and not interact further.

Ultimately, comments like these inspired Stephen and myself to seek third party, independent, lab validation of the EEG readings we were getting. We sought out 19-electrode professional/medical grade EEG equipment under the supervision of a doctor specializing in neurofeedback. We were happy to find our results confirmed, and we learned so much in the process. We feel gratitude to our critics for inspiring us to take this step.

Summing It up

So, to sum up, here's something you might try when you feel stuck in a negative mood or experience and can't seem to break free.

See if you can insert a mental pause, take a time-out, step back, and put your "Mindfulness Cap" on. Trace back through recent moments in time to the moment you began to feel the way you do now. To help you do this, you can keep going back until you find the most recent time when you felt better or at least different than you do now. Then, go forward to the moment your mood shifted. See what was happening in that moment. What was said or done, what happened that triggered the feeling you have?

See if you can observe this as a momentary event, rather than a chronic condition related to who you are, who others are, or how life is. Observe yourself and others in this moment with eyes of compassion. And, notice what you feel inspired to do.

Tracking a Recent Triggering Experience

Now, it's your turn. Think about a recent moment when the block you are working with was triggered and take yourself through the Tracking Triggers exercise.

1. Put your Mindfulness Cap on and recall a recent moment when you felt the uncomfortable feelings associated with your block.

2. Track back to the moment you were triggered.

3. Reframe the situation through the eyes of compassion for yourself and others.

4. Take appropriate action to resolve the situation skillfully. What do you feel inspired to do, if anything?

Now that you've rehearsed this process with a recent experience, you have a tool you can use in highly charged moments to move out of subconsciously reacting into mindfully responding. You can use Tracking Triggers right in the heat of the moment to step back and shift how you relate to what you are feeling and respond differently to what's going on.

--- --- ---

We've spent time exploring mindfulness and giving you simple steps to practice it when you feel triggered because, along with interoception, it is an essential skill on the path to raising your vibration and living from a state of Peace, Love, Light, and elevated Awareness. So, please take time to practice the exercises in this chapter. This will support your Subtle Energy Meditation practice as well.

Subtle Energy Meditation uses the skills of interoception and mindfulness as gateways to shift your state of consciousness and create a new way of being. With this in mind, it's time for the second meditation in our Subtle Energy Meditation Series.

Daily Subtle Energy Meditation Practice: 2. Five Gates of Mindfulness

The purpose of this meditation is to cultivate sustained concentration and deeper levels of mindful awareness. The Buddha said mindfulness is like a gatekeeper who grants entry into higher states of consciousness. Mindfulness guides attention to specific areas, remembers instructions, and initiates you into being awake, aware, and fully conscious of the present moment.

When you practice mindfulness, the First Gate into mindfulness and deeper states of meditation is being a witness in the present moment, observing with curiosity. The Second Gate is awareness of silence. The Third Gate is awareness of the breath. The Fourth Gate is awareness of the whole breath in every moment, sustained attention on continuous cycles of breathing. The Fifth Gate is awareness of Awareness itself. The meaning of these gates will become clearer as you practice them in the meditation.

When you pass through all Five Gates, you are able to sustain attention on one thing and hold it within the wider space of Awareness Itself. This is like a virtuoso violinist who masterfully plays his or her part while being aware of the performance of the whole orchestra. This state of being fully absorbed in sustained attention is called *samadhi*.

Practice the Five Gates of Mindfulness Meditation at least once before going on to the next chapter. Then, practice it once or twice a day until you feel confident with it before moving on to the next meditation in the series. Like the Relaxing Down Three Lines Meditation of Chapter 2, this meditation can be done at any time (morning, mid-day, or night), since it activates your natural relaxation response and supports a state of calm equanimity.

You can find the **meditation script** in the Appendices. You can memorize it, record it in your own voice, or follow along with the recording we've created, which can be found in the ROV Meditation App, available for Apple and Android devices in those app stores.

We suggest you continue to log your practice using the **Meditation Log** in the Appendices.

- For each session, log the day and time, and the name of the meditation you did.
- Add a brief description of the inner cues you found significant. (An example of this could be, "I am aware of the present moment, letting go the past and future.")
- Add a brief description of your inner felt experience of these significant cues. (An example of this could be, "I relaxed and felt the sensation of peace in my whole body.")
- Finally, rate your Energy, Mood, and Mental Clarity from 0 to 10.

Reflection & Insight Journaling

69

Take a moment to journal your response to this question: What have you learned about mindfulness that can help with your issue or block?

We suggest you continue to use your **Daily Mindfulness Check-ins** by pausing, noticing how you feel, and taking **One Conscious Breath** to refresh your state of mindfulness throughout the day. As you do this **ask yourself**, "Is it possible to look at myself, the events of life, and other people without commentary, without narrating a story about what's happening, without judgment, without labeling, and without taking sides? Is it possible to simply witness *what is*? This is mindfulness.

--- --- ---

In the next chapter, we outline the seven steps of Subtle Energy Meditation and dig deep into Step 1: Preparation of your body, environment, and intention.

4. The Seven Steps of Subtle Energy Meditation

Is it possible to cultivate your state of consciousness so that no matter what happens and no matter where you are, you feel safe, peaceful, compassionate, energized, and empowered? What we are talking about is not that you don't experience the whole spectrum of human feelings. Rather, it's how you relate to them. Is it possible to relate to all moments from a baseline of inner freedom, empowered energy, and expanded consciousness? In this chapter, you'll learn how Subtle Energy Meditation can take you there.

Over the next seven chapters, you'll discover seven essential steps to raise your vibration and live from this elevated state of consciousness in a way that fulfills your purpose and serves others. In this chapter, we explore Step 1 (Preparation), but before that, let's explore in greater detail the promise of subtle energy and the benefits of connecting to it through meditation.

Why Connect with The Realm of Subtle Energy?

There is a different world hiding right under our five senses—a realm that has a completely different feel—one that's more like a peaceful oasis, a realm of subtle energy that underlies this world.

Quantum physics tells us that the smallest particles of matter simultaneously exist as both waves of energy and points of information; as possibilities that flow into and out of existence as they are observed. They seem to arise out of a Formless Field, a Zero Point Field, and dissolve into this Field again. Reality, at the most fundamental level, exists as a Field of Potentiality, Possibility, Pure Consciousness, or Pure Awareness that gives birth to and supports Infinite expressions of Life. As we pointed out earlier, the flow of energy and information within this underlying Field is known by many different names. We will refer to it by the general term, subtle energy.

So how does this energy and information field relate to our levels of stress? When you're stressed, you're likely looking at life through the lens of your five senses, and the world seems to be rather solid and fixed. The demands you face may feel substantial. The pressure can feel overwhelming and unyielding, and your own capacities and resources can feel small and inadequate. When you have too much to do and not enough time, energy, and resources to handle it, you feel stress.

What if, on the other hand, you could see the world around you as more fluid and changeable? What if you could view your inner resources as more unlimited? What if you could perceive yourself as pure energy and awareness and the world around you the same way? What if you can change how you experience everything, so you feel safe, peaceful, energized, compassionate, connected, guided, and empowered? This is the promise of Subtle Energy Meditation.

The Promise of Subtle Energy Meditation

When you think about meditation, you might think of a technique for relaxation and focusing attention. Meditation is getting lots of attention these days for its ability to activate the body's relaxation response, while boosting mindfulness—the ability to pay attention, on purpose, in the present moment, non-judgmentally, like a curious observer.

These are indeed powerful effects of having a regular meditation practice. Practicing meditation gives you a way to release stress and become more relaxed, focused, intentional, and mindful. Through meditation, you learn to choose what you focus on and how you relate to it, so you can let go of seeing things in a stressful way and shift to feeling things from a calm, centered perspective.

These are invaluable skills. However, there is so much more available through a consistent meditation practice. Once you've learned to relax and focus your attention, deeper states of consciousness become available. You can learn to access the underlying Field of Awareness in a way that fundamentally transforms how you view yourself and how you relate to life! This is what Subtle Energy Meditation is all about.

Subtle Energy Meditation begins as many forms of meditation begin, by closing your eyes, letting go of external perceptions, and focusing inside. It then proceeds from very physical and tangible sensations such as posture points and breath awareness to more subtle sensations of subtle energy flow through points and paths within your body. It expands from these points and paths into sensing the entire energy field of your body and then into sensing the Infinite Field of energy and information within you and all around you.

Finally, it leads beyond all forms of energy and information. All forms dissolve into a formless Field of Potentiality, Possibility, and Pure Awareness. At this point, there's an experience beyond space and time, beyond the tensions of self, in a Formless Field of Being. As you rest in this Field, all the stress of living as an individual in a world of rigidly defined demands dissolves.

There is a feeling of complete freedom and ease. There is complete relief from pressures and demands. You feel as if everything is just as it needs to be.

As you rest in this transcendent realm, several things occur without effort. You naturally feel compassionate, the cells of your body resonate with this harmonious energy and begin to recover and heal, and you download information that guides you in how to navigate life skillfully. Peace, Love, and Light flow through the deepest energetic fibers of your being—and there is a Meta-Awareness that enables you to see beyond the confines of any perspective. This all happens naturally, as you attune with the underlying matrix of Pure Consciousness, Pure Awareness beyond form.

Start with Practicing Inward Sensing Daily

How can you gently ease into this Pure Awareness? It begins as you commit to a **daily practice** in which you set aside everything you think you have to do, let go of the outside world, and focus inside. If you truly want to connect with and live from this deeper state of consciousness, it takes a consistent daily commitment. Your ability to tune in to it requires the cultivation of finer inner senses—senses that are dormant if you are accustomed to only paying attention to input from your five outer senses.

During this daily practice of inward sensing, you'll need to have a quiet space, sit in a relaxed upright posture, close your eyes, and focus in on the sensations inside your body. You can begin by becoming aware of any tension in your body and using your mind to let go and relax these areas.

Next, you can focus on the sensations of breathing. A good place to do this is in your abdomen, noticing the subtle sensations of expansion and relaxation. It's important to really *feel* these sensations, as if they are the most fascinating event in the world. After all, breathing is sustaining your life. It's amazing how this happens without you having to pay attention.

However, when you do pay attention—and notice the entire cycle of your breathing, from the moment you begin to inhale, until you naturally pause, to the moment you begin to exhale, until you naturally pause—you start to feel at ease with this natural rhythm. Whenever your attention wanders, which it will, you recognize what grabbed your attention, release it, and return to feeling the sensations of breathing. As you do this again and again, you become completely absorbed in the sensations of breathing, and everything else fades to the background.

As you continue to tune in to these sensations of breathing, other sensations come to the fore. You may notice tingling, warmth, or other signs of subtle energy. As you focus in on these more subtle sensations, you notice they naturally expand to fill your entire body. You feel them throughout the entire space inside your skin. You become aware of the space around you, then of the Infinite Space extending in all directions.

As you rest in this Infinite Space, there is a feeling of complete freedom and ease, a release from the confines of self. There is complete relief from the sensation of pressures and demands. There's a natural lightness of being and a trust that all is well. You feel as if everything is just as it needs to be.

Naturally, effortlessly, Peace, Love, and Light flow through the deepest energetic fibers of your being—and there is a Meta-Awareness that enables you to see beyond the limitations of any perspective. You realize you are simply an expression of the One Life we all share. We are All One. This is the priceless pearl. You realize this is something you've always known. It's as if you've returned home.

As you continue to rest in this Infinite Space, compassion arises, as if it is just part of the nature of Reality. The cells of your body resonate with this harmonious energy and begin to recover and heal. You download information that guides and inspires you with the next steps on your life journey.

It's a beautiful state of consciousness, one you've always longed for, and now you experience it as always available—inside.

The Seven Steps of Subtle Energy Meditation

So, now you have some broad strokes about where we are headed. Over the years, we've honed in on seven steps that powerfully facilitate the process of connecting to subtle energy through meditation. In the rest of this book, we'll guide you through this process in-depth, in a step-by-step way, but first, we offer a brief overview of the Subtle Energy Meditation process, so you can get a feel for the path and the destination. Briefly, here are the Seven Steps:

- **Step 1. Preparation.** Prepare your body, environment, and intention for effective meditation.
- **Step 2. Initiation.** Initiate meditation by turning inward to activate interoception of body sensations and shift to an inner state of calm happiness using relaxation, posture, and positive energy cues.
- **Step 3. Concentration into Absorption.** Apply mindfulness to concentrate upon a focal object until you are completely immersed in and absorbed by that focal point and the effort of concentration falls away.

  For example, in the final meditation in our series, the Light, Love, and Peace Meditation (LLP), you begin the concentration phase by focusing on lower dantian breathing until you have this feeling of absorption. You then apply this concentrative absorption to cultivate Light, Love, and Peace.

  o **Light.** Focus up into the upper dantian and high above the crown, as if you are being pulled upward and "plugged in" to the energy of the Universe.

76

- o **Love**. Focus on breathing Unconditional Love through your heart and extending this Love outward to all beings and all of Life.
- o **Peace**. Focus down into a still-point in the perineum. Let go into stillness, silence, and spaciousness until you dissolve into Step 4.
- **Step 4. Transcendence**. Realization of the Universal Field, Pure Consciousness without form or content, awareness of Awareness itself, Nondual Awareness, Clear Light.
- **Step 5. Returning and Grounding**. Come back to body and environmental awareness.
- **Step 6. Reflection and Insight**. Recall important landmarks (peak felt sensations) of your meditative experience, inquire about the deeper meaning of these states, make connections, and apply your meditative experience to the events, circumstances, and relationships in your life. Keep a meditation log to record and process your experiences.
- **Step 7. Compassionate Action.** Carry your practice into the world in purposeful service.

We're going to guide you through these steps, one by one, chapter by chapter.

Step 1. Preparing for Successful Meditation

Let's dig into Step 1: Preparation. The main aspects of this step are:

A. Preparing your **body,** by building up your energy reserves;
B. Preparing your **environment** by creating a calm, peaceful, sacred space;
C. Strengthening your motivation and **intention**.

A. Increasing Your Energetic Power

Let's start with preparing your energy reserves, because to carry out these steps requires energy. If you are worn out from stress and can't imagine taking on anything more, it's going to be challenging to create something new.

So, the first step to raising your baseline vibration is to increase the overall energy you have. In Qigong Meditation (one of the primary styles of Subtle Energy Meditation, along with Kriya Yoga) the teaching is simple: **gather more energy than you expend.** When you look at this, it really is common sense. If you are expending all the energy you have, you deplete yourself. You have nothing left over. The mere thought of doing one more thing, such as taking 20 to 30 minutes to elevate your state of consciousness through meditation, is just too much.

Therefore, if you want to cultivate an elevated state of being, it's absolutely essential that you manage your time and energy output so you have a **surplus of energy**. One of the principles of Subtle Energy Meditation is to only use 70 percent of your available energy, so you have something in reserve. This surplus is what you will use to grow new possibilities or handle emergencies. Without this surplus of energy, you will always be trying to get by, trying to keep up, valiantly trying to get everything done, and trying to survive. Notice how much "trying" was in that sentence? Nothing will change without a surplus of energy to use for something new.

So, how can you create an energy surplus? Again, it's really common sense. It involves things we all know—but don't always do. The demands of the world compel us to give all our energy to work, tasks, and care for others. They push us to go against what we know is best for ourselves. The irony is that unless we take time to cultivate our own energy, we are less and less effective and useful to others and to the world. Gradually, we become depleted.

In light of this dilemma, gathering a surplus of energy will only happen when you commit to taking one or more small steps in this

78

direction every day. These little steps accumulate into large gains as you do them consistently.

Here are some simple ways to build your energetic charge. We suggest you **choose one or more that feel doable to you right now**:

1. Go to bed 30 minutes earlier than usual. Even an extra 30 minutes of sleep each night accumulates into a big energy gain over time.

2. Wake up 25 minutes earlier and center yourself using prayer, affirmations, or meditation. How do you feel when you wake up in the morning? No matter how you feel, you'll feel much better if you take the first few minutes upon waking to center your mind. What if you start doing this now, starting tomorrow? Meditating first thing in the morning is a powerful way to start your day in a relaxed, empowered, energized way. If you don't meditate first thing, it's likely it won't happen later, as you'll get involved in everything you need to get done in the day.

As a simple start, what if, as you lie in bed when you wake up, you think of what you are grateful for in your life? This instantly shifts your mood. If it aligns with your beliefs, what if you spend a few minutes expressing your thanks in prayer?

What if you take a few minutes to calm yourself by attending to the sensations of breathing? What if you find a place within you that is peaceful by focusing on sensing silence, stillness, and spaciousness inside your body? Each of these cues can take the edge off anxiety and connect you to a deeper awareness that is free from tension, worry, and fear.

What if you affirm the deeper qualities you would like to live from, such as peace, love, joy, compassion, and empowerment using simple, positive, present-tense statements. These could be, for example, "I am peaceful. I am loving and joyful. I am compassionate toward myself and others. I am guided and empowered to do what I am here to do today."

Doing any one or all of these first thing in the morning will center your state of consciousness and give you a positive reference point to start your day. This makes it easier to return to this state whenever you need to during the day.

3. Set a cellphone reminder to take a mindful pause. When you arrive at this mindful moment, check in with how you feel. Also, notice how others around you may be feeling. Then, take one conscious breath, paying attention to the sensations of breathing inside your body. Imagine your whole body fills up as you inhale, and your whole body empties out as you exhale. Consciously release any stressful thoughts, feelings, and tensions in your breath as you exhale. Extend compassionate awareness toward yourself and others.

As a suggestion, you might do this once in the morning, once in the afternoon, and once in the evening.

4. Consider everything you eat and drink in terms of how it adds to your energy and supports your health and well-being. Rather than mindlessly gulping, take your time and pay attention to everything you consume. Notice the tastes and textures. Notice how what you eat and drink makes you feel. Notice if you are eating and drinking for nutrition or to counteract something you are feeling. See if you can do this with the attitude of a curious observer.

At least once a day, interrupt an habitual unhealthy choice and choose something healthier instead. As a guideline, consider foods and beverages that are fresh, organic, moderate in size, and as close to their natural state as possible.

We both eat an organic, gluten-free diet, limit processed sugar and fried foods, don't drink coffee, and rarely have alcohol. Kevin's diet is vegetarian. Stephen has followed a primarily vegan and vegetarian diet since he was a teenager. He also, occasionally, follows a piscetarian diet, which is common living in Japan and recommended to him by dieticians there. Before any fish meal he prays "Fish of the sea, thank you for giving of yourself to me" and asks that the generations of fish before and after this one be liberated into infinite consciousness. All these habits support a high-frequency energetic vibration, as well as good health and energy.

While everyone is different, consider how what you eat and drink either supports or detracts from your health and energy, as well as how you think and feel. You can discover what works for you by keeping a log of what you eat and drink and noting your mood, energy, and mental clarity while you eat, and in the hour afterwards. Also, note how what you eat and drink affects your sleep and your meditations. Positive mood, energy, and mental clarity impact your ability to meditate effectively. In Subtle Energy Meditation, in particular, there is a sensitivity to inner sensations and a "lightness" of energy in the body that facilitates the process.

In the Appendices, you'll find a **Food & Mood Log** to keep track. We suggest you do this for at least three days to be able to notice correlations between your food, drink, mood, energy, mental clarity, sleep, and depth of meditation.

5. Consider everything you read, watch, or interact with in terms of how it adds to your energy and supports your health and well-being. Pay attention to how you feel as you consume this information. Notice the state of consciousness and mood they put you into. Notice if you are taking in this information for learning and well-being or if it is to counteract something you are feeling.

At least once a day, take a few minutes to read, watch, or interact with information that supports your mental-emotional-spiritual health and well-being.

6. Stand up and move your body once an hour. Exercise continuously for 20 minutes or more every day. Your body is made to move. Several physiological functions do not operate optimally without physical movement. Just standing up makes a difference. Even a 20-minute walk improves your health and energy. When you move, you circulate blood, which brings energy as oxygen to your cells. You improve digestion, which helps you absorb nutrients. And, you move lymph fluid, which clears toxins from your cells. Movement also stretches and warms connective tissue, which facilitates subtle energy flow. These are just a few of the benefits of exercise that raise your energy level. So, move in ways you enjoy daily.

As you commit to any one of the above, you'll find your energy level increases. You'll be on a path of managing and cultivating your vital energy, rather than overextending and exhausting yourself. With small repeated efforts each day, you'll begin to grow your energetic charge. This is your first step of preparation for Subtle Energy Meditation.

B. Preparing Your Environment

Whether it's a spare room, a closet, or a part of your bedroom, define a space that you dedicate to meditation. You can mark this space with a rug, a meditation bench, chair, or cushion. By meditating in the same space consistently, this space will come to represent "meditation" to you, and it thereby becomes a sacred space that supports you moving into a meditative state. After a period of time using this space for meditation, just sitting in this space will relax you.

To enhance the atmosphere of your meditation space you can set up a "shrine" or "altar" that represents what is important to you in your practice and your life. If the idea of having a shrine inspires you, it can take any form that pleases and motivates you. It can include photos, symbols, candles, flowers, offering bowls, statuettes, quotes, and so on. The basic idea is to put significant items here—ones that put you in a positive mindset for meditation and remind you why you are taking time for your practice. Create a sacred space.

If you use meditation to support your religious faith, place images or items that represent your faith on your altar. Kevin has symbols of several different spiritual traditions in his space to represent the Universal Spirituality underlying all faiths and traditions. He also has family pictures, pictures from Mount Kurama in Japan, and quotes that remind him of his higher intentions. Finally, he has an image that represents the Love, Light, and Peace Meditation you are going to be learning in this book in the center of the wall he faces as he meditates. Just gazing at this image supports and strengthens the felt sensations of energy flow. You can find this image on the cover of this book.

In a similar way to Kevin, Stephen has symbols of different spiritual traditions he has explored in his meditation space: a picture of Paramahansa Yogananda from Kriya Yoga initiations and the book *Autobiography of a Yogi*, ritualistic objects from his Avalokiteshvara initiation with the Dalai Lama, a heart crystal from his alchemical initiations with Tareth, and a wrist *mala* and statue of the Goddess Guan Yin riding a dragon from the Kiyomizu-dera Temple. Having objects imbued with energy and presence from various masters and teachers fills the room with an energy flow from those divine sources.

The most important quality of your shrine is that it represents what is important and inspiring to you in your practice. Meditation in your sacred space supports a meditative state by providing a meaning-filled, quiet, private, distraction-free environment. Once you've meditated in your sacred space for a while, you'll be able to take your meditation on the road and do it virtually anytime, anywhere—no matter what is going on around you. Even then, you'll really appreciate and value those times when you get to meditate in your sacred space.

C. Preparing with Intention: Knowing Your "Why"

Now, let's be honest. Especially when you're starting, you're not going to feel like meditating every day. You're not always going to feel focused and motivated. To carry you through these times and help spark the joy of your meditation routine, it's important to be clear on why you want to meditate. What is your intention for meditating? What do you hope to feel, change, or achieve?

Call to mind your answers to the Five Questions from our first chapter. No matter what you are working on, no matter what you want to create or release, meditation will help you. In fact, we would go so far as to say that meditation is the single most powerful technique you can use to recognize and release your inner blocks and grow what is most important to you.

What is it you want to release? What do you want to feel or create? How can meditation help you? Perhaps, you would like to journal your answers to these questions to gain clarity.

More Ways to Support Your Meditation Practice

1. Gently Exercise before Meditation

We both practice a series of limbering and stretching exercises prior to our morning meditation sessions. For Stephen, this takes the form of yoga asanas, Pilates, core, and energization exercises. Kevin begins with acupressure points on his head and neck, followed by rolling the soles of his feet on tennis balls, a stretching series for his whole body, and a face and head massage with cold water to wake up his brain, stimulate the vagus nerve, and promote circulation. He then does a Qigong movement sequence and Standing Meditation practice to open energy channels and prepare his body to feel the flow of qi more deeply.

While these are exercises traditionally suited to meditation, any form of mindful movement you enjoy will work. Many people like to take a walk, jog, or bike ride in nature to prime their body for meditation. Movement releases tension, stimulates circulation, releases endorphins, and prepares your body to relax and concentrate. Practicing mindfulness as you move, by paying attention to the felt sensations of movement, is a way to prime your mind for concentration in meditation by using an interesting, dynamic focus.

2. Create a Ritual Routine around Your Practice

Set a regular time for your meditation and a consistent routine that moves you into your practice.

To give you the best opportunity to practice consistently, make it a part of an established routine that you already do. For most people, the best way is to integrate meditation into their morning routine. This starts your day from a relaxed, clear, present, intentional perspective—and it ensures that you meditate before other events in the day get in the way.

Once you've decided on the time you will meditate, plan your day accordingly. If you are meditating first thing in the morning, make sure you go to bed early enough, so you can comfortably wake up early enough to practice without rushing. Set your alarm for an hour that gives you plenty of time to do your practice before you have to attend to the demands of the day. Consider practicing on an empty stomach as this facilitates undistracted focus.

Once you get up, design a routine that moves you into your practice. As mentioned above, we both follow a set series of gentle exercises to prepare mind and body for meditation. Having a routine that includes how you wake up makes the movement into your practice seamless and reliable. Over the years, we have both adapted and grown our routines as our needs, insights, and new learning have guided us.

The basic idea of having a ritual sequence makes waking up something you look forward to. It makes moving into your practice easy, natural, and enjoyable. As you include preliminaries that feel good and you groove your ritual routine, you'll find you look forward to waking up. You'll find you can't wait to revisit the good feelings of your preparation and your practice. Meditation will become one of the most treasured moments of your day.

No matter how you feel when you wake up, your ritual routine and practice sequence will shift your inner state into one of relaxed, positive, clear focus, and elevated Awareness. This a great state to be in as you start your day and a reference point that you can bring with you and return to anytime you need.

3. Create a Good Mental Space for Meditation

Kevin asked one of his students how his meditation practice was going, and he said it was a struggle. When Kevin questioned him further, the student said the road noise bugged him, his back hurt, he was sweating from the summer heat, and his mind was distracted by everything he had to do. Nevertheless, he sat there, agitated, and pushed through to complete his 20 minutes. Not an enjoyable experience.

Perhaps, you've had similar experiences trying to meditate? This student's experiences prompted a discussion about setting up for success. Kevin talked about putting a comfortable chair in his downstairs area, which is quieter and cooler. He also suggested that the student do a short exercise called "Shaking Your Body" to release tension, become "present in his body," and feel the sensation of vital energy before sitting down. He agreed these things would make meditation easier and more enjoyable.

As another example, Stephen does yoga and sings, chants, or repeats a mantra before meditating. The vagus nerve, which works through the parasympathetic nervous system, is connected to the vocal cords, and humming mechanically stimulates it. Repeating the sound "OM" before meditating stimulates your body's relaxation response, which supports a meditative state and boosts your health and immune function.

Consider finding an uplifting hymn, chant, or mantra you deeply connect to and use this to center yourself, define a sacred space, and inspire a feeling of awe and reverence that puts you in the right mental space for meditation.

Daily Subtle Energy Meditation Practice: 3. Seven Blessings

With the preceding preparation tips in mind, it's time to introduce the next meditation in our series, called "Seven Blessings." The purpose of this meditation is to cultivate postural alignment, spinal energy flow, and subtle energy awareness. We do this by applying interoception and mindfulness to concentration on the seven spinal energy centers or chakras.

What inhibits postural alignment is tension along the spine. This tension relates to issues stored in the seven chakras. So, in this meditation, we bring mindful awareness to the spine and note what arises at each chakra. We then bless the seven chakras by bringing liquid light, primordial sound, and the awareness of space to each one.

We recommend doing this meditation first thing in the morning or midday, but not at night, as it can be quite energizing. If you would like to do a second meditation at night, we suggest either one of the first two meditations in our series, "Relaxing Down Three Lines" or "The Five Gates of Mindfulness." Whenever you choose to practice, it's important to become familiar with this meditation before moving on to the next meditation in the series. The more you practice it, the better. You will become more adept at feeling the sensations as you go along. And, don't worry if you don't experience every cue just the way it's described or don't "get it" perfectly. Just follow the cues and do your best. Your inner sensing skills will grow through consistent practice over time.

You can find the **meditation script** in the Appendices. You can memorize it, record it in your own voice, or follow along with the recording we've created, which can be found in the ROV Meditation App, available for Apple and Android devices in those app stores.

We also suggest you continue to log your practice using the **Meditation Log** in the Appendices.

- For each session, log the day and time, and the name of the meditation you did.
- Add a brief description of the inner cues you found significant. (An example of this could be, "Become aware of all seven chakras at once, like a string of pearls from the base of your spine through the top of your head.")
- Add a brief description of your inner felt experience of these significant cues. (An example of this could be, "I felt an electric sensation up through my whole spine.")
- Finally, rate your Energy, Mood, and Mental Clarity on a scale from 0 to 10.

Reflection & Insight Journaling

What actions are you ready to commit to that will support you to have a surplus of energy? What can you eliminate that is draining your energy? What have you learned in this chapter that will help you in Step 1 of Subtle Energy Meditation: Preparation of body, environment, and intention?

We suggest you write down in a few sentences how meditation will support you to grow what is most important to you and release what is holding you back. Place this next to your bed, so you can review it first thing when you wake up in the morning to inspire your meditation practice. This can become part of your morning Ritual Routine after you Check-In by taking **One Conscious Breath.**

--- --- ---

In the next chapter, you'll learn the Step 2 of the Subtle Energy Meditation Process: Initiation. After good preparation, you initiate meditation by 1) Consciously relaxing, 2) Aligning your posture, and 3) Generating positive energy. We look forward to meeting up with you in the next chapter after you've taken time to practice the Seven Blessings Meditation. Enjoy your practice!

5. Relaxation, Posture, & Positive Energy

Stress Is an Inside Job

If you're like most of us, you probably relate the stress you feel to all the demands in your life. You've got work and family responsibilities, endless to-do lists, countless emails, texts, and social media invitations to respond to, as well as a constant bombardment of information, noise, and expectations of others all day long. If you are trying to counter this with a little self-care, by meditating, exercising, eating well, and giving attention to your spiritual life, these might feel like additional burdens on top of everything else you have to do.

No doubt, life these days is moving at warp speed and intensity—and it takes a strong committed effort to manage your time, energy, and resources, so you don't get overwhelmed and swallowed up by it all. However, did you know there's one key factor that is creating the stress that you feel? Learning to master this one simple thing will release you from the mountain of pressures that are weighing down on you.

Here's a psychological definition of stress that helps us understand what this one thing is:

"Stress is the perception of a threat combined with the perception of your inability to handle that threat."[18]

Basically, what it means is that the stress you feel is an "inside job." The stress you feel is not so much about what is happening "out there" in the world around you as it is about how you are relating to all of that—how you are perceiving what is happening. The **thoughts, feelings, and behaviors** that you are caught up in at any given moment determine the amount of stress that you feel.

For example, if you perceive something as a threat to your health, well-being, and success, and you doubt if you have the time, energy, skill, or resources to handle that, you'll feel stress. If you are looking at what you're facing as a "should" or "have to," you'll feel more stress about it. If you are looking at events, other people, or yourself and thinking that those events, people, or you "should be different," you'll feel stress. If you feel that what is happening is beyond your control, you'll feel stress. And, if you look at the challenges you're facing and think that you have to do it all on your own, all by yourself, you'll feel more stress.

In contrast, when you look at the challenges you're facing and think, "I have what it takes to handle that," "I can't wait to get to it," "Everything is set up perfectly for what needs to happen," and "I have abundant resources to handle this," you'll feel relaxed, positive, energized, and empowered to tackle those challenges.

So, the bottom line is this: **How you are thinking about the demands you are facing makes all the difference!** If you can look at what is happening in your life from a relaxed, empowered perspective, you immediately shift how everything feels. You are instantly able to think more clearly, be more productive, and enjoy your life more!

In 1975, Dr. Herbert Benson, M.D., released his groundbreaking book *The Relaxation Response*. He defined the relaxation response as a physical state of deep rest that changes your physical and emotional responses to stress, and he designed a simple meditation to elicit this response. Benson had people sit still in a comfortable position, close their eyes, relax their bodies, and breathe through their noses, silently repeating the word "One" with each exhale for 10 to 20 minutes.

Sounds pretty simple, doesn't it? Well, it is simple, but that doesn't mean it's easy. For many people, the simple process of sitting still and quiet, while sustaining a focus on breathing with "one" in mind quickly becomes very challenging.

At first, most people notice just how busy and distracted their minds are. It seems impossible to ignore distracting thoughts; they find themselves just sitting there worrying and/or wondering how this is supposed to be relaxing, calming, and quieting for their mind. Many people give up on meditation before they get far into it, thinking that they just aren't good at it or that it's just not for them.

As we've taught meditation over the years, we've discovered this is quite a common experience. Because of this, we've found most people do best following guided meditations, especially at first. In a guided meditation, you follow along with audio instructions, which helps you stay on track through your practice session. We've designed the progressive series of eight guided meditations that accompany this book and recorded them with that in mind. So far, we've introduced you to the first three of these.

Witnessing Responses to Stress: Our Experiences

Learning to consciously activate your body's relaxation response and observe the many different events that are happening in your mind and body are the first skills you develop as you practice meditating. So, how have we witnessed this for ourselves?

Kevin: I use the felt sensation of relaxing down through my whole body (like the feeling you have at the end of the guided meditation "Relaxing Down Three Lines") as a felt reference point throughout my day. Because I've practiced maintaining this inner sensing of my whole body, I can then notice when there is any change in this inner body sensation, observe its source, and take action to address what I need to do before I get dragged into a full-blown stress response. Having practiced this relaxed inner sensation for years, it is now part of my baseline state, as well as a go-to way to return to calm clarity.

Stephen: I use mantras during the day as a way of guiding my consciousness into relaxation anytime I sense the need. I especially like the Heart Sutra mantra, *"Gate gate paragate parasamgate bodhi swaha,"* which relates to an enlightened consciousness beyond the tensions of this world to remind me that we can carry the heart of relaxation within everywhere we go. The words of Avalokiteshvara (Guan Yin) from the Blessed Mother's Heart of Wisdom Sutra instantly trigger me into a slower breathing pattern that I practice whenever I say this mantra. This breathing pattern, along with the meaning of the words, initiates my relaxation response, and soothes away any feelings of stress.

How Stress Affects Your Body and Mind

Now, let's look a little more deeply into your personal responses to stress. By becoming conscious of your stress patterns, you can recognize when they are active and take steps to handle them gracefully. You can learn to achieve a state of balance in which you engage in optimal levels of challenge, novelty, and change without putting yourself into overwhelm by taking on too much.

Let's begin by briefly exploring the physiology of the stress response, and then we'll discuss some common ways that people cope with stress—some constructive and some, not so much.

When you perceive or imagine a potential challenge, demand, or threat, your hypothalamus, your brain's main switch for the stress response, signals your sympathetic nervous system to ramp up to meet the challenge. Your sympathetic nervous system does this by adjusting several physiological functions. Your heart rate elevates to pump more blood to your extremities. Your breathing becomes more shallow and rapid. Your blood pressure increases as blood is shunted away from your internal organs to your arms and legs.

As long as you perceive that you are facing a demand, danger, difficulty, or pain, your adrenal glands secrete corticoids (stress hormones), which help you gear up for the threat. At the same time, these hormones inhibit digestion, reproduction, tissue growth and repair, and immune responses. Your maintenance and repair functions shut down in favor of getting you ready for action.

This is important if you have a real, acute danger to deal with. However, if you are only imagining a threat or if you have a hyper-vigilant mindset that always sees life through the eyes of danger, anxiety, and fear, you may become locked in a chronic stress response. Chronic stress has severe consequences for your health and well-being, as well as for your mind's ability to make good decisions and stick with your good intentions. How severe these consequences are depend on which stage of stress you are in.

The Three Stages of Stress Identified by Dr. Hans Selye

In 1936, endocrinologist Dr. Hans Selye introduced the **general adaptation syndrome** to describe the three stages of stress response in the body: **alarm, resistance, and exhaustion.**[19] It's critically important that you don't let yourself get to Stage 3: Exhaustion, because it's hard to recover from this. It is possible to recover, but it will take a real committed effort—a really strong intervention on your part.

Let's explore these three stages in a little more detail. Understanding them will help you identify where you are at any given time, so that you can take appropriate action.

Stage 1: Alarm

When you first perceive a demand as a stressor and wonder if you have the ability to handle it, your mind and body go into "alarm mode." As we've touched upon, this initiates a cascade of physiological effects. These include your sympathetic nervous system activating, hormones such as cortisol and adrenaline releasing into your bloodstream, your heart rate, respiration, and brainwave frequencies elevating, muscle and connective tissue tightening, and blood shunting to your limbs for action and away from digestion and other maintenance processes such as immune response.

In addition, your ability to think at a "higher level" shuts down in favor of "survival" reactions and oversimplified "black and white thinking." Emotions such as doubt, self-judgment, fear, paranoia, and anxiety also tend to ramp up. All this happens immediately and subconsciously—and it impairs your ability to make good decisions and stick with your good intentions. When you are stressed, it's hard to resist that big piece of chocolate, bag of chips, or addictive behavior (such as obsessively exercising, checking your emails and texts, overworking, drinking, shopping, or surfing the internet).

If you end up handling the stressful situation effectively, your body returns to homeostasis (natural balance) as your parasympathetic nervous system takes over, sending a relaxation response throughout your body. This initiates a series of balancing physiological effects, including the release of good-feeling neurochemicals such as serotonin, calm coherence returning to your heart rate, respiration, and brainwaves, your muscles and connective tissue relaxing, blood returning to your digestive organs, and your immune response coming back online. Your mind returns to being able to think constructively and creatively, and feelings of confidence, self-esteem, willpower, and trust tend to increase.

This is the normal rhythm of a healthy life: you experience demands, find the resources to handle them, and then return to relaxation and recovery. **An empowered, purposeful, fulfilling life has a natural rhythm between periods of healthy challenge and recovery.**

Now, what happens if a situation overwhelms your ability to handle it? What if an experience is so traumatic that it leaves a lasting mark? Or what if stressors are so persistent and frequent that you cannot stay on top of it all?

Any situation that goes unresolved gets stored as tension in your body. This tension may go unnoticed as you move on to other events and experiences, yet it stays with you, subtly influencing how you think, feel, and behave in the future. As a situation remains unresolved and/or unresolved stressors pile up, your body moves into the next stage of stress response.

Can you think of a situation that is unresolved in your life at the moment? It could be something to do with your health, relationships, or money. These are three big ones for many people. Or it could be something else. What is unresolved in your life? What is a source of underlying tension?

Where do you feel this tension? In your gut? Your lower back? Your heart? Your neck? Your head? Just bringing awareness to this situation and seeing how it affects you is crucial. Awareness is a first step toward finding inner balance. Paying attention and gaining awareness helps you discern between healthy stress and when you need to set aside time to recover and resolve a situation. If you regularly take time for a check-in like this, you are much less likely to get pulled into the next stage of stress.

Stage 2: Resistance

In the Resistance Stage, your body fights to keep up with what it needs to do to maintain your health and well-being, as you try to handle the perceived demands you are facing and cope with stress that is stored in your system. Current research is beginning to show how stress that is not handled and resolved leads to chronic inflammation in your central nervous system that is a precursor to almost all serious and life-threatening illnesses.

In the Resistance Stage, you may notice yourself being persistently fatigued, more susceptible to nagging colds, slower to heal from injuries, and more emotionally on edge. You may find it easier to "fly off the handle," be subject to periods of "brain fog" in which you find it hard to concentrate, get caught up in cravings for salty or sweet comfort foods, and be more at risk for addictions to alcohol and narcotics that numb your feelings.

Getting some extra sleep, eating well, exercising, and consciously relaxing through activities such as meditation can help you stay afloat in this phase. By doing these activities, you can actively manage the Resistance Stage for quite some time—even for years.

If you are able to make significant life changes to prioritize your time, energy, and resources, engage in appropriate self-care steps, and take actions to resolve the perceived stressors you are facing, you can resolve Stage 2 and move back into a state of balance. By effectively handling stress, you become stronger and more stress-resistant and stress-resilient.

However, if you fail to take adequate self-care and do not resolve stressful situations effectively—and this happens for a significant period of time—you may crossover into Stage 3 of the stress response: Exhaustion.

Stage 3: Exhaustion

If you reach the point of exhaustion, you just cannot keep pushing forward. You've become depleted to the point that you must take serious recuperative measures to regain your strength, energy, vitality, confidence, and capability. At this point, self-care measures such as exercise, meditation, and eating well may just require too much effort. You may find yourself deeply depressed and unable to muster up enthusiasm for anything. You may find yourself in the grips of a serious illness, because your immune response is severely compromised.

At this point, extreme self-care is your only option. You absolutely must rest. It's essential to be kind and loving toward yourself and engage in gentle activities that nurture and heal your body, heart, and mind. Being open to receiving help and emotional support from others may also be extremely important. It becomes essential that you overcome the thought that you have to do it all on your own.

This is not a time for intense exercise, getting on top of your work, or trying hard to feel better. It's a time for quiet reflection and journaling, easy walks in nature, soothing herbal tea and healthy, easy-to-digest foods such as soups, steamed vegetables, and protein smoothies—along with lots of pure water. You may also benefit from supplements to support and heal your exhausted adrenal system.

Now, as with any system of categories, these stages are somewhat fluid. There are not necessarily firm boundaries by which you can definitively put yourself in one stage or another. However, understanding the characteristics of these stages is important, so you can identify what might be most helpful to you at any given moment in time. With this knowledge, you can take appropriate self-care steps to return to a natural balance and healthy flow in your life.

As you observe your own patterns of stress, see if it's possible to adopt a gentle, self-accepting, self-nurturing attitude—the calm, curious attitude of mindfulness that we practice in meditation. This mindfulness will help you more objectively witness your stress responses and more clearly see what you can do to manage your stress better. Awareness of your own stress patterns is job one.

It's also important to note that stress is not bad. Life is richer, more inspiring, and exciting when we face challenges and use them to grow into our full potential. A certain level of stress is positive.

However, it's vitally important to **discover your optimal levels and types of stimulation, see them as positive challenges, and balance them with rest and recovery.** This balance will vary from person to person. Some people are more geared to handle dramatic situations and spontaneous changes, while others need a little more ease and structure to feel right with life.

The very idea of balance contrasts with many common methods for handling stress. We live in a society in which we are encouraged to work harder and faster to get everything done in less time. As a result, many people bury their stressful feelings by consuming excessive alcohol, painkillers, stimulants, anti-depressants, fast food, TV, and entertainment. These strategies are short-sighted fixes that don't get to the root of the problem or begin to solve it. In fact, they make your stress worse. So, in addition to meditation, it's important to find ways to relax and unwind that don't feed patterns of stress or addiction.

How Do We Like to Unwind?

Stephen: I was involved with the entertainment industry for a long time through bands, dance, acting, and a television company. I found a way of balancing that kind of energy and stimulation with my natural need for easeful environments by becoming involved in spiritual and folk music, contemporary dance, children's musicals, and healthy lifestyle television programming. I love musicals, comedy, and Marvel comic superheroes (especially Thor), but cannot sit through horror or intense violence. I believe we all like to relax and sit down for a good movie or entertainment. So, it's important for everyone to find the optimal kind of entertainment.

Kevin: I like inspirational and comedy movies and reality shows in which people are overcoming inner obstacles and expressing themselves creatively or through physical challenges. I love to read, as well as take walks and hikes in nature. I also enjoy going out to family dinners at locally owned restaurants where there is interesting, healthy food, in a positive, uplifting environment, and where everyone knows each other's names.

What are the ways you like to unwind that feed your higher aspirations and cultivate what you want to grow in your life and in the world? As we suggested earlier, what if you view everything you do and everything you consume through the lens of what it supports in you, others, and our planet?

Tips for Becoming Stress Hardy

Researchers at the University of Chicago have found that "**stress hardy**" individuals have a proactive attitude toward stress.[20] These individuals "**view stressors as challenges and chances for new opportunities and personal growth** instead of as threats. They feel in control of their life circumstances, and they perceive that they have the resources to make choices and influence events around them."[21]

In other words, those who've become stress hardy adopt an empowered mindset and make choices to have more balance in their lives.

Dr. Herbert Benson found that in addition to having a positive outlook, stress-hardy individuals have good social support systems, engage in purposeful activities, exercise regularly, and eat a healthy diet.[22] They also have reliable ways to de-stress, which brings us back to our main subject—meditation.

Transforming Your Health, Energy, and Emotions

101

Many people come to meditation to learn how to de-stress, consciously relax, and unwind. Meditation is a highly effective tool to help you activate your body's natural relaxation response. It's a proven method to cultivate inner peace. It's also a powerful way to become more aware and accepting of yourself, others, and life in general. Yet, what if it could act on an even deeper level to transform the very structure of your body, heart, and mind?

On a physical level, what if it were possible to consciously program your genes, setting which genetic potentials were switched on and which ones were switched off? For example, what if you could switch on your genetic potential to neutralize cancer cells and stimulate your immunity in relation to any disease or virus? What if you could elevate your metabolism and increase your body's ability to burn fat and maintain a healthy weight? What if you could improve your brain function and start using more of your genetic potential?

We're not talking about gene splicing or genetic engineering in a lab. We're not talking about manipulations of genetic code that lead to unimagined and unintended side-effects. What we're talking about is optimizing your genetic code by activating and supporting the incomparable intelligence within your body, heart, and mind—which is an expression of the Greater Intelligence of the Cosmos itself.

Your Body as a Multi-Layered, Intelligent Information System

Think of your body as an infinitely complex, masterfully balanced, multi-layered, information system. Four primary types of information are transmitted through this system: nerve signals, biochemical signals, biomechanical signals, and subtle energy signals. Nerve signals are conducted through your brain, spine, and nervous system, while chemical signals are transmitted through your endocrine, digestive, lymphatic, and circulatory systems. Biomechanical pressures are transmitted through your muscles, bones, connective tissue, and respiratory system, and subtle energies flow through your connective tissue, meridians, and subtle energy centers.

Normally, all this happens beneath your conscious awareness. You just experience the surface feelings that sum up what's happening subconsciously. However, did you know you have a powerful impact on all this signaling activity by the thoughts and feelings you focus on, the food and drink you consume, and the behaviors you engage in? Have you considered the profound implications of your conscious participation or your lack of conscious participation in these processes?

Let's explore the positive role you can play in a little more detail. Then, you'll practice consciously signaling your body for optimum health and well-being using the Inner Smiling Meditation.

Two Modes of Being

In his groundbreaking book *The Biology of Belief*, epigenetic researcher Dr. Bruce Lipton describes a fascinating discovery he made with simple cells in a petri dish.[23] When Lipton introduced toxins into the petri dish, the cells would change their genetic expression into a "protective mode," walling themselves off from the environment around them and limiting their interactions with each other. When he introduced a nutritional substance into the petri dish, the cell walls opened, changing their genetic structure to a "growth mode" to absorb nutrients and engage in more cooperative interactions with each other.

He goes on to describe how, in the human bioinformation system of the body, heart, and mind, thoughts, feelings, beliefs, and behaviors alter the entire cellular environment determining if our cells are in "growth mode" or "protection mode." As a result, you feel relaxed, positive, empowered, and expansive or stressed, fearful, anxious, negative, limited, and contracted.

For example, the simple thought, "I'm no good at this" signals your body to slump forward. Slumping leaves you less space to take a full breath, so your breathing becomes shallow and restricted, and you take in less oxygen. Your abdominal space becomes cramped, which inhibits your digestion and absorption of nutrients. Your spinal muscles become lax, so lose your "backbone," your willpower, and your ability to stand up for who you are and what you desire. As a result of all of this, your mood, energy, and mental clarity dip, and you start thinking of ways to "survive" rather than to "thrive."

If this thought becomes a persistent pattern, and you are unaware of this, the associated posture chronically alters your breathing, digestion, and willpower. You lose your confidence and find it harder to be proactive with exercise, eating well, and getting the rest you need. All this compromises your energy and immunity even more and sets you up for illness and addictive behaviors to compensate for your poor mood, energy, and mental clarity. All of this makes it hard to think clearly, make good decisions, and stick with your good intentions. And, this chain reaction all started with a self-critical thought.

Further research into the phenomenon of how your mind affects your body has shown that thoughts and feelings quickly signal all the way down to the DNA level. This signaling immediately affects which of your genetic potentials are "up-regulated" or activated and which ones are "down-regulated" or turned off. When you consider that, at any given point in time, you are expressing only 1.5 percent of the genetic potentials stored in your DNA library, there is a tremendous opportunity for you to select different genetic expressions in a conscious way. You can consciously participate in switching on genes for optimal function and switching off genes for mental-emotional distress and physical disease.

Self-Generating a Positive Inner State

You can learn to send powerful positive signals through your body, heart, and mind by consciously adjusting your posture, breathing, emotions, and inner sensations to create a wave of relaxation and good feeling that affects you on a deep cellular and subtle energetic level. When you practice this consistently, you can create a baseline state of relaxed, positive, calm clarity that you can live from and return to whenever you need it.

That's not to say you will always feel the same—that you'll always feel relaxed and positive. That's not the way life works. We are made to have a variety of experiences and feelings. Life is always changing and requires many different responses. Yet, underneath it all, you can have a relaxed, positive, calm, and clear baseline state that enables you to "go with the flow" and thrive in the midst of whatever life brings your way.

The practice of Inner Smiling is a simple way to generate this state. The basis of Inner Smiling is actively self-generating a positive feeling of calm happiness in your body, heart, and mind. It begins by putting a subtle smile on your lips and then allowing the feeling of calm happiness to expand throughout your body.

Inner Smiling can lower your blood pressure, calm your nervous system, balance your hormones, and improve your brain function, while giving you a positive feeling of well-being. Generating an inner smile brings your parasympathetic nervous system online, which is your repair and recovery mode, your natural relaxation response. When your relaxation response is active, your levels of muscle tension decrease, you breathe more deeply, your digestive system receives more blood for absorbing nutrients and releasing toxins, and your immune system gets the energy it needs to function at a peak level.

These effects begin by bringing your breathing and heart rhythms into calm coherence. This, in turn, facilitates coherent brainwaves and integrated whole-brain function. As your higher-level brain functions come online, you will naturally find yourself better able to calmly observe what is happening inside and around you, make good decisions, and stick with your good intentions.

Pretty exciting stuff! So, how do you practice Inner Smiling?

Here are **four simple steps to practice Inner Smiling** anytime, anywhere:

1. Close your eyes and take several slow deep breaths, paying attention to the sensations of breathing inside your body.

2. Imagine you are breathing in and out through your heart to focus your attention there.

3. Put a subtle smile of calm happiness on your lips. Imagine and feel you are breathing calm happiness through your heart.

4. Each time you inhale, breathe calm happiness into your heart, and, each time you exhale, breathe calm happiness from your heart to every cell. Imagine and feel every cell is relaxing, opening, communicating with every other cell, and radiating pure, positive energy. Imagine every cell is smiling with calm happiness.

To help you generate Inner Smiling in your heart, and your body as a whole, call to mind someone whom you care for unconditionally, such as a parent, spouse, child, or pet. Or recall something you love to do or someone who makes you smile. Bring appreciation and gratitude for these people, pets, activities, or events into your heart, and then send this positive feeling outward into your whole body.

If you find this challenging at first, you might spend a little extra time focusing on breathing deeply in and out through your heart, while allowing any feelings of tension or irritation to dissolve in your breath, until you come to a feeling of "neutral." Then, imagine someone or something you effortlessly appreciate that makes you feel calm and happy.

See if it's possible to let go of "trying" to do anything and appreciate having a few moments of "just being." For a few moments, be grateful for what is, without striving to achieve anything. The bottom line is to allow the feeling of smiling to come easily and effortlessly, by putting a subtle smile on your lips and allowing the feeling of calm happiness to spread throughout your body.

Try this for a few moments now—and notice how you feel.

Can you imagine this positive feeling being with you consistently? What is it that interferes with this natural feeling of joyful vitality? Most likely it's how you interpret and deal with change.

Life is Movement, Renewal, and Change

Life is movement, renewal, and change. Nothing stays the same. All things arise, grow, linger, and fade. Only the time scales vary. When we stop moving, renewing, and changing, our bodies die. Each moment is new, and *you* are new each moment. Every cell in your body replaces itself every 7 to 10 years—and some renew much faster than this. Our stomach cells recycle every five days, and our skeletal cells recycle every three months. The raw material of the DNA changes every six weeks.

If you want to change the way your body, heart, and mind renews itself, you need to change your habitual thoughts, feelings, and behaviors, so you consistently send new signals to your cells. Changing the ways you interpret and respond to events in life is especially important when you feel stressed.

When events happen that feel threatening, you naturally want to stop the flow of life. You want to shut things down. You freeze or retreat. You seek refuge from the storm of emotions and try to stop them from flowing.

You may try to define things in ways that make them less scary, such as, "Life is safe if I just stick to what I know, who I know, and the places I know, instead of venturing out of my comfort zone." You may try to define yourself in ways that keep you safe, such as, "I am just not good at that, so I won't try." You define comfort zones of thinking, acting, and relating—and defend them against change. You try to keep things just the way they are.

Then, you naturally attach to these tightly defined boundaries of self, relationships, and events as if your life depends upon them. This creates tension in your body and mind. These tensions harden—and you harden to life. You lose your receptivity to change and diversity and your capacities for growth, healing, and renewal. You lose your capacity to "go with the flow."

Learning how to relax these tensions in a conscious way is the entry point to Subtle Energy Meditation, because tension is the primary cause of restricted energy flow.

The Primary Flows in Your Body

To better understand the importance of flow, let's use the analogy of blood flow. The flow of blood through our bodies is essential to life. Blood flow brings oxygen and nutrients to all our cells and clears toxins away from our cells. Without blood flow, our bodies die within minutes.

There are several events that inhibit blood flow. Stress and trauma restrict full natural breathing, leading to the constriction of blood vessels. Chronic stress, as well as toxins and certain foods and drinks, increase inflammation, which damages the walls of blood vessels leading them to scar, build up plaque, and become less flexible. Emotions such as fear, worry, and anxiety create muscular and connective tissue tension, which inhibits blood flow to muscles and internal organs, so they don't receive oxygen and nutrients and can't release toxins. These cells starve and become toxic. They are no longer able to renew and begin a slow death.

Life in our bodies requires the free flow of blood, as well as the free flow of lymph fluid, nerve signals, and subtle energy. Smooth flow is the essence of life—and tension restricts these flows. To improve flow, it's necessary to recognize and release tension and stored emotion, so these natural flows return. Fortunately, our bodies signal us when and where there is tension, so, if we're paying attention, we can take action to recognize and release these tensions.

However, for most of us, these tensions become so normal we don't even realize they are there. However, we can learn to recognize them by their symptoms.

Recognizing Tension

You can recognize inner tension from any of these symptoms:

- Muscle pain and stiffness
- Restricted movement
- Difficulty breathing
- Chronic fatigue
- Headache
- Congestion
- Indigestion
- Chronic illness
- Emotional overwhelm
- Brain fog and confusion
- Anxiety and worry
- Angry outbursts, agitation, irritation
- Harsh judgments of self and others
- Depression
- Feeling stuck
- Addictions
- Repeated poor results in your life, such as finances or relationships

Now, you might look at this list and say, "That covers just about every problem I could have. Can these all be related to tension?" The answer is, "Yes." Tensions in your body, mind, and emotions inhibit the smooth flow of blood, lymph, nerve signals, and subtle energy—and this contributes to all the above.

So, how do you recognize and release tension? Here is a simple but powerful process to work with tension and stress the moment you notice discomfort. We think you'll begin to recognize some similarities in these steps of mindfulness and interoception.

Steps to Release Inner Tensions

1. Pause when you notice any of the above, any sign of tension, distress, irritation, or discomfort.

For a moment, see if it's possible to let go of fear. For a moment, see if you can let go of catastrophizing what's happening and making it bigger. For a moment, let go of any stories your mind wants to tell about where these symptoms will lead.

2. Mindfully pay attention to the sensations inside your body. Notice the felt qualities. Is the discomfort located anywhere specific in your body? Does this area have a shape, size, color, texture, sound, and intensity? See if you can do this with curiosity and without judgment.

3. Allow a sense of space to surround the area. Gently allow a compassionate spacious awareness to surround the tense area embracing, infusing, and soothing it. Allow this space to expand in all directions, so the space feels large, and the area of tension feels small. Imagine this space radiates calm happiness and compassion.

4. From your point of view within the spacious area, **ask the tense area if it has anything to tell you.**

See if you can just float this question, listen, and feel without rushing to have an answer. Notice anything that arises, whether it's a thought, feeling, image, or sensation.

5. Breathe through the tense area. As you inhale, imagine and feel as if you are breathing love and compassion into the tense area. As you exhale, imagine and feel you are releasing the tension out of your body.

Continue breathing in this way until you have insight, feel relaxation, and/or notice a shift in what is happening. If you get distracted, bring your attention back to the area you're focused on and notice how it feels.

--- --- ---

These steps initiate a healing process that works over time. You may need to repeat this process many times with the same area or issue, especially if the tension is longstanding or relates to a dominant thought, feeling, or belief that you've held for a long time, such as the one you are working with from the Five Questions.

As you use these steps consistently over time, your body will begin to feel looser, lighter, and freer. You'll feel more joyful, inspired, and alive! Your energy and awareness will rise. You'll find yourself flowing with life, supported and guided by the current, and able to adapt to changes fluidly and gracefully. You will naturally begin to live from an elevated state of Awareness and resonate with finer frequencies of Peace, Love, and Light for the benefit of all beings and our whole planet. (In the next chapter, we'll help you understand how to activate these frequencies.)

You might consider implementing this practice as a prelude to your daily meditation routine, so you gradually release layers of tension that have stored up over the course of your life. This way of checking in with your body fits well with a morning or evening prayer or meditation practice, as well as being effective as a time-out in the midst of challenging moments during the day.

In our guided meditations, we Initiate the meditation process (Step 2) by using a series of cues to relax your body, align your posture, generate positive feelings, and prepare for deeper states of meditation. These will also help release the layers of stored tensions in your body.

Here are our meditative cues for relaxation, posture, and positive focus.

Cues for Relaxation, Posture, and Positive Energy in Subtle Energy Meditation

1. Set up a comfortable seat in a quiet private space. A good seat height sets your hips level with or slightly above your knees.

If you are able, sit upright on the front edge of your seat with the soles of your feet flat on the ground and parallel with each other.

2. Rest your hands, palms cupped, in your lap, right hand resting in the left, with the tips of your thumbs touching lightly in a gesture of composure and receptivity.

3. Look straight ahead, soften your focus, and open your peripheral vision. Gently close your eyes and keep them still.

4. Focus down into the soles of your feet and feel the sensations of your feet contacting the ground. Allow your feet to soften and relax, imagining that your feet are melting down into the ground.

5. Focus in on your palms and fingers and feel the sensation of contact with your legs. Allow your palms and fingers to soften and relax, imagining as if they are melting down into your legs.

As your hands relax, allow your arms and shoulders to relax down, releasing any tension in your shoulders and neck.

6. Imagine a string attached to the top of your head, drawing your spine gently upright, giving you a feeling of vertical spaciousness up through the core of your body, up through your spine, and through the top of your head. Imagine your spine is like a string of pearls or a stack of gold coins—aligned, tall, and dignified.

Tuck your chin in slightly, gently lengthening the back of your neck. Allow your shoulder blades to separate slightly and your elbows to separate slightly away from your body, as if you have wings.

7. Roll the tip of your tongue up to touch the roof of your mouth and lightly close your lips, so you are breathing in and out through your nose only.

8. Smile, a subtle smile of calm happiness.

Allow the feeling of smiling to relax your jaw and your eyes. Release any tension in your eyebrows and forehead.

Allow the feeling of smiling to wash down through your whole body, creating a positive inner environment. Imagine every cell is smiling, opening, communicating with every other cell, and radiating pure positive energy.

Go ahead and try these now. Read through this relaxation, posture, and positive focus sequence and follow along with your eyes open. Then, close your eyes and notice how you feel.

Do I Have to Sit This Way?

One of the most frequently asked questions we get about our meditation instruction is: "Why do I have to sit this way?" This is accompanied by several related questions, such as:

- Isn't meditation about what is happening in your mind?
- What does it matter if you sit, lie down, or stand on your head?
- Does it really matter if you sit cross-legged or in a chair?

- Does it make a difference if you sit back against a backrest or sit forward on the front edge of your seat?
- My back hurts when I sit that way, do I have to?

The bottom line is this: you *can* meditate sitting up, lying down, or standing on your head. You *can* sit cross-legged or in a chair. You *can* meditate resting against a seatback or not. Many people have done all these things with success. If you have a physical disability, you may *have to* meditate in a body position we wouldn't normally recommend as a general practice.

So, why do we make such a point about sitting upright on the front edge of your seat with your feet parallel and flat on the floor? The reason is this: for those who can meditate this way, there are many benefits. It may not be easy at first, but the positive results are worth the effort.

Upright Posture Supports Awareness

First, it's common to experience some back pain when you initially sit in an upright posture without back support. You may feel tension in your neck, between your shoulder blades, or in your lower back. Is this a bad thing? Why does this happen? If this is the posture we recommend, shouldn't it feel better? Isn't meditation supposed to feel good?

In our view, meditation is a complete system of personal development and spiritual transformation. Yes, it will help you de-stress, relax, and feel better—and it is so much more than this. It will help you calm your emotions, clear and quiet your mind, and connect with inner guidance. It will develop your ability to concentrate, visualize, and focus on strong intention. It will help you to be more conscious, integrated, and connected to elevated Awareness and the finer frequencies of Peace, Love, and Light. A powerful supporting factor in these results is posture training.

If you feel pain in your back when you meditate, this is most likely because of chronic tension along your spine, spinal misalignment, and/or weak spinal muscles. When you sit in an upright unsupported position consistently over time, you will strengthen your spinal muscles, release chronic tension, and come into better alignment. These postural effects will also carry over into your psychological and emotional experience.

Without sitting in this way, you may not be aware of your weak muscles, chronic tension, or misalignment. The posture cues bring these to the fore. As you become aware of tension, you can consciously let it go. In this process, you'll also let go of the mental-emotional holding patterns and past pain and trauma associated with them.

When you let go of tension along your spine, your spine will come into alignment. This alignment has more than just a physical impact. Yes, your nerve signals will travel more strongly and efficiently to your muscles and vital organs, and this will benefit your health and function. In addition, as your system works better as a whole, you'll experience a feeling of inner strength and integration, mental-emotional well-being, and subtle energy flow.

As you strengthen your spine, you'll become more physically capable of holding yourself upright during your daily activities. You'll also strengthen your "backbone," your ability to "stand strong," and follow through on your intentions. These common expressions are not mere metaphors. They are based in physical-energetic sensations.

All these benefits are supported by consciously sitting upright during meditation. Sitting with an upright spine enhances your ability to mindfully observe and accept your experiences as they arise (including back pain), let go of reacting to your experiences (such as by saying, "I can't do this," or "This is too hard for me," which creates suffering on top of pain), and maintain an intention (by maintaining your posture).

Seated meditation with upright posture also serves as an important barometer for your mind-body development. If you can sit still for hours and feel blissful the entire time, congratulations, your mind-body-physical-emotional system is likely in good shape. However, as is more often the case for the rest of us "mere mortals," the tension and discomfort that arise during meditation provide important information about where our weaknesses lie and how we can address them in meditation and in daily life.

Finally, upright posture during meditation supports alert awareness. This effect of your meditation practice will carry over into your daily activities, most of which require alert awareness in an upright position. Living a purposeful, self-responsible, conscious life is supported by having an upright, relaxed, aligned spine.

So, with all this in its favor, and admitting that it takes some training to achieve, our suggestion is to sit forward in an unsupported posture for at least a minute or two at the beginning of your mediation session. Then, move back against a seatback for the remainder of your practice time. Gradually expand the time you sit forward without back support.

Posture Affects the Body, Heart, and Mind

Besides the importance of sitting upright, here are reasons for the seated posture we recommend:

1. When the soles of your feet are flat on the ground, you are energetically "grounded" in the present moment. You are ready to "take your stand" in the here and now. The energetic points on the bottoms of your feet are activated, and the meridians running from the soles of your feet up through your legs are encouraged to be open, so that energy can flow smoothly and freely. The physical vitality centered in your lower abdomen, called the lower dantian, is

116

grounded and "fed" by connection with the Earth through your legs and the soles of your feet.

2. This posture encourages blood circulation through your feet and legs. In cross-legged sitting, many people find their legs "falling asleep." Sitting cross-legged can cut off feeling and circulation in your lower body (unless you grew up sitting this way and are used to it). Many people struggle with circulation in their legs already; there is no need for meditation to exacerbate this problem.

3. Having your feet aligned with your knees and hips is a biomechanically healthy position for your muscles and joints. Cross-legged sitting can over-stretch the muscles on your inner thighs and over-tighten the muscles on the outside of your hips. This can lead to chronic misalignment, tension, and pain, especially if you did not grow up sitting this way. Sitting in a chair with your feet, knees, and hips in alignment encourages good biomechanics and minimizes muscle and joint pain. Your feet, ankles, knees, hips, and lower back will thank you, especially as you grow older.

As a case in point, many years ago, Kevin had a client who was a well-known yoga guru who suffered from lower back and joint pain in his hips and knees because of prolonged sitting in a cross-legged position for many years. These were relieved as he did complementary stretching and strengthening and began sitting in a chair during meditation.

Your body is the vessel for your life journey. Contrary to thought in some spiritual traditions, it is not a hindrance to be avoided or escaped. Instead, your body is a sensitive instrument through which you can realize your full physical, emotional, mental, and spiritual potential.

The Buddhist teacher Naropa said, "The right physical posture is crucial to meditation" and it should be trained so that it becomes "comfortable, loose, and light," as then the body's natural channels and energies reach their natural condition.[24] If we meditate with poor posture, our mind will be distracted and it will be difficult for attention to stay still. If we meditate with a straight spine and still body, then our mind naturally becomes quiet.

In summary, maintaining an upright spine strengthens the spinal muscles, while supporting alert attention and the will needed for focused attention. Relaxing while maintaining an upright spine releases chronic tension and brings the spine into alignment. This relaxation enables the smooth and full transmission of nerve signals along the spine, through the three brains, and out to all your internal organs.

Enlightenment is a whole-body experience. Through attention to conscious relaxation, posture, and positive energy, you initiate effective meditation that leads to insight, discernment, and concrete feedback that inform your spiritual growth. You can take care of your body and enhance your evolution by being mindful to notice tension and consciously relax, while noting posture and returning to upright alignment and calm happiness, in meditation and throughout your life.

Daily Subtle Energy Meditation Practice: 4. Inner Smiling

The Inner Smiling Meditation helps generate a positive inner state and the health of your internal organs. In this meditation, you put a subtle smile of calm happiness on your lips and imagine a radiant spiritual sun shining down upon you. You combine the feeling of smiling with this warm, radiant, spiritual energy and allow it to flow like liquid light down three paths through all your internal organs and spine. You then experience yourself floating in an Infinite Sea of warm, smiling, liquid light.

The purpose of this meditation is to support the healthy function of all your cells and to train a calm, happy baseline state that you can live from and return to whenever you need. We think you're going to love how this feels!

This is a wonderful meditation to do first thing in the morning to start your day in a relaxed, positive inner state, as well as a good one to do in the evening to release stress and wind the day down.

You can find the **meditation script** in the Appendices. You can memorize it, record it in your own voice, or follow along with the recording we've created, which can be found in the ROV Meditation App, available for Apple and Android devices in those app stores. In the Appendices, you'll also find graphics to help you visualize your internal organs.

We suggest you continue to log your practice using the **Meditation Log** in the Appendices.

- For each session, log the day and time, and the name of the meditation you did.
- Add a brief description of the inner cues you found significant. (An example of this could be, "Smile into your heart. In your heart, this warm smiling energy becomes the color ruby red, a radiant ruby red.")
- Add a brief description of your inner felt experience of these significant cues. (An example of this could be, "I felt my heart open, soften, and glow with calm happiness.")
- Finally, give a rating of between 0 to 10 for your Energy, Mood, and Mental Clarity.

Reflection & Insight Journaling

What did you notice when you practiced the Inner Smiling cues for positive energy? Did you have any resistance to Inner Smiling? What might happen if you allowed yourself to be peaceful, calm, accepting, grateful, and happy? What would you need to let go of to allow yourself to feel calm and happy?

Where do you tend to store tension in your body? Is it in your jaw, neck, shoulders, hands, feet, lower back, abdomen, or elsewhere? What are some of your posture habits? How do these tensions relate to the issue you are working with from the Five Questions?

--- --- ---

In our next chapter, you'll learn Step 3 of Subtle Energy Meditation. After Step 1: Preparing your body, environment, and intention; and Step 2: Initiating meditation using relaxation, posture, and positive energy cues , you're ready to discover the power of Concentration to calm and focus your mind and activate the finer frequencies of Peace, Love, and Light. We look forward to joining you there after you've taken the time to practice the Inner Smiling Meditation.

Enjoy your practice!

6. Cultivating Concentration into Absorption

Why Your Ability to Focus Matters—And How to Improve It!

Do you find it challenging to stick with your good intentions or to filter what is really important from the sea of information that floods your senses and demands your attention every second? Do you find your ability to focus and remember isn't what it used to be?

You may have heard the idea that the average attention span is shrinking—that the average person pays attention to any one thing for only eight seconds before switching attention to something else. It's claimed that the average attention span has shortened from 12 seconds not so long ago. You may have heard that entertainment producers and advertisers know this and switch camera angles and breadth of focus every eight seconds to keep your attention. These "facts" are cited as evidence that your attention being pulled in different directions by technology and social media is damaging your ability to pay attention in a fundamental way. That may be so.

But the real issue is not whether your attention has a span of 8 seconds, 12 seconds, or 20 minutes. The real issue is control. It is "who or what" is controlling your attention and for what purpose. That may sound conspiratorial, but it's important to understand how this relates to the stress you feel and to what is blocking you from what you want to accomplish. What you focus on and how you relate to it determines the experiences you have.

Your ability to focus your attention on purpose is the most important inner skill you have.

You may recall from Chapter 3 that intentional focus contrasts with what your mind tends to do when you aren't intentionally focused, which is to wander to self-referential thoughts about yourself, your experiences, and your relationships with others. "Self-referential mind wandering" activates what is called the Default Mode Network in your brain. The DMN activates when your mind wanders in meditation, or when you daydream or ruminate. This contrasts with mindfulness, which is paying attention, on purpose, in the present moment, non-judgmentally. Mindfulness activates the Executive Control Center of your brain, which relates to intentional focus and choice. When meditating, there is a switching between mindfulness and the DMN until attention becomes fully absorbed in focused concentration.

Focused attention, or concentration, is an essential skill you can cultivate. To cultivate focused attention requires adopting a specific attitude and following known steps. This skill enables you to focus on what is most important, stick with your intended focus, and let go of the rest. Training your attention is the heart of any meditation practice. Training relaxed, focused, flexible, integrated, and conscious attention is the goal of Subtle Energy Meditation.

Training your attention through meditation has wide-ranging benefits, because regular meditation enables you to make long-lasting, positive changes in the neuronal pathways of your brain. These benefits can include:

- Getting better at holding your attention in the present moment.
- More detailed processing of sensory information.

- Better self-regulation of your autonomic nervous system and less stress.
- Becoming more intuitive and self-aware.
- Protecting against age-related memory loss and loss of brain function.
  25

In addition to these thoughts about the wide-ranging benefits of training attention using meditation, what does cognitive science tell us about our ability to pay attention on purpose? A prevalent model of attention from cognitive science describes two different ways the brain processes information—automatic and controlled. This is called the "dual processing model." When it comes to attention training, it is controlled processing that is responsible for self-regulation. So, after Preparation and Relaxation, the next step in meditation is about Concentration—controlling where you place your attention and sustaining it there.

Life on Automatic in a World of Distraction

While you may think you are generally in charge of your attention, for the most part, your attention is moving from one thing to the next as prompted by your environment, your schedule, and your routines. This is your brain in automatic mode, and as the name suggests, automatic processing happens without conscious effort. You react to what is happening inside and around you subconsciously, simply following learned habits. You wake up to your alarm, which initiates a morning routine. You don't have to think about how to brush your teeth, shower, get dressed, make breakfast, or drive to work because these are automatic behaviors that are well-grooved. You probably follow a pretty set sequence of these behaviors without giving them much thought.

There is an energetic value to having routines. They don't require conscious attention, so they are not "cognitively expensive."[26] In other words, they don't require a lot of energy. Automatic routines, however, also have their pitfalls. You probably don't remember most of what you do automatically, it doesn't deeply engage you, and these moments lack creativity and intention. They just happen to you and life passes by. Life on automatic is simply a reaction to subconscious internal and external cues.

If most of your life runs on automatic, you'll get stuff done, but life will feel repetitive and not particularly meaningful. Nothing will change, because you are simply repeating the same thoughts, feelings, and actions that give you the same perceptions of life and the same results. If your life is driven by automatic reactions to your environment, things also tend to get stressful, since what you attend to is outside your control. Your attention is driven by subconscious programs related to all the stimuli around you (work and family demands, social media prompts, news, advertising, noise, traffic, etc.) rather than being a conscious and intentional allocation of your time and energy. Furthermore, the stimulation and demands are not going to stop coming at you. You're not going to wake up one day with everything completed. So, you have to learn to take charge of your attention in the midst of all this busyness.

An Intentional, Purposeful Life

Fortunately, focused attention is a real skill you *can* learn. In fact, it may be the most important skill you can learn. And meditation is *the practice* dedicated to training your attention.

If you haven't consciously trained your attention in any disciplined sort of way, it can be a real eye-opener. When you're accustomed to running around on automatic, you're not fully aware of what you're doing. You may not be able to locate exactly where your attention is and why it's there.

Initially, it can be a real challenge to become aware of the automatic thoughts, feelings, and reactions that occupy your attention most of the time. It requires stepping back and observing, which is quite a different perspective. When you first start to pay attention to exactly where your attention is, it can feel overwhelming. Your attention can feel out of control—which, as a matter of fact, it is! Your mind goes from this thought, to that feeling, to some sensation in your body, to that person talking, to this advertisement, to the thunder in the sky.

When you first sit to meditate, it may feel a lot like that. For the first time, you may become aware of just how much is going on in your mind—and how random it is! You have probably heard the term "monkey mind" to describe this experience. Monkey mind is your attention on automatic, jumping from this point of interest to that, prompted by what's going on inside and around you. Monkey mind can feel pretty daunting because it feels like your mind has a life of its own, and it's taking you along for a wild ride. This is the DMN at work.

To get over this initial hurdle, you're going to need some powerful motivation. Gathering this motivation is the purpose of asking the Five Questions in Chapter 1. To generate the necessary enthusiasm, we want you to think about why you are reading this book and what you hope to gain from it. Remember your answers to the Five Questions or refer back to your Journal to find them.

To achieve any goal requires focusing your attention on what is most important to you and letting go of the rest. You have to learn to say "yes" to what is most important and "no" to the thousand other things that could occupy your attention. To overcome life on automatic, you've got to grow your ability to choose where you place your attention and sustain it there. To sustain attention requires energy and practice. It requires a simple technique and the right attitude. It's going to require a concerted effort on your part. However, rest assured it will be worth your effort. The steps are time-tested and well-defined. They are the steps, skills, and attitude you're learning in Subtle Energy Meditation.

Do You Know Where Your Attention Is?

The attitude for training attention is mindfulness: paying attention, on purpose, in the present moment, non-judgmentally—like a curious observer. Why is this important? It's important because mindfulness is what enables you to know where your attention is, and to be kind and gentle with yourself when you notice your attention has wandered off to some automatic thought, feeling, or behavior.

For example, let's say you want to start eating more veggies but find yourself magnetically drawn to a bag of chips. Moments like this are going to happen, especially if you're stressed or tired. The question is not if this kind of thing is going to happen, but how you respond when it does. You need to have a game-plan.

If you practice mindfully pausing to remember your "eating more veggies" intention and *why* it is important to you, rather than being sucked into an automatic, biochemically-induced behavior, you improve your chances of staying on track. Knowing and deeply feeling *why* you want something gives you the energy and motivation to make the effort.

The more positive emotion you associate with what you want to create or achieve, the more you'll feel drawn to it versus some other choice. Again, we come back to taking time to imagine what you want and how it will feel to have it. What difference will it make in your life? How will this feel? Strong emotion recruits and grooves mental-emotional circuits in your body and brain that support your new choice. The stronger your felt sense of "why," the more you feel the urgency of it, and the greater your chances of sticking with your good intention.

How Stephen's Journey with Mindful Practice Began

When I was 13 years old, my father, Derek, saw me practicing yoga one morning. Our interaction went something like this:

"What are you doing?" my dad asked.

"Yoga," I replied.

"What good is it going to do you?" said my dad.

"It's going to keep me healthy, young, fitter, and more flexible for longer."

"You'll have to keep doing it for a long time!"

"I'm going to!"

"Bet you won't."

"Bet I will!"

"How long?"

"Till I'm 90!"

"$1 says you won't."

"You're on!" I said.

My strong and sure intention was supported by this familial banter and the friendly sporting rivalry that I always enjoyed with my father. It helped bring forth my life-long practice of daily yoga. My daily practice continues to this day, some 45 years later.

The 3Rs of Focusing Attention

Stephen's story reminds Kevin of his "no muscle" experience in the school hallway that sparked him into life-long strength training that continues to this day. If you're lucky enough to have one of these "flip the switch" moments that is strong and lasting, that's great. Use it to your advantage.

However, if you don't have one of these "Aha" launch-points, you're going to need good strategies to keep yourself on track with your practice, especially when you're feeling stressed or worn out. At these moments, you'll likely choose the path that requires the least effort—which is most likely falling into an automatic habit that isn't good for you, rather than sticking with your good intentions.

To do something different in challenging moments requires more than just knowing what you want and feeling how good it will be to have it. You've got to train your attention to heightened awareness and establish a new routine that supports your new habit. You've got to establish attentional control.

You can train your attention using the 3Rs: Recognize, Release, and Return. Here's how this works: Whatever you want to create in your life requires repeatedly directing energy and attention to it for a period of time. During this focused time, you commit to doing this one thing and let go of everything else. You consciously and intentionally focus on what you want to achieve. You've got to do this if you want to create something new. There is just no way around repeated, sustained focus when you are trying to overcome life on automatic.

In this book, we're focused on learning and growing the skills of Subtle Energy Meditation. Meditation itself is the single most effective way to train your attention, and Subtle Energy Meditation trains you to have calm, focused, flexible, integrated, and purposeful attention within a high-vibration state of consciousness. If you really want to learn this—if you really want to raise your vibration and live in a state of Peace, Love, Light, and elevated Awareness—you're going to need to commit some time to this every day.

At the beginning, it's best to commit to a minimum amount of time that feels very doable. If you go longer, that's great, but commit to a minimum amount of time and schedule it. Scheduling is essential, because, otherwise, countless other demands for your attention will get in the way. Scheduling is part of good preparation.

You also need to define what you are going to do in a specific way. What will be your routine? If you don't define what you're doing, your attention will wander. So, it's essential to know the sequence of inner cues, the sequence of meditation prompts, that you'll follow. In this book, we provide eight specific meditation sequences. (You can find these scripts in the Appendices.) We've also created guided meditation audio mp3s (so all you have to do is push "play" and follow along).

When you arrive at your scheduled time to meditate, first call to mind *why* you want to meditate. Use this intention to focus your energy and attention. Then follow the specific steps of the meditation sequence you are practicing that day.

As you focus on being mindful during meditation, you'll notice moments when your mind drifts off to something other than your focal object. This drifting is going to happen. When it does, practice the 3Rs: **Recognize** what grabbed your attention, **Release** this, and **Return** to your chosen focus.

To do this requires energy and effort. You will have to bring your attention back to your chosen focus many, many times. This is normal. Attention wanders and gets pulled away. Our minds work by association and can be triggered by a multitude of internal and external stimuli. This happens automatically, without your control. If you don't consciously take control of your attention at these moments, it's going to be pulled into automatic grooves. This is going to happen, and when it does, practice the 3Rs—again, and again, and again.

Concentration into Absorption

As you practice the 3Rs, a shift takes place.

You start to be able to sustain your attention on one thing for longer and longer periods of time. You build the neural circuits of sustained attention in your brain. This is like building your concentration muscles. Meditation is like going to the gym and working out with your brain.

As you repeat a given meditation enough times, with strong feeling and focus, your attention begins to stick to your focal object and, at a certain moment, you cross over and become absorbed in it, as if nothing else exists at this moment. Your focal object becomes so infused with energy that it becomes a magnetic attractor that draws your attention into it. Your awareness merges with the focal object and becomes "one with it." When this happens, your mind quiets, your emotions calm, and you feel the deep inner peace of being completely and effortlessly absorbed in one-pointed concentration. The effort of focusing is no longer required. Meditative absorption takes on a life of its own and carries you along.

This experience of being carried along is different from just mindlessly following an automatic routine or drifting into distraction. It is infused with awareness. You are fully present and engaged in the focal object. Your inner senses come alive. Colors brighten and details sharpen. You are in the flow. It feels magical.

At these moments of deeply felt, highly concentrated absorption, your body and brain wire new neural networks that groove your meditative consciousness, so it becomes easier to return to and deepen. As you fully engage in your meditation practice with sustained focus, energy, and emotion, a meditative state becomes something easily remembered, easily repeated, and easily called forth whenever you need it. More importantly, calm clarity and elevated Awareness become part of your normal baseline consciousness. The state of meditation becomes a trait that endures.

The Three Dantians and Flexible Attention

In the Subtle Energy Meditation system you're learning in this book, we use energetic points, paths, and fields to focus your attention, build your concentration muscles, and cultivate a higher vibration. Most people find it easiest to focus on one point or small focal area first. Then, they are able to expand their focus to include pathways between points. And, finally, they can expand the breadth of their attention farther, so it diffuses into sensing a wider field.

For example, take a moment now to feel the tip of your index finger. This is focusing on one *point*. Tune in to sensory awareness of this single point. Notice how this feels.

Now, shift to feeling the path from the base of your index finger to the tip of your finger. This is feeling the *path* of your finger. Focusing on this path includes a feeling of connection from the base of your finger to the tip of your finger. Notice how this feels. Path focus is all about feeling connections and energy flow between points along a path.

Now, become aware of the space around your index finger. This is expanding your attention to a wider *field*. It is diffusing your awareness to take in "space." Imagine and feel this space expanding in all directions, so the space is infinite and your finger is tiny within this space. Notice how this feels.

Finally, fix your eyes straight ahead and let go of focusing on anything. This is attention without a focal object, just pure attention itself, also called "Choiceless Attention," because you are not aiming the arrow of attention at anything. You are not choosing a focal point, path, or field. You are simply resting in an open state of alert, present moment, attention. This is a bridge into transcendent states of consciousness, Nonduality, and Pure Awareness beyond content or form. Much more on this in Chapter 7 on Transcendence.

Each of these types of focus has a different purpose and feel to it. One-point focus is concentrated and targeted. It is saying "yes" to one thing and "no" to everything else. Focusing on a path is connecting and facilitates energy flow between points. Field focus is widely inclusive and diffused. Choiceless Attention requires letting go, simply being present, in an open state of attention. It is a wonderful way to release from being locked into any particular thought, feeling, or focal object and transcend the tensions of self-oriented focus. We cultivate all four types of attention in Subtle Energy Meditation.

Four Types of Focus/Attention

1. Point: facilitates concentration, gathering energy in one point, and letting go of everything else.

2. Path: facilitates energy flow and experience of connections within and with others.

3. Field: facilitates experiences of inclusion, belonging, Wholeness, and spacious awareness.

4. Choiceless Attention: facilitates letting go, nonduality, and Pure Consciousness beyond forms.

So, you can see that different focal objects generate different felt experiences and states of consciousness. Different focal objects give access to different energetic frequencies and patterns that show up on EEG readings with different brainwave signatures. When you train your attention to access these different states and integrate them as part of your baseline state, you can call upon them as needed in your life. Being able to shift between focal objects, attention styles, and states of consciousness at will is one of the gifts of the practice of Subtle Energy Meditation.

You may recall from Chapter 1 we spoke of three primary energy centers in your body (which can function like *points* for meditation) and a Central Channel which connects them (a *path*). You have, in effect, three brains that work together to shape your state of consciousness: the enteric nervous system in your gut, the cardiac nervous system in your heart, and the brain in your head. We call these the lower, middle, and upper dantian, respectively.

As we said previously, both the gut-brain and heart-brain communicate with the brain in the head through the vagus nerve. The vagus nerve originates in the medulla oblongata in the brain stem. It is responsible for regulation of wakefulness, alert attention, interoception, sleep cycles, respiration, heart rate, blood pressure, digestion, and levels of tension and relaxation in the body. The vagus nerve is also responsible for the parasympathetic response or relaxation response. It is, therefore, one of the first signalers of the shift into meditative consciousness as you initiate Subtle Energy Meditation using relaxation cues.

Relaxation sets the stage for Concentration. Concentration begins with focusing on one point or focal area, expands to focus on paths between points, and culminates with more diffused "whole-field" awareness. Fields can include the field of your body as a whole, the space around you, wider spaces and regions, the field of the whole planet, the Infinite Field of the Whole Universe, and the boundless field of Pure Consciousness itself.

As we said, point, path, and field awareness each have a purpose. One-pointed concentration enables you to selectively attend to one thing and let go of the rest. Concentration on paths between points enables you to experience connection. And, concentration on Fields dissolves boundaries and tensions, so you rest in a state of Unity Consciousness or Nondual Awareness.

This ultimate state of absorption is a diffused awareness that takes you beyond concentration into effortless immersion in the Field of Being. This state is generally identified with transcendence or liberation. In this state, you are released from struggles of self-focus and experience the blissful light of Pure Consciousness. In this state, your whole brain comes into coherence. Research on this state shows a movement toward total brain function, which improves mental-emotional-physical health, cognitive function, attentional stability, and sensory acuity.[27]

These stages of concentration are enabled by the activation of various structures within the body and brain, which relate to relaxation, focused attention, and will. The famed yogi Paramahansa Yogananda located the seat of our powers of attention and will in the center of the forehead and the entrance of Universal Energy into the body in the medulla oblongata.[28]

When we also consider the location of the pineal gland, nearer the medulla, and the pituitary gland nearer the third eye, we realize how important the structure of the brain is for supporting higher states of consciousness. The pineal gland is a neuroendocrine transducer capable of receiving and converting and sending chemical and electrical signals within the body and brain. The crystals act like cosmic antennae, giving us a portal to higher dimensions. Subtle Energy Meditation activates and integrates the function of these glands, which support our resonance with higher states of consciousness.

In meditation, our three brains can be activated and used to initiate meditation in an integrated fashion, by focusing on posture cues that activate all three: relaxing the feet on the ground (gut-brain, lower dantian), then relaxing the hands cupped in the lap (heart-brain, middle dantian), and finally imagining a string attached to the top of the head, drawing the spine gently upright (brain, upper dantian).

This final cue also activates the Central Channel that runs up through the core of the body, including the spine, from the perineum to the crown point of the head. The Central Channel is the "God Cord" that integrates all three primary energy centers within a shaft of light that connects Heaven and Earth through the human body. The microcosm of the three dantians in the body mirrors the macrocosm of the Heavenly Realm, Human Realm, and Earthly Realm.

In Subtle Energy Meditation, we work with all three primary energy centers by focusing on being elevated and infused by Heavenly Light from above in the upper dantian, transformed by Love for all beings in and extending out from the Heart (middle dantian), and grounded in Peace found in stillness in the lower dantian, which connects deep down into the Earth.

Each of these energetic frequencies adds to your baseline state of consciousness (the predominant state you live from) and gives you flexibility of attention, inner skills, and frequencies you can draw upon as needed. This powerful alchemical process can transform your state of consciousness. Through this process, you raise your vibration and are reborn as a being of Peace, Love, and Light. As you do this personally, you help to raise the vibration of all, because we are all part of One Life, One Body, One Shared Heart, One Consciousness—a vast, clear space of Pure Awareness.

Here's a summary of how this process works in Subtle Energy Meditation.

Enlightenment through Subtle Energy Meditation

Attention is energy. When you focus and concentrate attention on any area, it builds an electrical charge. As this charge builds, it becomes a magnetic attractor of felt sensation that draws your attention into absorption. The stronger the electromagnetic field, the stronger the felt sensation, and the deeper the absorption.

When the spinal energies are awakened, energized, and sensed (for example, by concentrating on the three dantians and their connection through the Central Channel), the spine becomes an electric pillar, like a rod of lightning, at the core of a strong torus field. This torus field is a standing wave of enlightened energy, a microcosm of the macrocosmic Field of Being.

In the culminating meditation of our Subtle Energy Meditation series (the Light, Love, and Peace Meditation), after Step 1 (Preparation) and Step 2 (Initiation), you move into Step 3. This step is Concentration, cultivated by focusing on breathing in the lower dantian to cultivate calm, mindful, concentration to build a charge of vital energy. You then use this vital charge as a foundation which energizes the next steps of the Subtle Energy Meditation sequence.

You draw energy from the lower dantian upward through the Central Channel to the upper dantian. Here you may feel a tingling, joy, warmth, or electric charge in the center of your brain, center of your forehead, and/or top of your head. You then allow your attention to be drawn upward through the upper dantian into a column of light above your head. Above your head is an energy center, the Soul Star, which contains information about your life purpose and energy to fulfill it.

As you breath into this energy center, you feel as if you are plugged into energy from the Source of Being. This energy feels like an electrical pulse. Concentrating into absorption here allows this information to download into your subconscious where it becomes available as inner guidance and inspiration. The high-frequency energy accessed through the upper dantian activates gamma waves in the brain, which improve focus, energize concentration, and integrate whole brain and whole body function. These waves feel as if they light up your body and brain with electrical charge.

Next, you allow the energy to flow down through the Central Channel into your heart. Here you access deeper connections to others as you concentrate into absorption on the felt sense of love expanding outward from your heart to all beings and the Whole of Life and back to you. The sensation here is a nurturing warmth that expands from your heart outwards.

Next, you allow this warm energy to flow down through the lower dantian into the perineum and connect deep down into the Earth beneath you. Here you access profound stillness and deep peace in the Earth Star, an energy center below your feet anchored into the ground. This peace feels rock-solid and immutable. Concentrating into absorption deep down into stillness and Peace, you access the primordial Field of Being.

The primary vibration and sound of this Field is OM. You could liken the sound and vibration of OM to the "hum of the Universe." It is like listening to the wind or the ocean in a conch shell or the purring engine of the Universe. As you listen to and feel the OM vibration, you become more deeply absorbed in the Primordial Field of Being. Your body resonates with this OM vibration, which integrates, heals, and transforms your entire being—so you become a clear channel of Pure Awareness, expressing the primary frequencies of Peace, Love, and Light. The Raising Our Vibration image in the Table of Contents is an illustration of this result.

This state of vast, clear, Pure Awareness is the end result of the process of Subtle Energy Meditation. It is a state of total brain and subtle energy coherence that supports you living your highest potential and inner purpose. We're excited to guide you into this state and to support you in practicing it, so it becomes your resident state of being—your dominant baseline state.

The path through this whole process begins with relaxation into concentration into absorption. You can become familiar with the three dantians and practice relaxation and concentration into absorption by doing the following breathing exercise. Before you do this, we want to first acquaint you with a mindfulness technique by which you can keep track of your attention while you're concentrating. This technique is called "Noting."

Recognizing Where Your Attention Is: Applying Mindfulness in Meditation by "Noting"

Noting is a way of noticing where your attention is placed, either because you've consciously placed your attention there or because your mind wandered there. So, you can use Noting either to become more aware of a focal object or to become aware that something has distracted you from your focal object.

According to mindfulness teacher Shinzen Young: "Noting usually consists of two parts: 1. An initial noticing, 2. An intent focusing on what you noticed. This intent focusing may last from a fraction of a second to several seconds. During this intent focus phase, you intentionally soak into and open up to the thing you noted. This is traditionally referred to as 'penetrating' or 'knowing' the focus object. Thus, noting consists of a sequence of noticing and knowing."[29]

Initial noticing is simply acknowledging where your attention is placed. You can do this in two ways. Either you can just make note of it or you can consciously label it by naming it. Noting can help you focus during meditation. For example, consciously Noting "breathing sensations in lower abdomen" can strengthen your focus there. You can use this initial noticing to lead you into the second level of Noting, a more intent focusing on what you noticed by paying attention in finer detail. This deeper paying attention, this deeper concentration, is what leads you to absorption in meditation.

You can also use Noting to handle distractions in meditation.

For example, if you are meditating by focusing on the sensations of breathing, and then you notice your mind has wandered away from the breath, you can simply recognize that you are no longer paying attention to your breathing and use this as a moment to refocus on breathing. This is initial noticing without labeling.

A second option is to notice the distraction and label what is distracting you in a precise way. For example, you might have found yourself thinking about something you said to your spouse the night before. You can label the distraction by thinking or mentally saying to yourself "thought" or "thought about what I said to my wife last night." "Mentally saying" means you intone it with a calm inner voice. This calm inner voice defines your mindful observational relationship to what you notice. When you mentally say something calmly, you're telling yourself, "it's no big deal."

Labeling is a way of putting observational distance between a distracting thought, feeling, or sensation and you, the observer of that. Labeling helps you get a handle on what distracted you, so you can consciously and intentionally set that aside and return to your focal object. The key to using labeling as a helpful tool is to use it with this attitude of mindfulness, as a curious observer. You notice, "Ahh, there's a worrying thought about what I said to my wife last night" and then release it, perhaps with a mental note to take care of it later, as you return to paying attention to the sensations of breathing. This is using the first level of Noting, initial noticing, with labeling related to a distraction.

In the second level of Noting, you inquire deeper about what distracted you. You use it as a focal object and seek to know more about it. For example, you might do this with a distracting pain in your back or neck as you meditate. As you note it in the first way, "Pain in right side of neck," you decide that you will inquire about this pain, so that you can release it.

You can ask this pain, "What do you have to show me? Why are you here? What brought you about?" As you tune in to the pain mindfully, just observing and noticing what arises, it may speak to you. Or it may present you with an image or a memory. Or it may begin to dissolve.

You may feel prompted to inquire further, "Pain, what do you need to resolve? Is there anything I need to do?"

As you continue to pay attention to the fine details of sensation, you may notice shifts in intensity, perhaps up or down. You mindfully notice whatever happens, as a curious observer, watching, listening, and making note of what happens. "Pain getting stronger . . . Memory of discomfort when I said that thing in conversation last night . . . New thought: it's OK, I can call and apologize this morning . . . pain diminishing . . . warm relaxed feeling . . . time to return to focusing on sensations of breathing."

Use this second, more penetrating, level of Noting when you have a nagging distraction that doesn't release with the first level of Noting or when you're seeking deeper healing, guidance, and insight. Otherwise, in general, use the first level of Noting, initial noticing (with or without labeling), to let go of distractions and return to your focal object in meditation.

You can practice Noting in the following meditative exercise.

Practicing Concentration Using Breath Awareness & Noting in the Three Dantians

The three dantians are powerful places to focus your attention because they are each home to specific frequencies. Each has its native energetic signature, which correlates with different brainwave frequency patterns as well. As we explored these three dantians and researched EEG studies, certain patterns have emerged. Concentration to the point of Absorption in the lower, middle, and upper dantian enables us to connect with and embody the Peace, Love, and Light that is accessed through each of them, respectively.

The lower dantian is home to the vital energy derived from digestion as well as to the feeling of deep inner Peace of being grounded in the present moment. Concentration here supports relaxing alpha rhythms in the brain and even deeper theta rhythms with long-term practice. The middle dantian is home to feelings of love and compassion that come from experiencing the deep connectedness of all beings. With practice, concentration here supports delta rhythms in which we let go of being an isolated individual self and

140

empathically merge with the One Life We All Share. The upper dantian is home to high-frequency light and the guidance available from the Source of our Collective Consciousness. With practice, concentration here supports gamma frequencies of elevated energy and Awareness.

When you put this all together, you get the Light, Love, and Peace Meditation sequence that you'll be learning after completing the six Foundational Meditations. For now, let's become acquainted with the three dantians using Mindful Breathing, Noting what arises in each of these three inner zones. Remember, as you practice concentrating on each dantian, anytime you lose your focus, practice the **3Rs.**

Exercise: Breathing and Noting in the Three Dantians
Sit in a comfortable seat, with your feet flat on the floor, and your hands resting palms cupped in your lap.

Begin by focusing in on the sensations of breathing in the lower dantian. Place your attention in your lower abdomen and become aware of the sensations of breathing here. See if you can stay present with the entire cycle of breathing, so you notice the moment you begin to inhale and follow the sensations of your in-breath until you naturally pause. Then, notice the moment you begin to exhale and follow the sensations of your out-breath until you naturally pause.

Pay close attention to the felt sensations in your lower abdomen. If this is an area of issue or block, for example, if your primary issue is related to fatigue, then be mindful when fatigue arises and label it "fatigue." If sensations such as peace arise, label them "peace" or "peaceful." Otherwise, continue noting whatever arises as you continue to breathe in the lower dantian.

After you have a good feel for what it's like to focus down towards the lower dantian and have noted what arises here, shift your focus upward to the middle dantian in the center of your chest, around your heart. Imagine and feel that you are inhaling and exhaling through your heart. Notice the sensations here and how you feel as you focus in on the area of your heart. Mindfully pay attention to whatever arises.

If this is an area of issue or block, for example, if your issue is related to frustration in relationships, you may notice uncomfortable sensations and related thoughts, feelings, or memories. See if you can note these mindfully, as a curious observer—without being swept up in any drama—just noticing, noting, and letting go.

After you have a good feel for what's it's like to focus in on the middle dantian and have noted what arises here, shift your focus upward to the upper dantian, in the center of your brain. The upper dantian is between your ears, directly under the crown point at the top of your head.

Focus in on breathing in the upper dantian. Imagine and feel as if you can breathe in and out through the center of your brain and pay attention to the sensations here. If this is an area of issue or block, for example, if your issue is related to confusion, then be mindful when confusion arises and label it "confusion." If sensations of calm or clarity arise, label them as such, "calm," or "clarity." Otherwise, continue noting whatever arises as you focus in on breathing in the upper dantian.

After you have a good feel for what it's like to focus in on the upper dantian and have noted what arises here, bring your focus back down to the middle dantian. Take a few slow deep breaths here. Then take your focus back down to the lower dantian and finish with a few, slow, deep breaths here.

Make note of anything significant that you would like to remember from this practice.

Keep in mind that your ability to concentrate on each of these areas and feel the energies grows through consistent practice over time. At first, you may notice you are more comfortable with one dantian versus the others. This is natural. One dantian or another may feel numb or uncomfortable. You may find it easy to focus in on one and close to impossible to keep your focus on the others. This, too, is natural. Just make note of whatever you discover.

If you practice interoception of breathing in the three dantians, with deep intention, commitment, and mindfulness, you'll learn to become deeply absorbed in these primary energy centers, so that everything else fades to the background. You'll know you've reached absorption when the effort of concentration is no longer required. Your focal object becomes like a magnet that attracts your attention. Your attention sticks to your focal object, is "one with it," effortlessly, without wavering.

In these moments of one-pointed focus you deeply absorb the frequencies of Peace, Love, and Light that make their home in these vital centers. Absorption in these frequencies starts to transform your body, heart, and mind so you resonate with Peace, Love, and Light throughout your life and can return to them anytime you need. We'll spend more time embodying these frequencies as we progress through the meditations in our series.

Daily Subtle Energy Meditation Practice: 5. Lower Dantian Breathing

Now it's time to practice the next guided meditation in this Subtle Energy Meditation Series. We recommend you do this at least once a day and up to twice a day for several days before going on to the next chapter. See the guidelines below.

The Lower Dantian Breathing Meditation cultivates strong, vital energy that supports concentration and vibrant health. You can practice this any time of day as it is a great meditation to relax, release stress, and connect with the inner peace of vital energy flow in your lower abdomen.

143

You can find the meditation script in the Appendices. You can memorize it, record it in your own voice, or follow along with the recording we've created, which can be found in the ROV Meditation App, available for Apple and Android devices in those app stores.

We suggest you continue to log your practice using the **Meditation Log** in the Appendices.

- For each session, log the day and time, and the name of the meditation you did.
- Add a brief description of the inner cues you found significant. (An example of this could be, "Imagine your breath is feeding this sphere, so it glows warmer and brighter, so it feels alive and full of energy. You are breathing in vital Life Force Energy.")
- Add a brief description of your inner felt experience of these significant cues. (An example of this could be, "I felt a fullness of energy in my lower abdomen, which felt peaceful and satisfying.")
- Finally, rate your Energy, Mood, and Mental Clarity from 0 to 10.

Reflection & Insight Journaling

How does running on automatic relate to the issue you are working with from the Five Questions? How can you become more conscious and intentional in this area of your life?

What did you learn that might be helpful for working with your primary issue from the exercise of breathing through the three dantians? Does this issue seem to relate to one of the dantians?

--- --- ---

In our next chapter, you'll learn how to step beyond yourself and experience Transcendence in the vast, clear space of Pure Awareness. We look forward to joining you there after you've taken some time to practice the Lower Dantian Breathing Meditation.

7. Transcendence

The Meditation Secret That Relieves Stress and Conflict

We live in a world in which stress is our common currency and conflicting points of view are deeply entrenched. Our world is set to hyperdrive and feels more polarized than ever. To deal with this, many like you, our readers, seek peace, calm, and clarity in meditation, while others find meditating just plain frustrating. In this chapter, we will share insights from the teacher J. Krishnamurti about how to free your mind. You'll also learn a meditation secret that can take your practice to the next level—and beyond.

Once you've learned:

> **Step 1. Prepare** your body, environment, and intention,

> **Step 2. Initiate** meditation with relaxation, posture, and positive energy cues, and

> **Step 3. Concentrate** to the point of Absorption, you're ready to

Step 4. Transcend into the vast, clear space of Pure Awareness.

This state of transcendence is the ultimate aim of Subtle Energy Meditation. It is a state of diffused attention immersed in the Field of Pure Consciousness that brings your body, heart, and mind into integrated coherence and optimal function. In this state, you are one with the flow of Life and attuned to the guiding light of inner purpose. You understand that beyond the variety of individual forms is a Universal Consciousness expressing itself through this infinite diversity. This One Life we all share is the Source and substance of all beings and all events. It is the doer of all actions. This transcendent Awareness gives us a whole new relationship with everyone and everything in life. It imbues every moment with the Light of Pure Consciousness, so that Peace, Love, and Light naturally flourish.

So, why don't we experience this? What keeps us stuck in stress and conflict? What is it that blocks Transcendent Awareness?

Be Careful with Organizing Truth

Krishnamurti told a story about a human tendency that is the root cause of stress (as well as all forms of conflict). He recounted this story on the day he disbanded the Order of the Star in the East, an organization that had proclaimed him as their messianic leader, the World Teacher.

In December of 1911, Krishnamurti, at the age of 16, was acknowledged as this World Teacher after a meeting of the Order in which all present experienced a rush of tremendous power flowing through him. On August 2, 1929, he gave a talk disbanding this organization after being its spiritual head for 18 years. He began by telling a story about a devil and his friend. In this tale, they were walking down the street when they saw a man pick something up and put it his pocket.

"The friend said to the devil, 'What did that man pick up?'

'He picked up a piece of Truth,' said the devil.

'That is a very bad business for you, then,' said his friend.

'Oh, not at all,' the devil replied, 'I am going to let him organize it.'"

Krishnamurti Foundation of America Bulletin[30]

Let this message sink in for a moment.

The Problem with "Things"

Our minds have a propensity for inventing and organizing "things." We like to label our experiences, name them as specific things, organize them into compartments and categories, and link them under hierarchies to explain and control our reality. This is a practical work of the mind, which has survival value. This activity of representing reality with labels, categories, and mental models gives us a point of view that helps organize our thoughts, inform our feelings, and guide our actions. Our mental representations give us structures to live and work in and maps to navigate our way through life.

Mental organization helps us manage the stress of uncertainty and feel safe. We keep things in labeled boxes to feel like we know what's going on. But, lurking in this categorical creation of "things" is a dangerous tendency—we tend to get very attached to the way we name and categorize things. We treat our mental models as more significant, substantial, rigidly defined, real, and permanent than they are. We tend to think that the lines on the maps we make are actually the territory they describe. We imagine our maps are Reality itself. When we see that others have different maps, we battle over which way of describing reality is the right one. We fail to see that the lines on our maps are fabrications made for their utility. They are not "the way things are."

Let's consider an example related to the stress that most of us feel these days. Meditation has become known as a "thing" that can calm the mind and help us find peace of mind. For this reason, many people are learning to meditate. If you've taken this plunge, you've likely learned there are a whole host of different meditation techniques. Which one should you choose? What's the best one? What's the best model to follow?

Finding the Right Meditation Technique

Perhaps, in your search for the best way to meditate, you decide to ask a friend who has meditated for years—and who seems very calm. This friend responds as if she has waited a lifetime for you to ask. She gushes forth about the wonders of Transcendental Meditation and how it completely transformed her mind and changed her life. It all started when she attended a weekend workshop and received her secret mantra, which she has repeated twice a day for 20 minutes for the past 30 years. She invites you to come to her meditation group and meet her teacher, who can give you your own secret mantra.

This all sounds appealing, except you've never really been a "group person" or someone who buys into the whole "secret" truth known by a select group of enlightened masters, so you thank her for sharing her experience and say you'll consider her offer after you do a little more of your own research.

Browsing online, you discover there are two types of meditation, those focused on concentration (like the mantra method) and those focused on open-monitoring of attention (mindfulness-based methods). You learn that concentration builds "attentional focus," the ability to control what you focus on, and mindfulness grows observational awareness, which has to do with how you relate to what arises in your mind. Each one has their benefits. So, you decide to try them both.

Doing a little more research on exactly how to practice these methods, you discover these are not the "real" two types of meditation. Instead, there is "active" or "passive" meditation. Even more confusingly, some put mantra meditation in the active category and some place it in the passive category.

More research reveals there may be 6, 7, 23, or even 80 different types of meditation—each suited to different personality types. It's recommended you choose the type best suited to your personality based on the astrological chart of your birth.

Now you're really in a quandary. You're not sure what you think about astrology and this isn't really what you're looking for. You just want some peace of mind, and meditation is supposed to be about that. Yet, what you find is a world of debate about what is the best meditation, what is true meditation, or any number of ways to discover the right meditation for you.

Hi-Tech Meditation to the Rescue!

About this time, Google has noticed your searches about meditation and has served up a solution. You see an online ad for a personal EEG brainwave sensor. This tech teaches you to meditate by monitoring your brainwaves and letting you know when you've got the right ones—the ones that signify your brain is meditating.

Tech solutions are appealing. It feels good that there's something measurable here. It's only $149, which is a lot less than the "secret mantra," which was going to cost quite a bit more.

In just two days from Amazon Prime, you excitedly open your new device, charge it up, download the app, and strap it on your head. The instruction is simple: just relax and pay attention to the sensations of breathing. If you do this well, you'll be rewarded with the sound of silence. If you do this really well, you'll hear the pleasant sounds of birds chirping. If your mind wanders or you tense up, you'll hear rain. If you really get off track, the rain pounds harder. It sounds like wonderful biofeedback.

Getting Started

Your first session goes pretty well. You focus in on feeling the sensations of breathing. Next, you notice some thoughts about breakfast, then remember you're meditating, and go back to your breathing. You hear some rain, then some silence, then some harder rain as your mind wanders to a meeting you have later today, which prompts you to relax and focus on your breathing again. You hear some silence—then, a bird chirps! You get excited. And the rain pours.

This is all pretty fascinating, because it's new. By the end of your session, you've heard some silence and a few birds, along with your share of rain. Overall, you feel more relaxed than when you began. At the end of your session, you have a score of 60 percent calm. Pretty good for a start. You feel good about this scientific way to meditate.

Over the course of a week, you find yourself with a variety of scores, some better than your initial 60 percent and some worse. Interestingly, they don't seem to correlate with your inner experience of calm. In fact, your most calm-feeling session gave your worst score. Hmmm. What's going on?

So, you go online to the Facebook community affiliated with this tech and discover the scores have a lot to do with something called "calibration." What the app rewards is a change from a stressed state to a calmer state. So, if you're stressed and scattered when you begin and are able to calm down and focus, you get a good score. However, if you're fairly relaxed and focused to begin, and you don't get much more relaxed and focused, you score lower.

In the online community, you discover a whole lot more. Some people, who are experts at using this tech, publish graphs with 90 percent calm plus every day. Others use a different app to see the actual brainwaves and get readings of gamma waves that are supposed to be associated with higher spiritual states than just relaxing and focusing. Others say that delta waves are the sign of "true meditation."

Which one is it? You're feeling confused. The whole thing seems focused on scores, graphs, and debate about the right practice and if graphs are showing "true" states or not. You're beginning to feel more stressed. This is definitely not what you had in mind when you thought you'd try meditation to find more calm and inner peace.

The Devil's in the Details

What seemed simple at first—learning meditation to become calm and peaceful—quickly became a tangled forest. Wandering through the trees of techniques to find the right one led you to get lost in this forest and the sounds of a thunderous storm. You begin to long for the spacious, clear, blue sky.

Krishnamurti had a lot to say about this point. Remember, he is the guy who disbanded his own organization because they were making both him and the organization into too much of a "big thing," while losing sight of what really matters—transformation of the mind.

Krishnamurti asked,

> "Is there a meditation in which there is no sense of comparison, or in which there is no reward or punishment? Is there any meditation which is not based on thought (which is measurement, time, and all that)?

How can one explain a meditation that has no thought, that has no achievement, that doesn't say: "I am this, but I'll become that?" . . . Is there a meditation that has nothing to do with will? . . . Is there a meditation that has nothing to do with effort at all? . . . in meditation which is absolutely no effort, no achievement, no thinking, the brain is quiet . . . And, being quiet, it has infinite space."[31]

Quiet brain. Infinite space. Now that sounds a lot more like calm and peace of mind.

How Do You Arrive at this Quiet Infinite Space?

Krishnamurti said, "One has to be choicelessly attentive, fully aware, and this state of choiceless attention is meditation."[32]

So, how do you arrive at choiceless attention, this Nondual Awareness, which is beyond techniques, effort, and striving to achieve or be some "thing?" The seeming paradox is that you begin with techniques. However, the key is not to end up imprisoned by the technique you use. The technique is used to transcend the technique. The aim is for the mind, for awareness, to be relaxed, focused, flexible, open, attentive, and free. In order to arrive at this state, it may be important to use a variety or sequence of techniques, so you aren't imprisoned by or attached to any particular one, or any particular state, thinking it is "the thing" you are looking for. Techniques are simply tools.

So, perhaps the "thing" is not the technique you apply, but how you relate to the techniques you are using. You are seeking a shift in awareness "beyond" the tendency to make events and experiences into "things" and judge them in relation to other things, whether that thing is your "self," "your achievements," "your mastery of a technique," or anything you might possess, identify with, and compare.

There is not one path to this shift into awareness. There is not one specific place you can focus on and go to. Rather, we seek an awareness of the origin of all paths, places, and points of view. This is an awareness of the formless matrix from which all experiences arise. This awareness can be discovered by applying mindful attention and diving deeply into any experience or climbing high to the top of any tree of technique. It is discovered when the mind becomes still, silent, and infinitely spacious. Sometimes this awareness will just come upon you spontaneously and take you beyond.

Certainly, meditation is a practice that can cultivate this awareness. The important thing is how you relate to your practice, how you relate to the techniques you use. Can you resist the temptation to bottle your method in a fixed formula and make it into a permanent "thing?" Can you use the steps of technique as stepping stones, without trying to pick them up and carry them with you forever? Can you use the map without thinking it is the territory?

Krishnamurti asks you to inquire with a mind free from preconceptions. A mind beyond the stress, conflict, and frustration you know—a mind that *welcomes the unknown*. This is the mind of meditation.

Could Your Dominant State of Mind Become Transcendence?

If you're not currently living in transcendent Awareness, what would you say is your dominant state of consciousness—the place you're coming from most of the time? Would you say you're generally loving life and feeling optimistic? Or do you feel overburdened and anxious? Are you generally, stressed or relaxed? Peaceful or frustrated? Open-hearted or protective? Or maybe you're any of the above depending on the moment?

What if there is a state of consciousness that is free from these ups and downs, free from struggle and suffering? Is such a state possible? Let's explore four cues that take you beyond the struggle.

In Buddhism, there is the promise of a state of being that is free from suffering. It's called "Nirvana." You take up residence here through dedicated meditation practice and insight into the nature of reality. Analogously, in the Christian tradition, St. Paul talks of having the mind of Christ. With the mind of Christ, you are "reborn," so you see life in a whole new Light.

As you learn to observe thoughts, feelings, actions, relationships, and events from this transcendent state of consciousness, you gain a new relationship with everything. This immediately releases you from stress and enables you to respond calmly and appropriately—with compassion and insight.

So, in what ways have we experienced this state of transcendence? And how did we get there?

Kevin's Story of Discovering Transcendence

Looking back, I realize that I discovered transcendence without knowing I was even seeking it. In August of 1984, I had just graduated from St. Joseph's University in Philadelphia and was inspired to take a backpacking trip out West. I was definitely a city-boy, hadn't done anything in the way of backpacking, and had never been west of the Mississippi.

For the month of August that year, I took a trip by car and on foot through Colorado, Utah, Arizona, and Wyoming with a friend. We explored the Canyonlands, the Grand Canyon, and Yellowstone National Park. We spent hours, day after day, in nature, without any TV, radio, news, music, or entertainment. The natural landscape was our primary stimulation.

The landscape began to shape my state of consciousness. What struck me most on this trip was the clear, spacious sky (you can see for miles in this part of the country), the silence, and the stillness. I absorbed these three qualities deep into my body and mind during that month. The outer landscape became my inner landscape.

To this day, I recall quite distinctly what I felt as I sat on the plane flying home. I had an overwhelming feeling of contentment. I was absolutely peaceful, my mind was still, silent, and spacious, and I felt no sense of worry or struggle. I felt completely free and at ease.

Out of this transcendent experience, three things became clear:

1. I discovered such a state is possible.

2. I found I needed to take a break from my busyness to arrive at this state.

3. I wanted to find ways to reproduce it, deepen it, and expand it. I wanted to cultivate this state as a reliable baseline to live from and return to whenever I needed.

This intention led me on a 30-year journey of learning, practicing, and teaching in the disciplines of T'ai Chi, Qigong, Reiki, meditation, Centering Prayer, Kriya Yoga, and other mind-body disciplines. From these years of study, practice, and teaching, I gathered specific techniques, including four cues, that reliably generate deep peace and calm clarity for me.

Kevin's story reminds Stephen that he arrived at these same four cues of "objectless imagery" along different paths. He experienced transcendence through his commitment to the practices of Devotion to the Divine Mother, Kriya Yoga, Buddhist Mindfulness, Reiki, and many other disciplines.

So, what are these cues?

Four Simple Cues to Realize Transcendence

If you work with these cues consistently, they do indeed renew your mind. Becoming familiar with them through practice gives you a baseline state of inner peace and calm focus that is ever-present and always available, so you can return to it when you wander from it.

These four cues grant instant moments of transcendence. They are described as "objectless imagery" because they contain no specific details or content. (You'll see what we mean when you practice them in a moment.) These cues give you a glimpse of what shifting beyond the confines of your personal mindsets feels like. Through consistent practice, you can build on these brief moments and cultivate a strong and unshakeable Nondual Awareness that releases all stress and conflict.

You can try each of the following techniques for just a few seconds or up to a few minutes—whichever you prefer. As you try them out, a few words of advice: see if you can let go of trying too hard or questioning what's happening. See if it's possible to let go of preconceptions and be open to what you can discover. Don't worry if you're doing these techniques exactly right. If one doesn't work for you at first, move on to the next one. Once you become familiar with going deeply into any one of them, the others become more accessible. Let's try out these cues, together, now:

1. **Stillness:** Feel the stillness underneath all movements in the center of your brain.
   - Focus in on the center of your brain—a point between your ears, directly under the crown point of your head, and halfway between your forehead and the base of your skull. Imagine sitting in a comfortable chair in this spot.
   - Once you are seated in the center of your brain, imagine and feel "stillness" here. Imagine sitting here as still as you can be. There is no thought in the center of your brain to disturb you. There are only sensations. Feel the sensation of sitting

still in the seat in the center of your brain. Feel the stillness here. Go ahead and give this a try for about 15 seconds now.

- Did your mind become still for a moment?

Let's add Cue 2.

2. **Silence:** Listen to the silence underneath all sounds in the center of your brain.
    - Sit in the center of your brain again and see if it's possible to listen to the silence underneath all sounds here. There are no thoughts, no inner voice, in the center of your brain, so it's very quiet. Listen to silence in the center of your brain for about 15 seconds or until you're ready to move on.
    - How did this feel? Did your mind become quiet for a moment?

Now, let's add Cue 3.

3. **Space:** Focus on the open, clear space in the center of your brain.

    - Imagine the center of your brain as open, clear, and spacious. Feel this space. Sense it. Go ahead and sit in the open, clear space in the center of your brain for another 15 seconds or until you're ready to move on.
    - Are you getting a feel for what it's like to transcend your normal thinking, feeling, and self-consciousness—if only for a few brief moments?

Let's add Cue 4.

4. ***Who* is having this experience?**

    - Sit in the center of your brain again and ask, "*Who* is having this experience?" Go ahead, give it a try, and see what you discover. Sit in the center of your brain and ask, "*Who* is having this experience?"

159

- For a few moments, did your mind go blank? Did your thoughts stop, for just a second or two? Interesting, isn't it?

It makes us both smile when we do this. It's like discovering a secret treasure! A clear, quiet mind.

If you'd like to experiment with these four cues a little longer to become more familiar with them, go ahead and spend as much time as you'd like practicing them now. What happens when you sit in the center of your brain, feel the still, silent, space here, and ask, "*Who* is having this experience?"

As you practice these four cues together, over time, they'll blend into a reliable baseline of still, silent, spacious awareness. If you prefer, you can also use them individually, especially if you find one of them that really works well for you.

Try this in moments of tension and stress by calling "time-out," going to a quiet private space, and letting these cues free your mind. Practice until you feel a release of tension and a shift into a state of awareness beyond the struggle. Then you can re-engage the situation from a better place.

Using Objectless Imagery to Move into Nondual Awareness

If such a renewal of your state of consciousness is possible for a moment, can you learn to live from it? Can this state of conscious become a stable trait of consciousness? If so, what difference would this make in your life, your relationships, and what you view as real and possible? Could this be the key to releasing your inner blocks and achieving the goal you set at the start of this book? In our own practice and teaching, we've arrived at the conclusion—*Yes!* The transcendent states cultivated in meditation can be become stable traits of the baseline consciousness you live from.

While each tradition has its teachings and practices, we propose that transcendence is an inherently natural process that unfolds as you learn to work with and master your attention—by choosing what you focus on and how you relate to it.

What you focus on creates your experience. Learning to choose your focal point and sustain concentration is the entry into being able to transcend all points of view and rest in a state of Nondual Awareness. Nondual Awareness is a state of consciousness free from the limitations of your habitual thoughts, feelings, actions, issues, and self-focus. It's a state beyond polarity, beyond tension, beyond me/you, us/them, inside/outside, now/then. . . . It transcends all organizations and models of reality. It is awareness of the Whole Field of Pure Awareness itself, prior to its manifestation into individual forms.

As we become aware of the Whole Field—and recognize individuality as movements of the Whole Field itself—a different relationship arises with everything. The Field is the doer of all actions. The individual is an event in the Field of Consciousness, like a wave in the Ocean of Being—arising, cresting, and dissolving back into the Ocean.

The practice of transcendence is to keep returning to awareness of this Infinite Field within which all events happen. This is especially helpful when you are struggling or when you see others struggling. If you shift attention to the Whole Field, then you simply "hold this space." This supports you and others to go through what you need to go through without judgment or needing to fix anything because you and others are simply the Field having an experience. Inspirations and skillful actions naturally flow as you hold this space of the Whole Field.

The purpose of meditation, then, is to train attention: to be relaxed, focused, fluid, flexible, open, clear, and spacious, to mirror the Field itself in our individualized consciousness. We become conscious and intentional about the whole process of attention—learning to tune in, connect, and let go into the Infinite Space of Awareness.

As we mentioned, in Buddhism, entry into the Infinite Space of Awareness is "Nirvana." This state is the cessation of all suffering. Suffering comes from identification with and attachment to "my" ways of organizing reality, my maps, my thoughts, my feelings, my beliefs, my actions, my relationships, my things, my experiences, and my body. Free from identification with all these "things," you discover that all things arise in relationship with everything else, then fade and dissolve into insubstantiality again. No "thing" is permanent and substantial. You gain this insight by observing the arising and passing of all thoughts, feelings, and sensations in meditation (and in life) and by applying insight to your experiences through reflection.

While transcendence can arise spontaneously, for it to become a dominant feature of your baseline state of consciousness requires disciplined practice. We've described the preliminary steps of this practice as:

Step 1. Preparation,
Step 2. Initiation, and
Step 3. Concentration into Absorption.

You've just experimented with the Four Cues that take you into Step 4. Transcendence—at least for a moment.

Let's explore what it's like to cultivate transcendence as a more permanent state of consciousness. For this, we return to the practice of mindfulness and repeat the journey through the Five Gates of Mindfulness into awareness of Awareness itself. After the Five Gates, we'll describe the experience of transcendence and its effects in several slightly varying ways, so it begins to shape your consciousness.

Reviewing the Five Gates of Mindfulness

You may remember that mindfulness is like a gatekeeper who grants access to deeper and more refined states of consciousness. Mindfulness means paying attention on purpose, in the present moment, non-judgmentally—like a curious observer. Maintaining mindfulness enables you to experience things with fresh new eyes, to dive into finer detail and depth, and notice the everchanging impermanence of all "things." This is why regular practice is so important. The more you practice, the more familiar you become with paying attention in finer and finer detail, which enables you to go deeper.

Your normal, everyday mindfulness is not as sharp or as powerful as what you need in meditation. Mindfulness in meditation is precise, detailed, flexible, and agile, able to move from one state to another, from one gate to the next. As you read the following descriptions of the Five Gates of Mindfulness, pause to practice along, so you enter each gate and understand it experientially with fresh new eyes in this moment.

1. The First Gate, the Foundation Keeper, is Present-Moment Awareness

To enter this gate, focus on what is happening now inside and around you. You might begin by becoming aware of the sensations of sitting or lying here, in this space. Notice your posture and how you feel right now inside your body.

Notice details of your present environment through all your senses. What do you see, hear, touch, taste, and smell? What do you sense about the energy of this space? Does this space have a feeling to it?

Notice when your mind wanders to thoughts of the past and thoughts about what might happen in the future—and return to what is happening now. Notice inner commentary—the narrative self. Notice the habit of describing, evaluating, and judging everything that comes into your awareness as something you like or dislike. This commentary is like an ever-present mental soundtrack for life, constantly putting words and labels on experiences.

Notice this commentary mindfully, then consciously let go of this background track of the thinking mind. In its place, re-engage a heightened sense of the sensory details of what is happening inside and around you. Become fully present, here and now, letting go of the need to narrate the experience. As you become fully present, notice a shift in your mind. The Second Gate of mindfulness opens.

2. The Second Gate is Silence

"I am silently aware of the present moment, letting go of commentary, resting in what is."

There is a silence underneath all sounds. Rest in this silence. Notice the deep relief. Subtle sensations arise in the silence, for example, the sensation of breathing.

3. The Third Gate is the Breath

"I am silently aware of the breath in the present moment, letting go of all other perceptions and thoughts."

Focus in on the subtle sensations of breathing. Really tune-in to the felt sensations, letting everything else fade to the background. This opens the Fourth Gate.

4. The Fourth Gate is Awareness of the Whole Breath in Every Moment

Find a place to focus your attention on the breath, such as in your lower abdomen, your heart, or in the entry to your nostrils, and stay present with the felt sensations here. Notice the moment you begin to inhale and follow this all the way through until you naturally pause. Then, notice the moment you begin to exhale and follow your out-breath all the way through until you naturally pause. Attend to these present sensations, here and now. Witness them. Feel them. Sense them. Whenever your mind wanders to anything else, practice the 3Rs—Recognize, Release, and Return to your breath.

Allow your mind to become completely absorbed in the gentle rhythm of breathing.

"I am silently aware of the ebb and flow of the whole breath, continuously, every moment. I am aware from the very beginning of the in-breath to the end of the in-breath and from the very beginning of the out-breath to the end of the out-breath."

In the Third Gate, you may still go off and observe other things, but in the Fourth Gate, the breath fully grabs hold of your attention. Your attention is anchored in the whole breath. Awareness is fully absorbed. There is only the breath and nothing else.

All your energy is concentrated in this one thing, like the sun of attention shining through the magnifying glass of mindfulness to make a fire. Or like a musician performing a flute concerto in front of a large audience where there is no other object of focus except for the notes being played, you realize this breath is truly the most important thing. Your attention gathers within this focal point and builds energy. It becomes a magnet that anchors your attention without requiring any further effort. Being present, silent, still, attentive, with sustained awareness on one thing is *samadhi,* complete absorption. You have let go and merged with the object of attention completely.

5. Absorption Leads to the Fifth Gate: Awareness of Awareness Itself

As energy builds, everything lights up. The breath becomes incredibly beautiful. Mindfulness powers up and generates deep insight and bliss that illuminates the three dantians (the three brains)—body, heart, and mind. Awareness arises like a fire that flows up through your spine, up through the space around you, across all space and time—and Beyond. You experience the Infinite Space of Awareness itself. Letting go into this space, you enter Choiceless Attention, Pure Awareness without content.

This is awareness without a specific focal object and without a specific seat of consciousness. Attention is not resting anywhere. It is everywhere and nowhere at once. This is attention without content, focal point, or commentary. It is the open, clear space of Nondual Awareness: awareness of Awareness itself. Experiencing Nondual Awareness is a release from the confines of self and an openness beyond any feeling or form.

Nondual Awareness

At this point in your practice, you experience a subtle shift into nondual states of consciousness. As described by Jenny Wade, "Nondual Awareness is a discrete shift in awareness, in which the consensual, apparently manifest reality of normal waking, adult sensory experience, is perceived to derive from a singular unmanifest source in a seamless whole."[33]

In Nondual Awareness, the division of "I" and "other" is transcended. In our practice of Subtle Energy Meditation, we've identified four subtle variations of this shift.

These may arise as distinct variations or may fuse together seamlessly:

1. Choiceless Attention, which is like an empty state in which nothing arises.

2. Infinite Spacious Awareness of the Whole Field of Consciousness.

3. Hearing the sound of OM (or AUM), the primary signal of Creation, the primordial vibration that brings forth and sustains all Life.

4. Clear Light, as the Infinite Space of Awareness brightens with bliss.

Each of these has a slightly different subtle effect.

Choiceless Attention is a complete letting go into "no-thing," so that no discrete experience congeals. This experience dissolves any attachments to self, and its thoughts, feelings, actions, and desires. Resting in Choiceless Attention, no experience forms. There is an empty space of Pure Consciousness that arises in stillness and silence.

Expanding the sense of spaciousness in all directions, there's a subtle shift into Infinite Spacious Awareness, an experience of the Whole Field of Consciousness, a boundaryless, limitless expanse. This gives an experience of Oneness beyond all forms; All is connected in a seamless whole that is aware or that *is* Awareness itself.

Sometimes, in this expanse, the Infinite Space brightens, a "Lightness of Being" spontaneously arises, a Clear Light permeates the Whole Space and brings indescribable bliss. A soft effervescent energy infuses the Field of Awareness with an eternally abiding peace and joy.

At other times, the OM vibration permeates this Infinite Space. Tuning in to the primordial Sound has synchronizing and healing effects. All is brought into alignment with Source Consciousness.

These primordial elements of Sound and Light attune you to the harmonious creative activity of Being itself. All events in life flow effortlessly from this attunement.

Here is how we cue these subtle experiences in the Light, Love, and Peace Meditation (Version 2), which is the final meditation in our Subtle Energy Meditation Series. It begins with the Choiceless Attention of stillness:

> "If you notice any movement of thought, feeling, body, or attention, let go into stillness. Imagine and feel this still point sinking deep down into the Earth, where it anchors a rock-solid, immutable, peace. Focus deep down into this still point. Let go. . . . Be still. . . . Let go. . . . Be still. . . . Let go. . . . Be still. . . .
>
> Feel the stillness underneath all movemen.t . . .
>
> Listen to the silence underneath all sound. . . .
>
> Sense the Infinite Space of Awareness. . . .
>
> Rest in the deep Peace of still, silent, spacious Awareness. . . .
>
> Within this still, silent, spacious Awareness become aware of the Entire Field of Being extending infinitely in all directions across all time. . . . You are a point of awareness within this Infinite Field.
>
> Become aware that the Whole Field is Aware. There is only Awareness. Infinite Spacious Awareness . . . Infinite Spacious Awareness . . . Infinite Spacious Awareness . . .
>
> Listen to, sense, and feel this Infinite Space of Awareness. You may notice it has a signature, a vibration, a subtle hum. You may begin to hear or feel the vibration of this Field, like the hum of the Universe, the OM.

Listen closer to this subtle sound under the silence. Tune in to this subtle vibration. It is the hum of the Infinite Space of Awareness itself. At first, it may feel like nothing at all.

Then, faintly, it is like listening to the wind, a distant ocean in a conch shell, or the gentle purring engine of the Universe. As you listen to, sense, and feel this OM vibration, you realize OM is the home signal, the signal from the Source, sustaining Life, supporting All. It is constant and unwavering. It contains the primary frequencies of Peace, Love, and Light and permeates the Entire Universe with Awareness.

OM . . . OM . . . OM . . .

Your body resonates with OM, which integrates, heals, and transforms your entire being—so you become a pure channel of Awareness, expressing the primary frequencies of Peace, Love, and Light."

Stephen's Mystical Experience of Nondual Consciousness

It is really so very simple. A thought arises. You stay with it, like a curious observer, non-judgmentally, happy to watch it as it plays, aware it is not you. If you watch for long enough, like watching a child's heart in play, great joy will arise at the play of the self. Then you become aware of the witnessing Presence that is watching. It is not the self that gave rise to the thought. Who then?

So, you watch the watcher. To do so, you must be very, very still. As you watch, many curious creatures arise, in the form of light and sound and space, as if you are sitting by a still pool gazing. And then, suddenly, as you sit so very still, there is an awakening as you become aware of Awareness itself. The stillness becomes rock solid and immutable—and you leap Beyond. Except that now there is no "you." Just pure expanded Awareness. And you know, without a

169

doubt, that this transcendent experience which has been spoken about in every holy book ever written, is true.

Recently, I was traveling home on the train, contemplating Presence and Awareness, when an experience of unshakable silence, stillness, and spaciousness arose. There was an awareness that I *was that*. There was an experience in this moment of everything as perfect exactly as it is. Nothing was missing. Everything was perfect in this moment.

Resting in the vastness, the emptiness, there was awareness of this emptiness, a vibrant, vital clarity, a luminosity, clear light, Presence.

I was aware of the spaciousness in my heart and mind, within and all around.

There was a union of space and unbound awareness, emptiness and clarity, warmth of presence, spaciousness.

Infinite Awareness, light. Spaciousness in the mind and heart, warmth, bliss.

I carried this presence into meditation later that day, resting in the vivid clear awareness of light. Awake and witnessing.

I made an intention before I sat, an intention for how I could be of highest benefit to this planet and its beings and dedicated my practice and enlightenment to their liberation.

Then, I watched and listened deeply. I watched the space in front of me. I listened, aware of the light and the incredible luminosity of being. I let the love in my heart expand out to embrace all humanity and dissolve into peace.

I stayed with an awareness of the subtle breathing and dived deep, riding the sound of OM and the inner light of Presence home.

Resting in the deep stillness of the body, silence of the mind, and spaciousness of the heart, awake and aware, I could not find anything when I looked. I could only find the mind, the one looking at the appearances. When I looked at the mind, I could only find emptiness, unbounded space. When I looked at the "no-thing" of this unbounded space, the emptiness, I was aware it was luminous, awake, a clear, clear light. I was able to rest there, observing the emptiness that is clear light and the clear light that is emptiness.

I was awake.

The Progression of Subtle Energy Meditation

In meditation, there is a progression from outer sensory perception, to coarse inner sensations, to subtle sensations, to objectless imagery, to Nondual Awareness. You first need to learn how to sustain attention on coarse meditation objects, like physical sensations of relaxation, posture, and breathing. This is a first inner layer of interoceptive awareness.

As you sustain mindfulness, the breath becomes the *subtle* breath: pure energy, light, love, and deep peace. This is a second, more subtle layer of interoceptive awareness—energetic awareness. Absorption in subtle energy frequencies leads to objectless imagery: silence, stillness, and spaciousness.

Immersion in silence, stillness, and spaciousness is formless awareness, a bridge beyond form and content. Sustaining this awareness requires the lightest touch of attention. It must be held and carried lightly, for trying to hold onto it chases it away. You must remain still, silent, and spacious. Waiting, listening, letting go, staying open, and paying attention—as transcendence beyond the "self" opens.

Resting in formless awareness, a subtle shift occurs: the one observing knows itself as that which is observed. Awareness aware of itself. There is only Awareness—Nondual Awareness, Pure Consciousness without division, form, or content, also known as

Clear Light Awareness. The Clear Light, formless emptiness, is also One, rich, vibrant, and full—a transcendent space from which all forms emerge. There is a luminous bliss in this awareness.

Emerging from this state and returning into a sense of individuality, there is a sense of connection with all other individualities as a result of our formless Oneness. This sense of connection is maintained as we keep the transcendent state as a background reference, the horizon within which we have experiences.

The process of Subtle Energy Meditation is like peeling an onion, beginning with using interoception to shift inward, under the layer of outer sensory awareness to inner sensations of relaxation, posture, and breathing. These lead to the next inward layer of subtle energy sensations, which lead to formless awareness of stillness, silence, and spaciousness. Patiently peeling away the last layer so that no form remains is entering the realm of Nondual Awareness, Pure Awareness beyond content and form.

Five Layers of Awareness

1. Outer Sensory Awareness using the five senses

2. Interoceptive Awareness of relaxation, posture, breathing, and other inner sensations

3. Subtle Energy Awareness of energy points, paths, and fields

4. Formless Awareness of stillness, silence, and spaciousness

5. Nondual Awareness beyond content and forms

Each layer of awareness unfolds naturally, as the previous layer is realized. So, don't move too quickly. Allow each layer to unfold fully, naturally, as you sustain mindful attention. Take your time. In time, you can experience transcendence in every moment, experiencing Nondual Awareness as immanent within each moment of Life. Life itself is aware. Life itself *is* Awareness—Pure Consciousness expressing, arising, and dissolving, in an infinite variety of momentary forms. Living in this realization transforms your experience of life.

Transcendence is freedom—freedom from doubt, stress, fear, struggle, and confusion; freedom from identification with thoughts, feelings, sensations, habits, memories, conflicts, traumas, labels, achievements, and all the ways you identify your "self"; freedom from any and every "thing"—so you rest in a state of Pure Awareness beyond form. Within this Nondual Awareness you engage with life in a whole new way.

Struck by the Light

Imagine one day you are sitting in your house, watching a video on YouTube, and responding to your social media inbox, when you are struck by a flash of lightning.

This is no ordinary lightning bolt. It is light from the Source above and goes straight down through your brain, heart, and gut through the Central Channel. This lightning ignites a Sacred Fire within you—the Fire of Illumination. You become aware of this Fire rising up within and all around you, across all space and time—and Beyond.

This is what happened to us. The social media is an analogy for the ordinary everyday world. The bolt of lightning is the experience of the transcendent that all of us have access to at any time.

Except that people don't attend to it. They just don't **see** it, **feel** it, or **sense** it.

When we met each other, we discovered a friendship that transcends the ordinary boundaries of space and time. We also discovered the qualities of transcendence in each other, just as they exist in you.

Do you ever feel you don't quite fit here? That the world and all its materialistic values are completely upside down?

A world that is based on physical, material values, will, like the physical body, collapse and die, no matter how good a shape you keep it in. A world founded in soul values will transcend the mundane and express the Infinite. But you cannot just give lip service to it. It isn't a matter of speaking the right words or thinking the right thoughts. The Infinite cannot be boxed in. It's a matter of Being.

What would happen if we suspended everything we're doing in this world, turned everything upside down, and began from a foundation of transcendent Awareness, of love and kindness, of compassion and wisdom?

What would happen if awakening our minds and hearts was the very first thing we taught our kids?

What if we gave equal value to understanding silence, stillness, and space as we do to the noise and activity of our human commerce and games?

Are we ready?

Consider what this would mean:

- We would give equal value to understanding the physical body through medicine and the subtle body through energy medicine.
- We would explore in our homes, schools, and businesses the power of the present moment through healing and meditative practices, creating new, unimagined opportunities and mystical, transcendent experiences.
- We would discover as a common humanity what it means to understand the body, environment, and time, as well as discovering what it means to get beyond the body, environment, and time.

- We would intimately know The Field of Pure Awareness, beyond space and time, just as we know our 3D world within space and time.
- We would equally understand our thinking and feelings, as well as subtle energy and consciousness.
- We would look with equal wonder at the esoteric secret paths of the masters and saints as avidly as we look at the paths of our sportspeople, celebrities, and scientists.
- We would get to know the heart-brain and gut-brain as well as we know the head brain.
- We would know the map of our channels and chakras in the energy body, as surely as we know the maps of our neighborhoods and the way to drive our children to the park.
- We would know how to activate the Inner Fire, the Sacred Fire, as surely as we can light our house by switching on the power.
- We would understand how to transform death as well as we understand how to transform life.
- We would know how to arise as Divine Beings as clearly as we know how to act as human beings.

Are you ready for transcendence? On the path to transcendence, we offer the next foundational meditation in the Subtle Energy Meditation series.

Daily Subtle Energy Meditation Practice: 6. One Shared Heart

The purpose of this meditation is to develop Concentration into Absorption and to cultivate love and compassion.

In this meditation, you direct your attention and your breathing to your heart, where through mindfulness of deep absorption in the breath of love, the energy of your being transforms into, and becomes, the purest Unconditional Love. You feel this love, like the warm embrace of a Divine Mother's Love in your body, then become aware of it extending outward to all beings, the whole Planet, and the entire Universe.

You can find the **meditation script** in the Appendices. You can memorize it, record it in your own voice, or follow along with the recording we've created, which can be found in the ROV Meditation App, available for Apple and Android devices in those app stores.

We suggest you continue to log your practice using the **Meditation Log** in the Appendices.

- For each session, log the day and time, and the name of the meditation you did.
- Add a brief description of the inner cues you found significant. (An example of this could be, "Feel the warm embrace of love expanding from your heart through your whole body.")
- Add a brief description of your inner felt experience of these significant cues. (An example of this could be, "My body felt warm, even glowing, and a great sense of calm and relief overcame me.")
- Finally, give a rating from 0 to 10 of your Energy, Mood, and Mental Clarity.

Reflection & Insight Journaling

What did you discover in the simple transcendence exercises in this chapter—the Four Cues and the Five Gates?

How can you apply these to what you want to achieve, create, and grow in your life? How can you use transcendence to release your inner blocks? What does transcendence mean to you?

--- --- ---

In our next chapter, we'll talk about how to return from transcendent experience, ground back into the body, and integrate Nondual Awareness into your life. We look forward to joining you there after you've taken the time to practice "The One Shared Heart" meditation. Enjoy your practice!

8. Returning and Grounding

While some use meditation to escape this world, the purpose of Subtle Energy Meditation is for your body, heart, and mind to resonate with the finer frequencies of Peace, Love, and Light, so that you can live in an elevated state of Awareness in this world and in your transition Beyond.

To achieve this, it's important to follow the three steps we've outlined leading into Transcendence—Preparation, Initiation, and Concentration—as well as the three steps leading out of Transcendence.

The first of these three steps leading out of Transcendence is Returning and Grounding.

To highlight the importance of Returning and Grounding, we share a brief anecdote about a humorous alert to residents who live and work near a prominent meditation center in Iowa. According to local lore, residents are advised to be cautious when driving near the center when a group meditation lets out. Apparently, some of those streaming out of the meditation—perhaps in a state of meditative bliss—are prone to getting into fender benders.

Whether traffic records back this up or not, it's important to watch out for this tendency to use meditation to "bliss out" and avoid life in this world, rather than to heal, transform, and mindfully engage. This tendency is natural if you discover a blissed-out state in meditation and find this contrasts with challenging experiences here on this planet. Who wouldn't want to stay there, rather than be here?

However, this is not what we are looking to do with Subtle Energy Meditation. We are looking to live in an elevated state of Awareness filled with Peace, Love, and Joy that is grounded and integrated in our bodies and physical reality. In this way, we transform the way we live and the way the Collective Consciousness operates, so that we are more attentive and present; so our whole lives become a meditation, radiating mindfulness and compassion.

Step 5, Returning and Grounding, is this bridge from a period of meditation back into life, so there is a continuum of awareness. Meditation is not so much a separate experience apart from life, but a time of connection to the Transcendent Awareness that underlies and permeates life. We then bridge from this experience of transcendence to awareness of this world by grounding our meditative consciousness in our bodies. This is a crucial step before you rush off into the activities of your day. Without this step, your meditation becomes a forgotten memory and your life will tend to return to running on automatic programs and reacting to outer demands unconsciously. Your meditation may have been a nice experience, but it will have little impact in your life and the lives around you. It will be like a brief holiday, an experience that is lost as you jump back into the fray of worldly pressures and obligations.

So, Returning and Grounding is about merging your inner meditative experience with your outer experience in the world, so they integrate as a unified whole; so, there is no separation. Awareness infuses the body. There is a recognition of the fact that Awareness infuses Life—and you experience this through the sensations in your body.

Returning and Grounding also prepares you to do conscious work from your meditative state, such as reflection and insight, healing, and manifesting. All of these actions within a state of meditative consciousness transform the way you relate to yourself, others, and Life.

There is Nothing Better Than Here and Now

Meditation helps you to recognize and be aware of the inherent completeness of every moment. Events are the result of a chain of specific causes, so nothing "should be" other than it is. Things are the way they are because of what created the conditions of "now." This doesn't mean you don't make efforts to change situations that are harmful. Instead, you learn to free yourself from limiting thoughts, feelings, and beliefs about these situations, so that you can see things clearly and take insightful, skillful actions to move forward. Meditation is being aware of "what is" here, now. Returning and Grounding brings this awareness into your body and records it in your cells, so it becomes part of your experience here in this world.

The Dalai Lama constantly encourages us all that our practice is not just for us. Every time you sit to meditate, whether you are aware of it or not, it is for the benefit and welfare of all living beings. Being conscious and intentional about this service of your practice gives it even more power.

Returning and Grounding your meditative awareness helps you to be aware of this intention to assist others here and now, rather than get carried away to some other world for your own benefit and achievement. The inherent completeness of grounded awareness guides your actions throughout the day. Grounding keeps you in touch with your moment-to-moment experience and assists you to experience life directly, free of distorted views, rigid forms, and divisions. You remain rooted in the Field of Awareness, which is inherently pure and compassionate. When this purity of Awareness is unobstructed, it expresses through you effortlessly. It flows naturally and guides surely. Returning and Grounding is how you begin to bring the state of elevated pure Awareness into the world.

Cues to Ground Meditative Awareness

After you've discovered transcendent awareness of Awareness itself and rested here for a while, your task is to return consciously and intentionally. Take your time with this step, as it's the key to meditation transforming your everyday state of consciousness—the baseline state you live from. It's the key to shifting how you view yourself, others, and Life in a more permanent way.

Your body is the bridge for this return. Your body is both a bridge to transcendence Beyond and a bridge back into this world. A first step on your return is to feel your body as a whole from the inside, to sense the entire space inside your skin. Spacious awareness is a bridge to transcendence and now it's a bridge back into the body as you return to sensing the space inside your body.

Next, you can notice how you feel both emotionally and physically. As you did when you began your meditation session, take a moment for a check-in and notice any shifts as a result of your practice session. How do you feel now versus when you began? If you could sum this up in a word, phrase, or image, what would this be? Consciously recording this word, phrase, or image along with your felt experience can become a landmark that solidifies the felt experience in your conscious mind. Remembering this landmark will help you return to a meditative state more easily in the future. So, when you recall the feeling you have at the end of your meditation and pair it with a word, phrase, or image, it becomes a strong memory that motivates you to practice again and serves as a bridge back to the experience you just had.

For example, at the end of your meditation, you might feel lighter, freer, more relaxed, peaceful, clear, and compassionate. By noting the feeling you have, labeling it, and recording it deeply in your mind, heart, and body, you groove a neural network associated with this experience. This neural network grows stronger each time you practice with strong intention and emotion.

Smile as you record your word, phrase, or image to strengthen the positive emotion and encode it deeply in your body, heart, and mind. Positive emotion amplifies the grooving of neural networks, so they are more memorable and easier to recall.

The next step is to set an intention to bring this feeling with you into your life. You might even imagine yourself in a situation that is coming up feeling the way you do at the end of your meditation, so you can associate your meditative state with this situation. This will prime you to respond with more mindfulness, presence, compassion, and awareness when you arrive in this situation.

After setting your intention, slowly half open your eyes and take in the space around you. Sense the space inside and around you, with your eyes open. This begins to link your inner and outer experience. Again, recall the word, phrase, or image that summarizes your feeling at the end of your meditation, this time with your eyes open. Opening your eyes is the next bridge from meditation into life. Do this slowly. Gradually allow your inner and outer experience to merge.

Now, feel the sensations at the top of your head . . . in your hands in your lap . . . and in your feet on the ground . . .

These three sensory cues ground the energies of the three dantians into your present-moment bodily awareness.

Continue with your intention to take this feeling of meditative awareness with you wherever you go and share it with those you meet. You've now made a complete return from your inner experience to your outer experience and grounded meditative awareness in your body. However, before you rush off into your day, it's important to take two final steps in the Subtle Energy Meditation process. These steps further transform your consciousness and support a permanent shift in how you approach life. They help you use your meditative state to overcome inner blocks and manifest your deeper soul desires and purpose. We look forward to sharing them with you in the next two chapters.

Now, it's time for the first version of the meditation that integrates the whole of our Subtle Energy Meditation sequence in one complete practice. We call it the Light, Love, and Peace Meditation.

Daily Subtle Energy Meditation Practice: 7. Light, Love, and Peace (Version 1)

The purpose of this meditation is to integrate all the steps and inner skills we've explored, while empowering you to resonate with the finer frequencies of Peace, Love, and Light and realize a state of elevated Awareness.

Special Note on the Light, Love, and Peace Meditation

The Light, Love, and Peace Meditation (LLP) is the culmination of all the foundational meditations you've practiced up to this point. It is a joyful embodiment of Nondual Awareness, permeated by the finer frequencies of Peace, Love, and Light. If you look at the cover image of this book, you see a visual representation of this meditation. Take a few moments to gaze at this image and imprint it in your mind. This will help you imagine and feel the energy and form when you practice. Consider gazing at this image each time before you practice the LLP.

In this meditation, after good Preparation (Step 1), you Initiate the meditation sequence (Step 2) by: relaxing, aligning your posture, and generating positive feeling. Then, you focus into the breathing in the lower dantian to build vital energy here. Once your Concentration is strong and absorbed (Step 3) and you feel the energetic charge, you draw energy up the spine, through the upper dantian, to the crown, and above into the Soul Star, an energy center several inches above your head. The Soul Star contains energy and information related to your life purpose. Resting your attention here, you take in high-frequency Light. Imagine you are downloading Divine energy and information about *who you are* and *why you're here* into your subconscious, where it will inspire and guide you.

This high-frequency energy infuses and transforms your mind. You can know your vibration is raised to this frequency by tingling sensations of electrical charge above your head and in your brain, and perhaps descending down through your whole body. We have come to note these sensations as increased gamma readings on EEG sensing devices.

Then, allow this energy to flow down into your heart, where it transforms into the purest Unconditional Love, the Love of a Divine Mother who embraces you unconditionally. You experience this Love in your heart and become aware of it extending outward to all beings and the whole Universe. Imagine and feel this Love flowing through One Shared Heart. Inhale this Love through your heart, extending it to all beings and the whole Universe. As you exhale, feel this Love flowing back through your heart. You can know your vibration is resonating with this frequency of Unconditional Love by feelings of warmth and connection extending outward from your heart. We have come to note these frequencies as either elevated gamma readings or elevated delta readings on EEG sensors.

Finally, allow the energy to flow down to your perineum, where you ground it in stillness, experiencing the deep inner peace of letting go. Rest in still, silent, spacious Awareness until you feel Transcendence of self (Step 4) into this vast clear space. You can know you are resonating with the frequencies of deep Peace, stillness, and Awareness itself by a release from all tension, thinking, focus, and emotion into a formless resting in Pure Awareness. The sense of being an individual body and an individualized self dissolves. There is only Awareness—open, clear, spacious Awareness. We have come to associate this state with elevated theta frequencies, along with spontaneous arising gamma frequencies as the Whole Field brightens with Awareness.

After spending time in this space of Awareness, you'll follow cues for Returning and Grounding and complete the final steps of the meditation, which we discuss in the next two chapters.

Through the course of this meditation, you experience different frequency bands of the Universal Life Force, each with their particular purposes. Light focuses, illuminates, informs, energizes, elevates, and inspires. It helps to release lower-level energies and perspectives and provides inner guidance. Love brings a warm, soothing experience of harmony, unity, and connection that comforts and nurtures. Experiencing Love flowing through your heart facilitates compassionate relationships with yourself and others. Letting go into the deep Peace of stillness grounds the energy, while calming your system and releasing any effort, movement, or tensions of self. In stillness, you dissolve into formlessness and open to Pure Conscious awareness of Awareness itself—Nondual Awareness.

As you spend considerable time in Nondual Awareness, you begin to experience several subtle variations of this state: Infinite Spacious Awareness, Choiceless Attention, the Bliss of Being, and the Clear Light that permeates All. This moment in meditation is like returning to a state prior to Creation, the Zero Point, from which all forms emerge and into which all forms dissolve.

In a sense, we are recapitulating the process of Creation and Returning to Source: Light and Love express through embodiment and then return to formlessness, the state prior to Creation. By letting go into formlessness you dissolve attachment to any aspect of this process. Through this meditation, you are reborn as a being of Light, Love, Peace, and elevated Awareness. You are an expression of Life itself becoming Aware of itself in the process of Creation and Returning to Source.

You can find the LLP1 meditation script in the Appendices. You can memorize it, record it in your own voice, or follow along with the recording we've created, which can be found in the ROV Meditation App, available for Apple and Android devices in those app stores.

We suggest you continue to log your practice using the **Meditation Log** in the Appendices.

- For each session, log the day and time, and the name of the meditation you did.
- Add a brief description of the inner cues you found significant. (An example of this could be, "Rest in still, silent, spacious Awareness.")
- Add a brief description of your inner felt experience of these significant cues. (An example of this could be, "I felt as if 'I' dissolved and there was only Infinite Space. There was a softness and lightness that was deeply peaceful—a complete freedom from tension, pain, and struggle.")
- Finally, give a rating from 0 to 10 of your Energy, Mood, and Mental.

Reflection & Insight Journaling

What did you learn from this chapter that can help you integrate your meditation experience with your life?

Why is it important for you to take time ending a meditation session rather than rushing off into everything you need to get done? What happens if you don't do this? How does this relate to the primary issue you're working with and what's blocking you from having the experiences that your soul desires?

--- --- ---

In our next chapter, we'll guide you to reflect on your meditative experiences and help you to use your meditative state to gain insight,

187

solve problems, heal, and manifest the experiences your soul desires. We look forward to joining you there after you've practiced the Light, Love, and Peace Meditation (Version 1).

9. Reflection and Insight

How to Use Meditation to Change Your Life

Once you've learned to cultivate a meditative state, you might be inclined to just hang out there and enjoy the relief from over-thinking, tension, and stress. You might want to bask in the calm that comes as you find a place of peace beyond the intensity of life. You may want to savor the feelings of relaxation in your body.

It's good not to rush back into life and lose this meditative experience in the busyness of the day. It's important to soak it in and absorb it fully, and to register it in every cell and fiber of your being, so it becomes a reliable baseline of peace, calm, and awareness to live from. As you do this, meditative awareness will begin to permeate every aspect of your life.

You can also use your meditative state to do conscious work to transform any aspect of your life. It's possible to use a meditative state to gain insight and wisdom, solve problems, heal, and manifest the experiences your soul desires. In this chapter, we explore several ways you can use a meditative state to improve the quality of your

189

life and relationships in very specific ways that are important to you at this moment. Ultimately, Subtle Energy Meditation is about the transformation of consciousness, so you resonate with the finer frequencies of Peace, Love, and Light and live in an elevated state of Awareness.

What Exactly Is a Meditative State?

Before we move into things you can do from a meditative state, let's revisit exactly what we're talking about. What do we mean by a "meditative state?" As we've learned, this is a progressive series of steps, layers, and states of consciousness.

When you first begin to meditate, you learn **relaxed, focused, mindful attention**. You learn to pay attention, on purpose, in the present moment, non-judgmentally—as a curious observer. This is a skill you can apply to every moment of your life to be more attentive, aware, relaxed, calm, and free. No matter what happens, you can learn to be present with it, rather than consumed and overwhelmed by it. In this state, your non-stop thinking, analyzing, comparing, and "doing" mind quiets down, and you feel a relief from tension and stress.

This state of relaxed, mindful awareness is characterized by relaxed alpha brainwaves and steadily focused beta waves. In this state, your mind can observe what is happening, consciously choose where you focus your attention, notice distractions, and return to focus. You can also use interoception to openly monitor your inner state and notice where your attention *is* without feeling compelled and pulled by inner tensions and attractions.

As you learn to sustain focused attention, you move toward **one-pointed concentration** in which your attention is unwavering. This state is characterized by brainwaves synchronizing and moving tightly together in unison. We've noticed, with focused breath awareness, in particular, a pattern of overriding alpha over a triple band of theta/beta/delta over low gamma brainwaves in this state. When you are deeply concentrating on something, so that everything else fades to the background, you have entered one-pointed concentration. Concentration builds the energy you need to access deeper states of meditation.

From one-pointed concentration, your focal object becomes highly energized, and it draws you like a magnetic attractor into **absorption.** At this point, you lose the sense of being separate from what you are focusing on. You are "one with" the object of your attention, and the effort of focusing concentration is no longer necessary. You are fully immersed in it. For example, if you are focused on breathing, you become one with the breath, as if "it is breathing you." There is no longer "you" doing something called "breathing." There is just "breathing."

Athletes and artists call this "being in the zone." In this state of effortless flow, you lose all sense of time and are carried along in the activity itself. In this state, sensory details seem richer and brighter. These moments have a magical quality. It feels as if everything is exactly as it is meant to be. In this state, theta waves (related to deeper access to your subconscious), and delta waves (related to your unconscious connection to All of Life), rise toward alpha waves of relaxation and beta waves of focus.

Meditative absorption facilitates a crossover into **Transcendence**. In Transcendence, you move beyond the *content* of awareness into still, silent, spacious awareness of Awareness itself—the Field of Pure Consciousness beyond form, the matrix from which all experiences emerge and into which all experiences dissolve. This may appear as a luminous clarity, a blissful Nondual Awareness. This state is beyond description by its very nature. Any attempt to describe it makes it a "thing" with prescribed boundaries. It is no-thing, as it is the Source of all things. It is the Unmanifest prior to form.

This stage of meditation is a venture beyond the known and into the unknown, the Source from which everything emerges. This experience is available through meditation or may spontaneously arise in transcendent moments in nature, art, or relationships. However, it arises, it is a state of consciousness characterized by increasingly prevalent theta waves that signal you've stepped "beyond" the world of known "things." In these moments, gamma, delta, or theta waves may rise, as you resonate with superconscious high-frequency Light, the collective unconscious through Love, or the deep stillness of Peace, and merge with awareness of Awareness itself.

Why Is a Meditative State Useful?

Now, you might wonder why these meditative states, especially this last state of awareness of Awareness itself, are useful at all? How can they change your life?

Each one is useful on its own and as a part of a progression. It's useful to cultivate the ability to move fluidly between different states of consciousness, as well as to be able to call on them as situations require their attributes.

For example, in a state of relaxed, focused, mindful attention, you can observe your own and other's states of thinking, feeling, and behavior without overreacting and being overwhelmed by them. With the skill of mindful attention, you are more calm, aware, intentional, insightful, cooperative, and effective.

Cultivating concentration is essential, because attention is pulled in so many different directions in our information-overloaded culture, saturated with advertising and social media. The skill of concentration enables you to choose your focal point, focus on what really matters, and let go of the rest.

Absorption enables you to rise above the mundane and everyday into a magical world of connection, creativity, and performance beyond the limits of time and space. It enables you to break free from the limiting thoughts, feelings, beliefs, and perspectives within which you may normally feel confined.

Transcendence is the ultimate liberation from all tensions and divisions, in which you experience the sublime Clear Light from which we are born and into which we dissolve. Experiencing this vast, spacious, Nondual Awareness makes anything here in this world seem small, inconsequential, and transient by comparison. Transcendence is a release from self-focus and an awakening to Infinite Eternal Presence.

Finally, entry into any level of meditative state is important for how you can use it to do other conscious work. Even the first level of relaxed, focused, mindful attention is free from the tensions and stresses of non-stop thinking, analyzing, comparing, and doing, which enables you to engage deeper capacities and inner skills.

Seven Ways to Use a Meditative State to Change Your Life

Here are several ways you can work with a meditative state. Any or all of these are ideally done after a period of meditation, in which your mind is quiet and focused, your emotions are calm, and your body is relaxed. In this state, other capacities and inner skills are readily available. A meditative state gives you access to intuition, empathic understanding, insights, subtle perceptions, visions, and healing that can change your life.

1. Landmarks

One of the simplest and most important things to do at the end of meditation is to make note of how you feel, record this sensation in your body, and label it with a word, phrase, or image. This helps you remember this state of consciousness, so that you can bring it with you, and return to it any time you need it. These landmarks become reference points you can use to return to a meditative state.

The end of meditation is also a time to review your meditative experience for any particularly poignant moments or insights and write them down. This solidifies these moments in your conscious awareness, so they become more meaningful and memorable and have a greater impact on your life outside of your meditation time. Using a journal to record these moments is useful to remember, process, and integrate them in your consciousness.

2. Healing

A meditative state is a powerful state from which to heal your body, mind, and emotions. In this state, you activate your parasympathetic nervous system—your relaxation, recovery, and repair mode—which naturally facilitates healing. In this state, you feel less engaged with and compelled by superficial thoughts and emotions, so you can access deeper subconscious holding patterns and resources. The relaxed, empowered feeling of a meditative state enables you to observe deeper tensions and stored traumas and related emotions without reacting in fear.

It's particularly powerful to use healing imagery to access subconscious information and set in motion your innate healing systems. For example, as we did in the "Discovering the Message in Your Body" exercise in Chapter 2, you can ask your body where a particular issue is stored and what sensory qualities it has, such as shape, color, size, texture, sound, or taste. You can ask what message this issue has for you and what it needs to heal. You might be surprised at the information you receive. Any healing modality is more effective when accessed from a meditative state.

3. Insight/Problem Solving

As you let go of your thinking, doing, comparing, and analyzing mind, you open the doors to deeper intuitive resources. Depending on the depth of your meditative state, you can tap into information from your subconscious or even from the Collective Consciousness of the whole human race and beyond. Even in a light meditative state, you can float any question you have, let go, and allow information and associations to flow. Again, you might be surprised at what arises when you allow answers to come to you rather than trying to think your way to them. Writing a question in your journal and freely writing whatever comes to mind is one way to access this information.

4. Manifesting

A meditative state is conducive to rewiring your body, heart, and mind to receive new experiences. This is based on the premise that your subconscious mind doesn't differentiate between "real" and imagined experiences. Both groove the same neural networks in your body and brain that make subsequent real or imagined experiences easier to reproduce. Interesting studies show that mentally rehearsing an experience is highly effective and sometimes even more powerful than practicing in physical reality. Brain imaging studies show that mentally rehearsing any activity grows the same parts of your brain that physically practicing the activity does.

Your imagination is powerful, especially when you combine it with "feeling" as if you are actually doing the activity. The basic idea is that by imagining and feeling what it's like to have an experience, you establish a neural network that is conducive to and supportive of this experience. Mentally rehearsing a desired experience primes your body, mind, and emotions to more easily welcome similar experiences in your real life.

So, if you have something you would like to grow or experience in your life, spend some time mentally rehearsing this experience at the end of your meditation practice. We suggest that an even more powerful way to look at manifesting is to ask this question: "What does Life want to manifest through me right now?" This immediately takes you beyond self-focused self-interest and connects you to the flow of The One Life We All Share. Your deepest inspirations and aspirations are the inspirations and aspirations of Life itself.

So, what does Life want to manifest through you right now? You can know this by your soul's deepest desires. What is your soul's most prominent desire right now?

Picture the experience you desire (or that Life desires) and imagine yourself stepping into this scene and living it in full sensory detail. Make the sensory details rich and bright and feel the powerful positive emotion of what it is like to live in this experience. Play the scene forward in your mind as if you are really doing it and feeling it. Fully absorb the experience in your body, heart, and mind. Notice how you feel.

If you don't feel great, you can change any aspect of the experience in any way you desire, so it feels even better.

Finally, record an image of this experience and the associated feeling in your mind and body. Absorb the image and felt sensation deeply into your memory and your cells.

Then, be on the lookout to notice similar opportunities in your real life.

5. **Wisdom**

In a meditative state, you are receptive to deeper wisdom about the nature of self and life. The end of your meditative practice is a good time to reflect on what you learned.

For example, the simple act of paying attention to the ebb and flow of your breath can teach you about impermanence, about how all things arise, linger for a while, and dissolve—including your body, possessions, and achievements. Observing the arising and fading of your thoughts and feelings can teach you about their impermanent and insubstantial character, as well. They aren't as big, real, and substantial as they might seem. This can help you let go of the ones that do not serve you or others.

Touching something deeper or transcendent in meditation can teach you there is more to life than meets the eyes or is available through your five senses. There is a realm beyond this 3D world from which everything arises. The end of your meditation is a good time to reflect on what deeper wisdom you contacted.

Stephen's Meditation Insights into Suffering

As I sat down to write this, I was flooded by the knowledge of many lives, of the many lives we have, and the suffering inherent in that. I wept. I couldn't hold back the tears and I wept for myself and all others who have not seen the deep insight that comes from direct knowledge of these lives and the extraordinary dimension of *samsara* (the cycles of life).

We struggle with life and suffering primarily because we only see the part of life we are dealing with right now. Unless we are deep in present-moment awareness, this view of life is a very small part of life as a whole and yet we focus on it as being the whole of reality.

It is like looking at the stars we can see and saying that is the universe. The section of the night sky we are seeing is a very small portion of the whole. We eliminate birth and death, past and future lives, out of our conscious awareness and instead focus on a very small part of our life and make an assumption about reality based on this small scope of awareness.

We are not living in consciousness of the full picture, the entire universe as it were, and so our understanding mostly begins and ends with what is happening to us now.

When we commit to truth and freedom, we can use practices like meditation and the profound insights that come from it to embrace the whole picture.

From the deep insight of many lives to deep insight in the present moment, we see that the present moment, if we are still, silent, and spacious enough, contains the full consciousness of all life, with its births and deaths, joys and sorrows, fortunes and misfortunes.

We see that wherever there is birth, there is suffering. We see and feel the immeasurable expanse of all these births and deaths deeply in our being. If birth is the beginning of suffering, and we feel it deeply, then we also see the possibility of being free of suffering, by freeing ourselves from the continuing passage of births and deaths. As we become free, we open up to a deeper happiness, one free of all suffering.

When we meditate deeply, new undiscovered parts of our being reveal themselves through *jhana*. Jhana, or subtle states of consciousness, arise when we have deep concentration on a single object like the breath. Clarity, joy, and bliss that we never knew before spontaneously arise. We realize a different kind of birth, a rebirth from within.

When we are deeply still, silent, and spacious, we connect to the inner space of Being. When we are agitated, the ego occupies this space with thoughts. When we are still and silent, clarity, joy, and bliss emerge. These may be accompanied by signs of freedom, like sound and light. These signs or *nimitta* are a confirmation of the ever-increasing freedom found when resting in the space of Being. These states are unforgettable, undeniable, indefinable, and timeless. The experience is so profound that we naturally want to inquire about where this newfound clarity, joy, and bliss comes from. They appear naturally, woven into the very fabric of Life itself.

How then can we become free from suffering?

Let's take the example of agitation. Perhaps it comes from fearful thoughts about a physical problem we have. When something doesn't feel good in our physical body, our mind goes to work, imagining all sorts of things it might mean. Is it serious? Is it lasting? What will happen to me?

I have a body that is very sensitive, so when I get under stress, it trembles. When a person is angry around me (even if it is not at me), my body trembles from the stress of the emotions I feel from that person. In that sense, I am very empathic. Meditation has been such a boon, a tremendous gift, in dealing with this sensitivity. Here is how it works for me when I am agitated by an angry person.

The first thing I do is sit still. I become aware of the trembling. When my mind is agitated, it is difficult to stop. So, I connect with the physical experience of stillness and I breathe, usually with a long exhalation. Just this kind of breathing and stillness. Amazingly, even if there is a strong involuntary tremor or spasm in my body, it calms down with simple breathing and stillness.

Then, I listen to the silence. Silence is the quieting of the inner voice. When I can rest in the silence and the stillness, then the thinking mind is quiet, and I reach a space of emptiness. Emptiness is the dissolving of whatever was agitating. It is no longer substantial. It's no longer a "big thing."

Next, I feel into the space of open awareness. It is like looking up into the sky at night and seeing and feeling beyond it into the vast spaciousness of the universe itself. I see and feel into the universe and let go of any boundaries. The universal consciousness awakens in me, breathes through me.

When the spaciousness is all around me, within me, and beyond me, I rest in this space. I am free.

The reason we suffer is we don't see the whole picture, the big picture. We focus on very tiny parts of our consciousness, such as what we are anxious about, who is bothering us, why we don't have enough money, and what our future will bring.

When we meditate, we let go into the silence, stillness, and spaciousness of Universal Consciousness, where we don't hang onto the self with its needs and thoughts. For a short time, we are free in the boundless space of Infinite Awareness. Just for a moment, we go beyond this 3D world and touch the Transcendent—pure Being. Pure bliss. Pure consciousness.

This wider vision transforms consciousness.

6. Liberation: Some would say the whole point of meditation is liberation—to be free from the tensions, preoccupations, and illusions you identify with. Meditation can show you what you are ready to let go of, so you can live more openly, freely, acceptingly, and lovingly—so you can live from greater awareness and a much larger vision of Life. What are you ready to let go of because it no longer serves you or others?

If you experience Transcendence in meditation, you come to understand liberation as a profound, palpable, felt experience you never forget. This experience transforms how you relate to everything. Make note of your moments of Transcendence and describe them as best as you can so you can imprint them in your mind.

My Faces Before I Was Born: Stephen's Liberation Experiences

When I was little, my dad managed an intravenous unit at the main hospital in the city and mum was the matron of another hospital. I got to help dad on my holidays by delivering IV solutions to the patients (with their doctors) and helping them to cheer up. They all seemed to welcome a young boy with a big smile and stories that would help them through their long days in hospital beds.

When my grandmother was dying, my mum nursed her at our home, and I helped. Because I was involved in her care, when Nana passed I felt it was natural—part of the life and death cycle of the human body. I knew her spirit had gone somewhere else. Mum was an Irish

Catholic. So, for her, Nana had gone to Heaven to be with my grandad, Poppy. Dad was a scientist. So, for him, Nana was part of the great energy cycle of the universe, where nothing is created or destroyed. Energy just changes from one form to another. I grew up with these two fundamental ideas. They nurtured and sculpted my mind and heart, until I saw them as co-existing principles of a Universal Consciousness.

The other thing I spent most of my time doing was observing space. I was fascinated by the stars and intuited that what we could see was a remarkably tiny portion of what actually is in terms of the entire universe and beyond. I was curious about what lay beyond what we knew and how we could venture there and make contact. I wrote to NASA when I was five, asking if I could be on the first trip to Alpha Centauri. I figured that might be a useful place to start in the search for other consciousness like ours.

This curiosity about the body, spirit, space, and what lay beyond led me to inquire deeply into the nature of existence. This led me to meditation; this and one other experience from when I was very little.

As a child, my earliest memory is a dream I had every night from the time I was two until I was three. In this dream, I was a Tibetan monk who died defending my spiritual leader on a bridge. I fell from the bridge into a chasm, surrounded by cosmic sound and light.

This dream made me deeply curious about our "continuum of lives" and particularly the consciousness I seemed to be carrying, containing a continuum of lives devoted to liberation. It gave me an insight into the continuum of consciousness itself. It made me want to explore this practice called meditation, so that it might liberate me into what lay beyond the physical world.

Insight after meditation takes many forms, depending on the depth of your experience and the focus of your inquiry. Interestingly, when you look at the Buddha's own enlightenment under the Bodhi tree, the first area of deep insight was into past lives. One might question the validity of past lives. The Buddha said that one who holds the view that there is no other world and no rebirth has a wrong view. So, how can you verify the truth of rebirth for yourself?

There is an ancient Tibetan meditation that can take us back to our time of birth to see what we arrived with and what we bring into this world. It is called "The Faces Before You Were Born." This meditation is also practiced in many Zen traditions. In it you reflect not only on the lives you lived before this one, but also your support at birth, your life lessons, support at death, and your faces after death.

When I first practiced this meditation, I experienced emptiness. Nothing arose in the space of awareness, so I went for a drive. Driving down country roads and walking in our nearby forest are especially good for me when I am seeking insight. As I was driving, I spontaneously heard a voice. It said, "The faces before birth are *bodhisattva* faces connected to Maitreya." This realization came in waves of energy that confirmed its truth. I had to pull over and park—it was so strong and overwhelming.

As you begin to understand how to access early memories, even ones before you were born, you can continue to suggest clearly to your mind, "Earlier, earlier" and then return to the inner silence with no expectations.

If you quietly attend to the present moment and your absorption is deep enough, the memories will come. When they come, you'll feel an absolute clarity and certainty that it is a memory from an earlier time, like the bodhisattva faces connected to Maitreya. It was goosebump-spine-tingling stuff.

Meditation Exercise: The Faces Before You Were Born

To begin, settle yourself into a meditative state using whatever simple method works well for you. Perhaps spend a few moments relaxing and focusing on the present-moment sensations of breathing in your body.

Concentrate on the point of your life's beginning. Know it as the point of the beginning of your "death." See that both your life and "death" are manifested at the same time. One is a continuum of the other; one cannot exist without the other. See that the existence of your life and "death" depend on each other. Birth is the foundation of "death," just as the birth of a star already swings into motion the "death" of that same star. You are at the same time your life and your "death." The two are not opposites, but two aspects of the same reality.

Search for your true face before birth. This is who you truly are and what you bring to this world in service. See who you arrived with at the moment of your birth and what support you brought to enable this service to humanity. See what lessons of life you agreed to and how you decided to play out this lifetime. Then, concentrate on the point of your life's ending.

Search for your true face after "death." Keep the deep sense of who you truly are and what you bring to this world in true service, as you "die," transition, or ascend. See who you depart with and what support you have always had with you to enable this transition into the next life, world, or dimension through the process called "death."

See the ending point of this manifestation of both your life and your "death" and that there is no difference between before birth and after "death." There is a natural continuum that a deep part of you has been aware of through this incarnation on this planet.

Search for the many faces of the pure consciousness that you are. Realize that, "I am never born and can never die."

You are not the body. When you identify with the body, you think about birth and death. When you know you are the pure consciousness, existence, and bliss beyond the body, you know the truth of this realization, "I am never born and can never die."

7. Compassionate Service: Some would say the purpose of meditation is to cultivate a more compassionate life. From a meditative state, you are less attached to self-focus and all the things you identify with and hang onto, so you are more able to consider the well-being of others. Becoming more aware of your inner life through meditation tends to engender self-compassion as well, as you directly face your various thoughts and feelings. This naturally leads to compassion for others and what they go through.

A meditative state frees you from tension and fear so that you are truly more able to care for yourself and those around you. When you realize we are all born from and return to the same Source of Being, compassion for the well-being of All naturally arises. We share One Life. The well-being of one contributes to the well-being of All. From a meditative state, you might consider what ways you feel inspired to be of compassionate service in this world.

With these thoughts about how to use a meditative state to do other conscious work, it's time to practice the final meditation in our Subtle Energy Meditation series.

Daily Subtle Energy Meditation Practice: 8. Light, Love, and Peace, Version 2

In this extended version of the Light, Love, and Peace Meditation (**LLP Version 2**), you'll be guided deeper into Transcendence. You'll spend time experiencing the felt sensations of still, silent, spacious Awareness. Then, you'll shift deeper into Infinite Spacious Awareness and become aware of "Who is aware of this space?" You'll realize that the Infinite Space itself is Aware. There is only

Awareness, Infinite Spacious Awareness. This Infinite Space resonates with a primordial vibration, the OM. Allowing the OM to resonate throughout your being liberates, heals, and enlightens. It carries you Beyond.

You can find the LLP2 **Meditation Script** in the Appendices. You can memorize it, record it in your own voice, or follow along with the recording we've created, which can be found in the ROV Meditation App, available for Apple and Android devices in those app stores.

We suggest you continue to log your practice using the **Meditation Log** in the Appendices.

- For each session, log the day and time, and the name of the meditation you did.
- Add a brief description of the inner cues you found significant. (An example of this could be, "You may begin to hear or feel the vibration of this Field, like the hum of the Universe, the OM.")
- Add a brief description of your inner felt experience of these significant cues. (An example of this could be, "I felt as if my whole being was absorbed in the OM vibration, as if it was supported and cradled in this soothing vibration, which took me beyond myself into the Infinite Space of Awareness.").
- Finally, give a rating from 0 to 10 for your Energy, Mood, and Mental Clarity.

Reflection & Insight Journaling

As you consider the seven ways we've suggested to use a meditative state to change your life, which one jumps out at you? Which interests you the most right now? How might you incorporate this into your meditative practice?

Experiment with any one or all of these techniques to transform your meditative state into a vehicle to change your life and Our Life here on this planet.

--- --- ---

As we've said, ultimately, Subtle Energy Meditation is about the transformation of consciousness, so that you resonate with the finer frequencies of Peace, Love, and Light and live in an elevated state of Awareness. This begins as you learn to access different states of consciousness in meditation and it grows as you reflect on these states and gain insights about yourself and the nature of life.

These insights include realization of **compassion** for yourself and all beings, as you mindfully accept the diversity of your own inner life; **impermanence** as you recognize that all things arise, linger, and dissolve; and **non-substantiality** as you see that you, others, and Life's experiences always exceed any words you try to find. Other insights include **Oneness** as you contact the underlying Field that is the Source of All Life, and **Bliss** as you discover the Clear Light of Being that is always present underneath everything that happens.

As you embody these states and insights, your life transforms. You become a new being and contribute to raising the vibration of our Collective Consciousness. The final step is to fully embody this new way of being in acts of compassionate service. In doing so, you realize and fulfill a higher purpose in being here, now.

--- --- ---

In the next chapter, you'll discover the inner treasure of deeper meaning, purpose, and service you are here to share with the world. We look forward to joining you there after you've taken the time to practice LLP2 several times.

10. Compassionate Action Takes Us Home

The Inner Treasure of Meaning, Purpose, and Service

Have you noticed you operate on different levels of consciousness simultaneously? Here's what we mean. There is one layer you might call "surface consciousness," which is what you are aware of being focused on. If you don't dig any deeper, you might live on this level of consciousness most of the time. On this level of consciousness, you think things like, "I'm tired, I want a cup of coffee." If you don't go any deeper than this, you'll find yourself constantly reacting to life and repeating the same patterns of fatigue, stress, and frustration again and again.

Then, there is a deeper layer underneath, which houses a more primary, emotional, or spiritual need. Here is how Matthew Fox puts it: *"Deep down, each one of us is a mystic. When we tap into that energy, we become alive again and we give birth. From the creativity that we release is born the prophetic vision and work that we all aspire to realize as our gift to the world. We want to serve in whatever capacity we can. Getting in touch with the mystic inside is the beginning of our deep service."*

Christian Mystics: 365 Readings and Meditations 34

This is what you need to access if you want to transform your life and find what your soul truly desires. For example, underneath a "coffee moment," perhaps your soul wants something more—an experience beyond your normal state of consciousness—transcendence. Accessing and living from a transcendent state of consciousness is the ultimate goal of Subtle Energy Meditation. Perhaps, this is what your soul truly desires, when your surface consciousness is looking for a little more stimulation.

Perhaps, your soul is saying: "I want to do more than just get through this day. I'm tired of the pressure to get so much done. I wish I could do what I really want to do. I want to feel more alive! I want to break free! I wish I could be on fire with meaning and purpose! I want to make a difference! I wish I could transcend my 'self,' be free of tension and stress, and immerse in the flow of Spirit—making a powerful positive contribution to help others and raise the vibration of our planet!"

Now, that's a whole different dimension of being alive! Perhaps, coffee was a surface attempt to fill a deeper need. If you could find this deeper need and fulfill it, coffee may or may not call to you. You'd feel so purposeful and alive that Spirit would carry you on a magic carpet ride through the day.

In this chapter, you'll revisit the Five Questions we've been using throughout this book and add a sixth that will bring it all home. You'll discover the inner treasure of meaning, purpose, and service you are here to share with the world.

Let's begin by revisiting the Five Questions. Now that you know how to access deeper meditative states, you can inquire into the Five Questions from this deeper state of intuitive knowing and take the next step into your greater purpose here and now.

Five Questions to Dig Deeper

We encourage you to take a few moments to revisit each of these questions and write down anything that comes to mind. Each time you ask these questions is an opportunity to discover something new and fresh in this moment. Sometimes, what you discover is just for this moment. Sometimes, your answers carry you forward on a new path. Asking these questions from a state of deep meditative awareness might surprise you and take you to a whole new place in your life. At the same time, don't worry about answering these "correctly." See if you can float these questions in an open space of mindfulness, without rushing or judging what comes up.

Imagine each question is a fishing line you are casting deep into your subconscious. Wait patiently for a tug on the line. The tug could be very subtle or it could be strong. See if you can just notice what arises. Note any discomfort as well as what "sparks joy" (to borrow a wonderful phrase from Marie Kondo).[35] "Sparks joy" means something that makes you smile and feel good, something that feels just right and comes with a sense of deeper meaning and purpose.

You'll know you've hit upon something significant by a sense of knowing, a tug of emotion, or a gut feeling of "yes, that's it." The more often you ask questions like this, the more your intuitive sense of a deeper knowing will awaken and become a sure guide. If nothing comes to you with a particular question, you can move on to the next one and return to it at the end. You can also just write down something, even if it doesn't seem exactly right. This "something" may turn out to be more than you initially think it is. Sometimes, what initially feels "off" is just different from your usual mind about things—and this difference is the key to take you to a new place.

Before you cast these lines, we suggest you close your eyes. Take note of how you feel right now. Then, use this seven-point checklist to touch in with the meditative or Nondual Awareness you've cultivated through Subtle Energy Meditation:

Checklist for Nondual Awareness

1. Close your eyes (Read each step first. Then, close your eyes as you practice them).
2. Check in with how you feel right now, here in your body. If you could sum this up in a word, phrase, or image what would this be?
3. Focus in on your felt sensations of breathing. See if you can notice the moment you begin to inhale. As you breathe in, see if you can follow the sensations of inhaling until you naturally pause. See if you can notice the moment you begin to exhale. As you breathe out, see if you can follow the sensations of exhaling until you naturally pause. Follow your breathing until you feel completely absorbed in it. Then, allow the breath to become quiet, subtle, and soft, so you barely notice the subtle sensations. Become aware of the stillness at the beginning and end of each breath. Become aware of the beautiful feeling of the breath itself. Enjoy the beautiful breath.
4. Become aware of the entire space inside your skin, the inner field of still, silent, spacious awareness.
5. Imagine and feel this space within filled with light. Become aware of this light surrounding you and extending infinitely in all directions, so you are immersed in an Infinite Field of Light. This Infinite Field is the space of Consciousness itself, the Infinite Light of Pure Awareness. This Infinite Space is Aware.
6. Breathe in the Light of this Infinite Space, imagining as if this Infinite Space is breathing through you, is breathing you into life. The Infinite Space is breathing in, breathing out. The Infinite Space is breathing you. Feel the light of this space filling your body, making it glow. Feel it. Feel the being-ness of this energy field. You are one with this Field. It is your Life. You are an expression of this Field, this One Life we all share. You have shifted awareness beyond self,

time, and form. There is deep, still, silent, spacious, Nondual Awareness—and a natural peace, joy, love, and compassion that is woven into the nature of Reality itself—the formless, timeless, nameless realm of Being from which all forms, all inspirations, and all answers arise.

7. Slowly half open your eyes and feel the space within you within the space all around you. Notice how you feel. If you could sum this up in a word, phrase, or image what would this be?

Now, you are ready to revisit the Five Questions and then add the sixth question of deeper meaning, purpose, and service. We suggest you go through these slowly, mindfully, and write down your responses.

Five Coaching Questions

Question 1. What is your biggest need/frustration/issue/challenge right now in your life?

Question 2. How do you want this to improve? What result do you desire?

Question 3. What is blocking you?

Question 4. What do you fear will happen in the future if you don't resolve this?

Question 5. How will you know you've achieved what you desire? What will you feel?

So, how did it go revisiting these questions? Did you discover anything new that helped you dig under your surface thoughts and feelings?

These questions initiate a process of self-inquiry that is essential if you're going to find the deeper treasure you're really seeking, yet they stop short of the most important question which completes the puzzle. These questions are all about "you." If you want to get where your soul really wants to go, you're going to have to get over your "self." Answering the following sixth question transcends the struggles of self-focus and takes you all the way home.

The Sixth Question: Meaning, Purpose, and Service

What if your greatest gift and service to the world comes from the desire you most want to fulfill, which in turn comes from your biggest struggle in life? So, for example, feeling that "I don't fit in" gives a desire to fit in, to be part of a family or group in which you feel you belong, and this gives you a purposeful mission to create community where people feel like they belong. In this way, your deepest hurt becomes your greatest gift and service in the world. We sum up this transformation in our sixth question, the question of meaning, purpose, and service:

Question 6. How can you use what you've been through and the skills and resources you've gained to serve others and raise the vibration of our planet?

Let's explore this question in more detail. So, what would you say is your biggest struggle? This struggle gives you a specific strong desire that can become a powerful path of service. This sixth question is really a multi-part question that digs down to the soul level. Let's go through the steps together. We suggest you write down your responses:

Based on your responses to the Five Questions above (which relate to the present and future moments in your life), what would you say is your deepest hurt, pain, or struggle over the course of your life as a whole? What is an old hurt that you seem to carry with you to this day?

Based on this hurt/pain/struggle, what is your deepest desire?

212

For example, if you were ridiculed as a child for being weak, you might want to become strong. If you loved to sing and were told you were no good at it, you might want to become a world-class singer. If you felt isolated, misunderstood, and alone, you might want to find a community in which you can express yourself. If you felt lost in school, you might want to learn as much as you can in a subject you love, so you become an expert. If you felt anxious and overwhelmed by life, you might want to find a peaceful place that is free from pressure and stress. If your parents argued all the time, you might have a strong desire to create harmony between people. If you have been sick, you may have a strong desire for health. If you were abused, you may have a deep desire for healing. If you didn't have the resources you needed, you might have a strong desire for abundance . . .

Again, what is your deepest pain and your resulting desire? Cast one of those fishing lines into your deeper mind . . .

Now, it's time for the turning-point question. Previously, you may have thought of your pain as a hindrance, a stumbling block, and something that limits you, frustrates you, or holds you back. The turning point comes when you see what you've been through as a gift. This is how you move from being a victim to an empowered contributor to the well-being of others. This move is what takes you all the way home.

How is your deepest pain and desire the source of your greatest gift? What have you learned, developed, or grown as a result of what you've been through? What skills, talents, or resources did your deepest pain and desire ask you to cultivate?

If you feel you haven't yet grown these gifts, how might you do so?

And, finally, how can you offer this gift to others? In what ways can you use what you've been through and the skills and resources you've gained to help others and raise the vibration of our planet?

When you discover this deeper meaning in what you've been through, your feeling state immediately elevates. You rise up and flow in the currents of Spirit. Your life becomes that mystical carpet ride of your deepest dreams. You live beyond your small sense of self, beyond the pressures of time—effortlessly carried on a marvelous journey to unknown destinations that make life feel rich and meaningful. You feel purposeful and fully alive!

Now, all this may seem like a lot to ask from spending a few minutes contemplating on a deeper level. Yet, our hope is that it sparks a deeper level of ongoing inquiry under the surface consciousness of your life. Moments of discomfort can transform into moments of insight and compassionate action that elevate your life and the collective life of all of us together.

So, when you feel the tug toward coffee, or any other way you might hope to shift your inner state into one that's closer to "sparks joy," what if you pause and ask some deeper questions like the ones suggested above? When you do this, moments of surface tension become moments of inquiry that bring deeper resources online to guide your way. In particular, the sixth question opens you to a world beyond self-focus in which compassion is your sure guide.

Let's look at how to practice compassion in a variety of important relationships and settings beginning with yourself.

Practicing Compassion in Different Relationships and Situations

We live in a world in which we often feel vulnerable—and that vulnerability can make us afraid. Fear can make us want to defend ourselves, strike back, or put the blame on others. It can lead to knee-jerk reactions that end up making situations worse rather than better. Or, it can make us want to turn away or hide, rather than venture out to live fully, with courage and compassion.

214

However, the solution to every challenge begins by recognizing, accepting, and appreciating your own vulnerability, your own suffering, as well as the suffering of others, rather than turning away from it. Healing and transformation comes through accepting your own imperfections and thereby having compassion for others. Only by facing what is happening with loving kindness will you heal yourself and create a safer world.

Now, it's natural not to want to spend much time embracing your imperfections or acknowledging your suffering or the suffering of others. It's uncomfortable to feel this vulnerable. Sometimes, it's hard enough just to get through all you have to do in a day—much less having to face more uncomfortable feelings. However, by recognizing the vulnerability in yourself and others, you open the door to being stronger and more resilient and to supporting others and feeling more connected to them.

Approaching vulnerability and suffering mindfully can bring about great compassion—and compassion is the secret to personal resilience and interpersonal connection. Compassion begins with yourself, then naturally extends to others.

Three Steps for Self-Compassion

Dr. Kristin Neff, who runs the Self-Compassion Research Lab at the University of Texas, in Austin, says that self-compassion has three elements: self-kindness, common humanity, and mindfulness.[36] Here's how she sums this up:

1. Self-kindness is the quality of being warm and understanding toward ourselves when we suffer, fail, or feel inadequate, rather than ignoring our pain or self-criticizing.

2. Common humanity is recognizing that suffering and feelings of inadequacy are part of the shared human experience—something we all go through rather than something that happens to "me" alone.

215

3. Mindfulness is non-judgmentally observing negative and uncomfortable emotions without being swept up in them or carried away by them. By mindfully observing vulnerable feelings we release stored tension and pain around them and open ourselves to the healing, gifts, and connections that are available in them.

As you practice these steps of self-compassion, you may discover that you naturally feel more compassionate toward others. To deepen this compassion, while also observing and learning about your own reactions, we suggest this next compassion practice.

Sacred Listening

What would you say is the foundation of compassionate communication? Though there are probably several good answers, the practice we're going to focus on is **Listening**. Not just listening as in hearing what someone else is saying, but **Sacred Listening**.

Sacred Listening is listening to another with "unconditional positive regard" (to borrow a phrase from psychologist Carl Rogers).[37] You respect another for who they are without trying to change them in any way. In Sacred Listening, you act as an open receiver in a conversation. You put all the focus on the other person and what they have to say. You mirror back to them without offering your commentary or point of view. The conversation is "all about the other person."

When you practice Sacred Listening, you accept the other person completely, just as they are.

Sacred Listening merges the interoceptive awareness that you've cultivated in Subtle Energy Meditation with your sense of hearing. It attunes your sense of hearing to mindfulness, so you listen to others with that attitude of nonjudgment, acceptance, appreciation, gratitude, and compassion. In this way, you re-train and refine your sense of hearing. Sacred Listening creates a supportive environment

216

of unconditional acceptance and appreciation within which another feels free to speak as they are at this moment.

So, how do you do this? We suggest you choose at least one conversation every day in which you will be a sacred listener. You can tell the other person that you are building your listening skills and would like to hear what they have to say. You can also do this without the other person knowing what you are doing. The other person will probably simply appreciate being heard. However, if the situation would be awkward, let the other person know what you are doing.

After choosing your opportunity and informing the other person (or not), you can initiate the conversation by asking the other person an open-ended question such as "How are you feeling about such and such?" Encourage the other person to relate their feelings versus simply recalling events.

As they talk, let them know by your body language that you are truly interested in what they are saying. Sit facing them or at least turned in their direction. Make eye contact when appropriate. Smile with acceptance. Soften your eyes with understanding. Relax your hands in your lap.

At appropriate breaks in their speech, you can mirror back to them what they just said in their words or your own, whichever feels natural. This will clarify that you are paying attention and encourage them to elaborate. You could say something like, "So, what you're saying is _____," or "Would you tell me more about _____," or "So, you are feeling _____, is this what you're saying?"

If the other person asks for your opinion or your advice, gently turn the conversation back to them by saying something like, "Can you tell me more about _____." Most of the time, people would rather be heard and come to their own solutions rather than getting advice. It's helpful to have someone really listen. Listening provides "an open space" in which the other can discover their own solutions. You are simply "holding this space."

Being listened to in this way is a true gift. You offer the other person an environment in which they can be themselves without fear of critique or judgment. Sacred Listening creates a safe haven.

When you practice Sacred Listening, you learn more about the other person and more about your habitual response patterns. You may notice how quick you are to jump in with your opinion, or your agenda, rather than really hearing what the other person is expressing. You may notice how you try to turn conversations in the direction that you want them to go. You may notice how you try to wrap up a line of conversation, so that you can get on with what you want to do or say. You may become aware of your own reactions when you stop them and keep the focus on the other person.

You may also come to appreciate the other person in ways you never have before. Listen for their interests, passions, hurts, and desires. Listen for their unique talents and the perspective they bring to the world. Tune in to what is good and sacred in them. Through Sacred Listening you support the other person to discover and be who they are at this moment. By Sacred Listening, you say "Namaste" to another: "The Light in me bows to the Light in you."

When you listen to another with the sole intention of understanding their point of view, you develop compassion. Compassion is the ability to "walk in another's shoes" and understand where they are coming from. It is the ability to understand their suffering along with the desire to help relieve this suffering. It overcomes separation and turns "the other" into a sacred partner in this moment.

Compassion is the basis of your ability to truly care for another. Without knowing another's needs, hopes, and desires you have no basis for offering support. Through compassion, you offer support that comforts another's pain and nurtures their highest aspirations.

Often what we offer to another is what *we want* to see them do. We look at another through our own point of view and offer what we would do. We try to move them toward our agenda. Even though we may have good intentions, we are imposing our will.

Sacred Listening opens you to truly enter the world of the other. You set aside your agendas and your desires, so that you can understand another's context, the world they're living in. You get inside their pain and suffering along with their aspirations and highest truth. You hold a protected interpersonal space which encourages *their* plans to emerge from within *their* own experience. Sacred Listening is a foundation for compassion.

Stephen's Story of Compassionate Parenting

Here I would like to share about bringing compassion into our roles as parents, though it applies to bringing compassion into any relationship.

I often talk about meditation and life with my four-year-old daughter, Maia. We talk about life through questions. Every dinner time is question time. She asks my wife and me about our day, and we ask her about her day. We ask things like, "What did you dream last night, and what did it show you?" or "What did you learn from today?"

If we listen compassionately, truly valuing the unique perspectives children have, we can gain a lot from their clarity and insight. Often, they'll say things in unexpected ways that shed new light on what we take for granted. My daughter is a natural dream yogi. She had a dream of my wife. In the middle of her dream, she woke herself up because she knew, "It wasn't the real mama."

My daughter often reminds me of the simple lessons in meditation. When she was only one, we were at our local Shingon Buddhist

---

temple doing a Goma Fire Ceremony, when a camera crew arrived. There were a lot of people there. The temple is revered for the immovable indestructible presence and manifestation of the Buddha. The interviewer asked Maia to point out the Buddha to her. Maia pointed straight to the young woman's heart. "Babu (her name for Buddha) is there, inside your heart."

Meditation is like this, letting the mind and heart be, quite naturally, like a child. It is simply about feeling the way you feel and letting the mind and heart be as they are and gaining insight into how they are in this moment. It takes compassion to do this for yourself and for others. Though it may seem like nothing, it is quite a practice to live from this place of acceptance and non-judgment:

Silent, still, and spacious. Sitting in compassionate awareness for yourself and others exactly where you are at this moment.

Sometimes, "where you are" is angry and frustrated, like a child. My daughter had some real blowouts and tantrums as a three-year-old. My wife and I struggled to be with her in these moments. We worked hard to breathe with her and embrace what she felt. This is a practice. We've gotten better at it. As we are able to breathe, let go, and accept the moment as it is, it helps us and her to calm down.

My daughter puts things in simple ways. She once asked me why I didn't get angry like other people. I told her I was practicing compassion. "Oh," she said, "That makes you a Buddha." "What about you, Maia?" I asked her. "I'm an angel," said Maia.

As you sit in meditation, you take your attention to simple things— like the breath. We are all breathing together. The Universe is breathing through us. Your children are within this breath. Your parents are within this breath. Your neighbors and coworkers are within this breath. All beings and the whole planet are within this breath.

Children know, in very simple terms, this power of interconnectedness. They are related to us, their parents, and, by nature, also related to everything else through us. Everything contains everything else. And everything is changing. Children know this. We can re-learn it by paying attention to how they see things.

From a child's point of view, their rapidly changing world deeply enhances an appreciation of impermanence, as does their openness to so many new experiences. We know how vulnerable they are, how precious little babies are, yet we often take this for granted. In compassionate listening, we are present for our children in their world, as it appears to them, along with all their hopes and fears.

What if we could approach each person, every being, as a child of the One Life we all share? This is the heart of compassion.

Applying Compassion in the Moments You Really Need It

Compassion is one of the primary fruits of meditation and mindfulness practice. We've looked at a few skillful ways to cultivate it, and to make it more ready and available as part of your baseline state of consciousness.

One of the purposes of having a guided meditation, such as the Light, Love, and Peace Meditation, is to train new ways of thinking, feeling, and being. It expands the range of states of consciousness available to you. It teaches you to consciously relax and embody upright posture, which supports alert mindful attention. It guides you to concentrate with one-pointed absorption in the finer frequencies of Light, Love, and Peace and let go in transcendence beyond content and form into the bliss of Pure Awareness. It encourages you to reflect on this elevated Awareness and gain insight into how to live a life of compassionate action.

Compassion offers an alternative to the mind of stress. It grants access to a wealth of resources that you can't see when you feel you've got to do this alone. Your experience of stress is the result of how you are thinking about the demands you're facing. In general, you'll feel more stress if you think that the challenges in front of you are big and your resources are small. You'll feel more stress if you think you've got to do this all on your own. Most of us tend to do this to some extent.

We tend to exaggerate the magnitude of our challenges and underestimate our own resources. We tend to think of ourselves as separate from each other and separate from Life itself.

For example, you'll feel lots of financial stress if you are constantly thinking that you "never have enough money" and "it's all up to you." You'll tend to get sick if you think the world is a toxic place teaming with unhealthy germs and underestimate the power of your immune system and social support system to handle it all. As a result, you don't empower your immune system with the support it needs to do its job.

You'll feel more stress if you're always thinking about the countless things you have to do, instead of focusing on the one thing that is in front of you to do right now—that you *can handle*. If you have a habit of putting yourself down or thinking you are "never enough," your life will be a constant struggle against overwhelming demands that you never seem to overcome.

Thoughts are powerful. The thoughts you entertain and focus on are critical to your health, happiness, and success. Therefore, how you *work with* your thoughts is one of the most important keys to relaxing deeply and mastering the stress you feel. You can learn to work with your thoughts effectively and transform any stressful situation into an empowering opportunity for compassionate action.

Three Steps from Stress to Compassion

Here are three simple steps using the skills you've learned in this book. You can practice these steps whenever you feel stress, anger, anxiety, fear, frustration, or any tension or discomfort that blocks you from a compassionate response.

Step 1. Pause and mindfully observe your thoughts without being caught up in them.

Notice the chain reaction that starts with how you're perceiving the situation you're in. If you can insert a mental pause in your moment of stress, you can interrupt this chain reaction of thinking, feeling, and behavior. Then, you can make conscious choices that support compassionate action, instead of what you may feel reactively compelled to do.

When you feel stress rising up, notice the words in your head. Then, notice how you feel when you think this way. And then, notice what you feel compelled to do when you are thinking and feeling this way.

Practice witnessing your thoughts with calm acceptance and self-compassion, as if you are a curious observer looking on from the outside. See if you can observe what you are thinking, feeling, and doing without judging it as "good" or "bad." Simply notice it with a gentle curiosity. If your inner critic rises up, notice this, too. "Hmmm, that's interesting. I see that."

This observer's perspective, this gentle acceptance of yourself and of "what is," takes your stress down a notch and gives you some mental space to witness your automatic reactions without feeling compelled to follow them. As you gently accept "what is," it becomes easier to allow experiences to come and go naturally. It becomes easier to "rest in what is" and allow yourself to trust and let go. You may be surprised at how well this works, especially when you follow it with Step 2.

Step 2. Consciously relax your body and resonate with finer frequencies.

After inserting a mental pause and calmly observing your thoughts, feelings, and behaviors, you can use the relaxation cues you've practiced in our meditations and summarized in the "Checklist for Nondual Awareness" earlier in this chapter to take your stress down another couple notches. You can sit upright, relax your feet and hands, breathe consciously, smile inside, feel inner-body sensations of open, clear, spaciousness awareness, and allow your whole being to resonate with the finer frequencies of Peace, Love, and Light. Once you are deeply relaxed and attuned to Nondual Awareness, you can move on to Step 3.

Step 3. Find a Compassionate Response from Inner Guidance

From the perspective of Nondual Awareness, **ask your inner guidance how to move forward compassionately**. There's a Core part of you that is connected to deeper intuitive wisdom, to the Universal Field, to the One Life we all share. When you are deeply relaxed and tuned to higher frequencies, you are better able to hear and choose compassionate action, instead of the automatic reaction you felt compelled to do before initiating these Three Steps.

Once you've paused your automatic reaction and created some mental space by observing it with detachment and acceptance in Step 1, then deeply relaxed your body and aligned with Nondual Awareness in Step 2, you are in a whole different space from which you can much more easily and naturally tap into inner guidance. From the relaxed centered space of Nondual Awareness, you'll most likely find it much easier to discover the "opportunity for compassion" that is available in the "challenge" you're facing.

You can ask very simply: "**What is a compassionate response to this situation?** What can I do that takes into account the needs of myself and others and moves us forward in a way that provides what each of us needs?"

Let's discover just how well this can work, right now. We suggest you practice the Three Steps using a recent stressful moment. By practicing on a memory of a stressful situation, you can grow your inner skills so that you can use these steps in the heat of stressful moments, when you really need them.

So, if you will, call to mind one stressful experience from this past week. Think of a time that put you on edge and challenged you. It could be a moment in traffic, a deadline you faced, being late for an appointment, an argument, or an interpersonal conflict.

Once you have one event in mind, follow the **Three Steps from Stress to Compassion:**

1. Pause and mindfully observe your thoughts without being caught up in them.

2. Consciously relax your body and resonate with finer frequencies.

3. Find a Compassionate Response from Inner Guidance

Notice how following these steps shifts your perspective and your experience. We encourage you to do this mental exercise now, so you can witness the power of how it shifts your perspective and opens up new vistas of compassionate action.

As you get good at the Three Steps, you can begin to use them proactively, before upcoming potentially stressful situations, to shift how you approach the situation before you even get there. To do this, simply imagine a potentially stressful future situation and follow the Three Steps.

Notice what happens as you bring compassionate action into every moment and every relationship in your life.

Daily Compassion Practice With Journaling

In addition to continuing your daily meditation practice, how can you incorporate compassion practice into your life? Perhaps, you feel inspired to do the Sacred Listening or the Three Steps from Stress to Compassion exercises. What can you do to remind yourself to come from the mind and heart of compassion? We suggest you journal the results of your compassion practice to record, process, and integrate the experiences deep into your consciousness.

Daily Meditation Practice

It's time to think about **designing your daily meditation practice**, so it becomes a powerful tool to transform your consciousness, how you relate to others, and the way you live. Consider the eight meditations in this course. Which one or ones did you connect with the most? We've listed them below.

Choose one or more of the Subtle Energy Meditations to work with as a daily practice. Perhaps you want to cycle through them all again and use them as a series? Each of them has a particular purpose and they work well as a progression. The Light, Love, and Peace Meditation puts the key elements of all these meditations together in an integrated sequence. The LLP is also the longest meditation in the series, especially Version 2. If you find it challenging to fit this into an everyday routine, you might do the longer meditations on the weekends and shorter ones during the week.

As you memorize the sequence of cues, you can also do the LLP Meditation internally self-guided for whatever length of time feels right. The important thing with self-guiding is to make sure you spend enough time in each section to really *feel* the cues and become absorbed in the experience before moving on to the next section.

Also, consider what is the best time or times for you to meditate. Commit to a time or two for your daily meditation practice. Many people find that meditating first thing in the morning helps to start the day from a calm, centered, intentional place and meditating last

226

thing before bed helps wind down the day and prepare for a good rest. Find the time or times that work best for you and commit to them.

Remember, your meditative skills and depth of your inner state grow through consistent practice over time. Think of meditation as a life-long discipline that progressively changes your baseline state of consciousness and the quality of your life and relationships. How do you feel inspired to use these meditations? Design a routine that works for you.

Here is a brief summary of them all:

ROV Subtle Energy Meditations, Their Purposes, and Chapter References

1. Relaxing Down Three Lines (Interoception and Conscious Relaxation), Ch. 2: Interoception

2. Five Gates of Mindfulness (Concentration and Deeper Layers of Mindfulness), Ch. 3: Mindfulness

3. Seven Blessings (Postural Alignment and Chakra Awareness), Ch. 4: Preparation of Body, Environment, and Intention

4. Inner Smiling (Generating a Positive Accepting Inner Attitude and Cultivating Health), Ch. 5: Generating A Relaxed, Aligned, Positive State

5. Lower Dantian Breathing (Concentration and Cultivating Vital Energy), Ch. 6: Concentration

6. One Shared Heart (Concentration and Cultivating Love), Ch. 7: Transcendence

7. Light, Love, and Peace Version 1 (Cultivating Light and integration of all the above in one sequence), Ch. 8: Returning and Grounding

8. Light, Love, and Peace Version 2 (Extended Version: Focusing on Transcendence: Awareness of Awareness, Choiceless Attention, and Clear Light Bliss of Being), Ch. 9: Reflection and Insight

227

You can follow along with recordings of all these meditations in our ROV Meditation app. Enjoy your practice!

Reflection & Insight Journaling

Take a moment to reflect back on the question of meaning, purpose, and service. How can you take your struggle and desire and turn this into a gift you can share with others? What compassionate action do you feel inspired to take? How can this become part of your mission and service in the world?

--- --- ---

Next up, in the final chapter of this book, we look at how to engage in your practice in a world that is moving so fast and asking so much that you feel as if you just can't fit in another thing. After all, compassionate action is not just something you do during a set time each day, like during meditation. It's a way of life that changes how you relate to everything, every moment—especially when you feel as if there's too much to do and not enough time.

11. Bringing Awareness to Life

Staying Mindful of Your Practice

When was the last time you said, "I am *so busy*. I have *way too much* to do!"?

Honestly, this is like a badge of honor we wear proudly in our "get it all done yesterday" culture. We take pride in how busy we are and how much we can get done—and this creates a habit of impatiently rushing—even when we don't have to. Then, we end up stressed-out, sick, or exhausted and wonder what happened.

In this final section, we explore how you can release the stressful habit of impatiently rushing around getting things done, so you can be more mindful, present, intentional, and compassionate in what you focus on and how you get involved. In the end, you might find you're loving life a lot more and engaging with the people and events that matter most, rather than just ploughing through another stressful day.

I Do It, Too: Kevin's Story

Here's how I've learned to shift from feeling like I have to get it all done right now!

I have to admit, I can fall prey to the habit of impatiently rushing. Maybe it's because I was born a Capricorn and love to get stuff done. Or, maybe, it's the effect of growing up in a capitalist consumer culture, in which the measuring stick for our lives is **more** and **more** productivity, effort, and things . . .

Over the past few years, I've cut down on my commitments, so I can focus on what is most important to me, what feels like my strongest passion and service. Yet, I can still get caught up in creating a long to-do list and then rushing around impatiently trying to get it all done today.

This year, I caught myself doing just that with Stephen and my new teaching venture, "Raising Our Vibration." Stephen and I had created a to-do list of sequential steps to get started. We'd already identified our community of meditation practitioners interested in spiritual transformation, outlined our core content, defined our mission and purpose, begun writing a book together, and designed our logo. We were ready for the next practical steps.

Certain things, like getting an LLC registered, needed to be done before getting a bank account, credit card, Facebook page, PayPal account, domain name, designing an app to deliver our content, and so on. Then, there was the online course based on the book and the library of content for the app to support our community of participants.

The Next Step

I was sitting at my desk working on the next step, registering the LLC, and I wanted to get it done in an hour, so I could get to the bank, open an account, get a credit card, register the domain, and start working on the FB page and app. LegalZoom said I could register the LLC in 10 minutes, so surely in an hour I'd be off to the bank and ploughing through my list.

Sparing you the details, 21 days later, I was still waiting for the revised structuring of our LLC to go through. What I had thought was our best business structure was met with a different idea from the bank. So, I went to another bank and another, until I realized it was time to reorganize. Why wasn't I told this before, when I asked the bank, my accountant, and LegalZoom? It really doesn't matter—and it turns out, it was for the best.

On that day, I thought I was going to wiz through the next nine steps. Completely on my own, without pressure from anyone else, I got myself caught up in feeling impatient and stressed about completing all those steps in one day. I was excited and wanted to get going—but honestly there was no rush. There was no reason I needed to get all nine of those steps done in that one day. Three weeks later, that became clear. Looking back, it's also clear it was best to take our time.

We had been busy working on our book together and talking about the best ways to support our participants. We had set up a Core Founding Group of members and had been able to chat with them about our ideas and get their feedback. We had taken them all through our 10-module course. All of this was essential to be able to provide the best service for our community. By going slower—because I was forced to—we've been able to go about this project more mindfully. We've learned more and had more good experiences with our community members than we could ever have imagined.

Lesson Learned Again

Over the years, I've learned this lesson again and again. Proper timing is important. Rushing is unnecessary and usually counter-productive. There's a right timing and sequence for each step. Each step completed gives more insight for the next step.

Rushing through the steps has consequences. First, I miss out on the experience itself. When I am rushing, I am less present in what I am doing, because my mind is trying to be done with a step, so I can get on to the next one.

If I am not fully present in what I am doing, not only do I miss the experience itself, I also miss out on what I might learn that will help me when it is time to take the next step. I miss paying attention to details that matter.

Third, when I am impatiently rushing, I miss out on the enjoyment of interacting with others. One of the greatest joys of doing anything is enjoying the exchanges of energy, camaraderie, love, and information in relationship with others. When I am rushing, I am unlikely to ask questions to get to know the other person or share about myself. When I am strictly task-oriented, I miss out on the connections to others in anything we are doing together. I lose the heart of compassion when I am consumed with getting everything done.

Finally, when I am impatiently rushing, I feel unnecessary stress. This is stress of my own making. If I simply focus on what I am doing now and engage in it fully, I feel the excitement of it, but it is not stressful. It is simply the joy of involvement and creativity and the excitement of being alive and interacting with others in the process of what we are doing.

There may be moments of tension, but these are just part of the process of discovering the path forward. These moments of creative tension lead to new insights, skills, information, and interactions that unfold naturally. It's the unfolding of what is not known that gives the greatest joy and satisfaction, rather than checking off boxes on a to-do list of what *I think I know* about how I think things *should* go.

Moving Forward One Step at a Time

The process of writing this book and the accompanying course with Stephen and our Core Group taught me once again to relax and stay present in what is happening now; enjoy the people and the process of working together; and trust, be open, and relish the unknown as it unfolds. Life has bigger plans than what I know. There is a better sequence and timing than I know ahead of time. And—everything doesn't have to get done today.

If I focus on what is most important right now and fully and compassionately engage with others and with this step, I can be sure that everything will be done in the best way possible and it will exceed what I could have imagined. This isn't just a wishful thought. Life has proven this to me again and again.

Remembering What's Most Important

There's a strong momentum to go faster and do more. We have to watch out for the habit of impatiently rushing (remembering it's just an unproductive habit) and step in with mindful pauses every step of the way. In these mindful moments, we remember *why* we are doing what we are doing and what we hope to share to help and serve others. We feel the energy of our mission and purpose—and trust that all is well. With this mindset, we are open to opportunities for relationships, insights, and experiences that we would never have if we are just ploughing through everything we think we have to get done today.

So, if you find yourself impatiently rushing, what happens if you insert a mindful pause, activate Nondual Awareness, and ask: "What is most important at this moment? What is life asking me to pay attention to and do right now?" "How can this moment be one of deeper meaning, purpose, and compassionate service?"

A Practice from Stephen: Living in Presence

Let's talk together about Awareness. Deep Awareness and Presence arise out of stillness, silence, and spaciousness. How can we open to stillness, silence, and spaciousness? As you read this, allow your mind to absorb the words deeply. Surrender and allow space for the silence at the end of the sentences.

Pause for a moment right now. Take a long calm breath as you are reading this and exhale with an even longer breath.

Be still.

Take your attention to the space in your heart.

Go right to the core of your heart.

Be still here.

Listen to the silence. Pause. Be still and silent. Listen.

Feel this space of your heart.

Do you feel it? Can you feel a shift in your awareness as you feel this space?

There is a subtle shift into Presence, even as we do something as simple as focusing into still silence in the space of the heart.

Let us consider our present awareness a little more deeply, awareness of what we bring, here and now, to the present, to this moment.

When we consider this moment carefully, we see that all is not as it seems.

Look around you now at your surroundings.

The space that surrounds you is filled with energy, consciousness, and information. It is alive.

The body you exist in and the space within you is also filled with energy, consciousness, and information.

You sense this.

The space within you and all around you is alive with energy.

You witness this.

Yet, you are not anything in your environment, nor are you the body.

We all know that, at some point in time, our body will cease to exist, just as everything in our environment will.

Right now, there is a witness, an observer, a presence within you that knows.

You are awake.

This awareness arises because you are becoming still.

Be still and know Presence.

We are so conditioned to our body and our surroundings that we believe this 3D reality defines us.

Yet there is something greater, a power, a knowing within.

A deeper Awareness.

You feel it.

This is why we are here, gathered together on this planet.

Let us experiment together in this Awareness.

Go into the body now, feel it.

Feel the space within you.

Notice how you *feel*.

Generally speaking, it is easier for you to *feel* and *be in* your body with the "soft" part of you, the aspect we call the feminine in us all, which is naturally aligned with Being and Presence. It is this aspect that yields, surrenders, opens to *what is*, and embraces in compassion.

Many ancient cultures chose female figures like Isis or Guan Yin to represent this formless transcendental reality. The Tao in the *Tao Te Ching* is described as the infinite, eternally present, mother of the universe. Prajnaparamita in the *Heart Sutra* is described as the Mother of All Buddhas.

So, to feel in this way is to embody the unmanifested, the transcendent, the feminine within, whether we have a male or female body in this lifetime. To connect with Presence, Being, or Source requires surrender, grace, non-judgment, openness, and compassion—the feminine.

Opening the Heart to Create Space for Stillness, Compassion, and Non-Judgment

So, how can we act with presence and awareness, instead of reacting from thinking and suffering? It's all about letting go—surrender. Surrender creates space for stillness. How can we do this practically? How can we create space for stillness? The openness and surrender that creates space for stillness is found in non-judgment.

A simple practice is to look at our judgments. Through compassion, we can translate our judgments into needs and connections. This is like the deep listening of Guan Yin, the Mother of Compassion— the power of listening with deep empathy.

Let's take an example. Most of our agitation in life comes from a need for deeper connection. Let's say someone says something we really don't like. They might talk about someone else as stupid or impulsive or something else. Our dislike creates a reaction and we drop into judgment: "How could you think that?"

Now, when we feel this energy of judgment, which is usually preceded by agitation or discomfort, if we are aware enough, we can notice the agitated energy. We can notice this signal that we are disconnecting from compassion. You might notice this when you're in a hurry driving in traffic. Can you catch the moment you shift into judgment?

Or, perhaps, it happens when you disagree with someone at the office and you have to be very direct with them. This can create tension and ignite judgment as you "steel yourself" to be strong. You find yourself feeling adversarial, rather than cooperative and inclusive. When you become aware of this, you can slow the conversation. You can slow your thoughts down, move towards stillness, silence, and spaciousness, and let the defensiveness and judgments drop away. Naturally, clarity, insight, and inclusion arise.

This is the power of empathy, deep listening, caring, and the kindness of presence. In the split second you are able to notice your judgments and shift your focus to the needs we all have for connection and clarity, an "Aha" of great insight can arise. The whole situation can be transformed. If you practice this, you can bring all your unconscious judgments into the Light of Consciousness.

Choiceless Attention

Stillness, silence, and spaciousness open your mind and heart to choiceless attention. Choiceless attention has no preferences. It is non-judgmental—clearly seeing *what is*. This is a type of attention you inherently have from the time you were a child, prior to being caught up in thinking. It is the attention that develops by practicing meditation to the point of transcendence, in which you realize

Nondual Awareness. Nondual Awareness is the basis of your ability to exercise choiceless attention.

Try this: Focus in on what is going on inside of you right this moment. Ask yourself, what is going on inside of me? Now watch. Who is watching? Who is having this experience? Don't try to analyze it. Simply let your attention rest in this question. Allow your mind to become quiet and still. When your mind is quiet and still, you can exercise choiceless attention to see things as they are prior to evaluations and judgments.

Practicing Presence is another way to bring you into choiceless attention.

A Practice of Presence

Breathe. Feel the sensations of breathing.

Feel the energy of the body, the emotions.

Become very present in what is happening here and now.

Open yourself to the inner energy field of presence within the body.

Be very still.

The body is a portal of Presence, the doorway into Being.

Presence is this beauty, joy, and grace of Being.

Presence arises in stillness.

You discover stillness in the gaps between busy-ness, in pausing during moments of stress and frustration. You find a space in the confusion that speaks a deeper wisdom.

As you listen, feel, and pay attention, what needs to be done calls to you, and the rest fades into the background until its time arrives. You find yourself released from self-focus and enter into the timeless abode of Nondual Awareness—an effortless inspired flow.

Being present in this primordial flow, you resonate with the finer frequencies of Peace, Love, and Light and live in an elevated state of Awareness in which we all thrive.

Subtle Energy Meditation is a powerful tool to take you into the Space of Presence, Stillness, Silence, and Nondual Awareness. We believe strongly in this tool and hope that you've learned how to make it a transformative part of your life.

The Seven Steps of Subtle Energy Meditation Practice

How can your meditation practice have more of an impact on your life and relationships? How can it raise your vibration, so you resonate with the finer frequencies of Peace, Love, Light and live in an elevated state of Awareness? Remember these Seven Steps of the Subtle Energy Meditation Process to enhance meditation and cultivate deeper states of consciousness that are life-changing for us all:

- **Step 1. Preparation.** Prepare your body, environment, and intention for effective meditation.
- **Step 2. Initiation.** Initiate meditation by turning inward to activate interoception of body sensations and shift to an inner state of calm happiness using relaxation, posture, and positive energy cues.
- **Step 3. Concentration into Absorption.** Apply mindfulness to concentrate upon a focal object until you are completely immersed in and absorbed by that focal point and the effort of concentration falls away. For example, in the final meditation in our series, the Light, Love, and Peace Meditation (LLP), you begin the concentration phase by focusing on lower dantian breathing until you have this

239

feeling of absorption. You then apply this concentrative absorption to cultivate Light, Love, and Peace.

- o **Light**. Focus up into the upper dantian and high above the crown, as if you are being pulled upward and "plugged in" to the energy of the Universe.
- o **Love**. Focus on breathing Unconditional Love through your heart and extending this Love outward to all beings and all of Life.
- o **Peace**. Focus down into a still-point in the perineum. Let go into stillness, silence, and spaciousness until you dissolve into Step 4.

- **Step 4. Transcendence**. Realization of the Universal Field, Pure Consciousness beyond form or content, awareness of Awareness itself, Nondual Awareness, Clear Light.
- **Step 5. Returning and Grounding**. Come back to body and environmental awareness.
- **Step 6. Reflection and Insight**. Recall important landmarks (peak felt sensations) of your meditative experience, inquire about the deeper meaning of these states, make connections, and apply your meditative experience to the events, circumstances, and relationships in your life. Keep a meditation log to record and process your experiences.
- **Step 7. Compassionate Action**. Carry your practice into the world in purposeful service.

It's essential to prepare your body, environment, and intention before you meditate, to give yourself the optimum conditions and focus for your practice to thrive. Make sure you have a routine of steps to follow and at least one focal cue to concentrate on. Otherwise, your practice may be fragmented, and you may spend a good portion of your practice session "spacing out." When you do lose focus, simply make note of this and return to your practice sequence using the 3Rs. See if it's possible to pay attention to the finest details and shifts in states of consciousness during your practice. Your sensitivity to these sensations and shifts will grow as you practice consistently.

After your meditation sessions, take time to remember and deeply enjoy key moments, so you can establish landmarks that can help you to live from meditative awareness and go even deeper the next time. Taking time to reflect on your practice gives you opportunities for insight that you can carry into your life and relationships. Meditation becomes so much more than just a nice break in your day. It becomes a practice that transforms how you think, feel, and interact!

At the end of each session, take time to journal with detailed attention, so you can gather information to help you process and integrate your experience and record it deeply in your body, heart, and mind.

--- --- ---

Congratulations! You've set a solid foundation for lifelong practice by completing the exercises in this book and following the series of guided meditations. However, this is just the beginning. From here, let your daily practice be your teacher and guide. **Design a daily routine of meditation and Mindfulness Check-ins** that support you in resonating with the frequencies of Peace, Love, and Light, and in living in a state of Nondual Awareness.

Whether you are listening to the guided audios or memorizing the cues and practicing in a self-guided way, design a daily meditation routine that works well for you. As more and more of us engage in this practice together, we will raise the vibration of our Collective Consciousness and transform life on this planet!

We hear from many of our students that it's challenging not to be disturbed from the finer frequencies of Peace, Love, and Light by the stresses and turmoil of our world. One of the things we hope we've shared with you experientially in this book is that underneath all disturbances, the most fundamental fabric of Reality is always vibrating at the frequencies of Peace, Love, and Light. Nothing disturbs this. A deep inner peace is always available—every moment. It's just a matter of tuning in to it. Disturbances are always on the surface, like waves in the Ocean. The Deep Ocean is undisturbed. What we are doing in Subtle Energy Meditation is learning to tune in to this Deep Ocean (or this Infinite Space) so we resonate with these finer frequencies.

As this becomes our baseline state, the surface waves no longer disturb these frequencies. Instead, these deeper frequencies begin to entrain the surface frequencies, so our Collective Consciousness resonates from this plane. It's a matter of where our consciousness resides and abides. Do we allow our consciousness to be swept along on the surface currents or do we anchor deep into the fundamental frequencies that give rise to this Universe—the frequencies of Peace, Love, and Light carried in the fundamental carrier signal of Reality— the OM vibration, the Divine Presence?

The choice is yours every moment. To live from these finer frequencies takes practice, because we are conditioned to other states of consciousness. If you want to experience a fundamental change in your state of consciousness and therefore in what you contribute to our Collective Consciousness, you need to set yourself up for success in be consistent in your practice. We hope you've learned the keys to do this in this book.

Most of all, remember this practice is about being lighter, freer, more peaceful, joyful, compassionate, connected, aware, and alive. So, savor your meditation time.

Thank you for your practice!

Reflect on Your Experience

Take a few moments to reflect on your answers to the Five Questions with which you began your journey through this book. What new insight have you gained? Have you noticed any shifts? How might you continue to use Subtle Energy Meditation to let go of stress, release inner blocks, and live the life of deeper meaning, purpose, and service your soul desires? Write down your responses in your journal.

You also may want to revisit the MAIA Questions to see how your sense of interoception has shifted since the first time you asked yourself these questions.

The MAIA Questions: Using a Six-point Likert Scale

1. Noticing ("I notice where in my body I am comfortable.")
2. Not Distracting ("I distract myself from sensations of discomfort" – reverse scored: 1=always, 6=never.)
3. Not Worrying ("I can notice an unpleasant body sensation without worrying about it.")
4. Attention Regulation ("I can return awareness to my body if I am distracted.")
5. Emotional Awareness ("I notice how my body changes when I am angry.")
6. Self-Regulation ("When I bring awareness to my body, I feel a sense of calm.")
7. Body Listening ("I listen to my body to inform me about what to do.")
8. Trusting ("I feel my body is a safe place.")

Has your total score changed? Which question has shifted the most? What inner sensing cues work well for you to maintain and return to a state of calm clarity and elevated Awareness throughout your day?

--- --- ---

We are so happy you've embarked on this journey of Subtle Energy Meditation. This is a powerful lifelong practice that will continue to teach you as you engage in it day by day over time. For ongoing support, join our **Raising Our Vibration Community** page on Facebook and download our **ROV Meditation app on Android or iOS**. We also offer a **10-Week Subtle Energy Meditation Course** online via videoconferencing, which guides you through these meditations with personal coaching and group support. For more information visit: **http://raisingourvibration.net**

You'll find more resources in the Appendices:

Suggested Reading

ROV Meditation Scripts

Brainwave Graphs

Food & Mood Log

Meditation Log

About the Authors

Notes

Appendices

Suggested Reading

Mindfulness, Bliss, and Beyond by Ajahn Brahm

Hands of Light by Barbara Brennan

The Way of Qigong by Kenneth Cohen

Kalachakra Tantra: Rite of Initiation by His Holiness The Dalai Lama

The Open Focus Brain by Les Fehmi and Jim Robbins

The Awakening of Intelligence by J. Krishnamurti

Clear Quiet Mind by Kevin Schoeninger

Diary of a Yogi by Altair Shyam

The Untethered Soul by Michael Singer

The Royal Seal of Mahamudra: A Guidebook for the Realization of Coemergence by The Third Khamtrul Rinpoche, Ngawang Kunga Tenzin

Awakening the Mind: A Guide to Harnessing the Power of Your Brainwaves by Anna Wise

Autobiography of a Yogi by Paramahansa Yogananda

The Science of Enlightenment by Shinzen Young

Subtle Energy Meditation Series Scripts

1. Relaxing Down Three Lines-Liquid Light Version

Before you begin, arrange your **environment** so it's conducive to meditation. Set up a comfortable seat in a quiet private space and turn off the volume on your phone. A good seat height sets your hips level with or slightly above your knees. Consider the lighting, sounds, visual images, and scents, so you create a sacred space.

In this meditation, we focus on the sensation of warm, soothing, liquid light flowing down three lines: from your shoulders to your hands, from your hips to your toes, and from the top of your head down your spine. The purpose of this meditation is to activate your body's natural relaxation response and awaken your inner sense of interoception, your ability to feel inner sensations.

As you follow this meditation, practice **mindfulness** by paying attention, on purpose, in the present moment, non-judgmentally— like a curious observer. If your attention wanders, practice the **3Rs**: recognize what has grabbed your attention, release this, and return to following the guided cues. Do this as often as your attention wanders.

Let's begin by sitting comfortably upright with the soles of your feet flat on the ground and parallel with each other. If you are able to, sit far enough forward so you feel some weight in your feet, perhaps all the way on the front edge of your seat, so you feel the weight of your feet firmly on the ground. If you need back support, you can sit back against a seatback.

Rest your hands palms down on your thighs. Lightly close your eyes.

Take a moment for a Mindfulness Check-in inside. Notice how you feel right now. If you could sum up this feeling in a word, phrase, or image, what would this be?

Bring to mind your intention for your meditation practice.

246

Now, focus down into the soles of both feet. Feel the sensations of contact between the soles of your feet and the ground. Allow your feet and toes to soften and relax, as if they are melting down into the ground.

Focus in on the sensations in your palms and fingers. Feel the sensations of contact with your legs. Allow your hands to soften and relax, as if they are melting down into your legs.

As your hands relax, allow your arms and shoulders to relax down, releasing any tension in your neck and shoulders.

Imagine a string attached to the top of your head drawing your spine gently upright, giving you a feeling of vertical spaciousness up through the core of your body, up through your spine, and through the top of your head. Notice how you feel when you sit nicely upright. You may feel more purposeful, alert, more empowered and intentional.

Tuck your chin in just slightly, gently lengthening the back of your neck.

Roll the tip of your tongue up to touch the roof of your mouth or touch the tip of your tongue to the gumline behind your upper front teeth, whichever is more comfortable. Soften and relax your tongue here. Smile, a subtle smile of appreciation and gratitude, of calm happiness.

Allow the feeling of smiling to relax your jaw, relax your eyes, and release any tension from your eyebrows and your forehead. Allow the feeling of smiling to wash down through your whole body creating a positive, nurturing inner environment. Imagine every cell is smiling, relaxing, opening up, communicating with every other cell, and radiating pure positive energy. Calm happiness.

Now, focus in on your right shoulder. Allow a feeling of warmth and relaxation to fill your right shoulder. Imagine and feel warm, soothing, liquid light slowly flowing down into your upper arm, inch by inch, down through your right elbow, into your right forearm, through your right wrist, into the palm of your right hand, and out through your fingers. Feel your right arm as a whole, from your shoulder through your fingers, filled with warm, liquid light, and completely relaxed.

Now, focus in on your right hip. Feel the sensations of contact with the seat underneath you. Allow a feeling of warmth and relaxation to fill your right hip. Imagine and feel warm, soothing, liquid light slowly flowing into your right thigh, through your right knee, and down, down through your shin and calf, down through your right ankle, your right heel, through the arch of your right foot, the ball of your foot, and out through your toes. Feel your right leg as a whole from your hip through your toes, filled with warm liquid light, and completely relaxed.

Now, compare your right side with your left side and feel the difference.

Now, focus in on your left shoulder. Allow a feeling of warmth and relaxation to fill your left shoulder. Imagine and feel warm, soothing, liquid light slowly flowing down into your upper arm, down through your left elbow, into your left forearm, through your left wrist, into the palm of your left hand, and out through your fingers. Feel your left arm as a whole, from your shoulder through your fingers, warm, filled with liquid light, and completely relaxed.

Now, focus in on your left hip. Feel the sensations of contact with the seat underneath you. Allow a feeling of warmth and relaxation to fill your left hip. Imagine and feel warm, soothing, liquid light slowly flowing into your left thigh, through your left knee, and down, down through your shin and calf, down through your left ankle, your left heel, through the arch of your left foot, the ball of your foot, and out through your toes. Feel your left leg as a whole from your hip through your toes, warm, filled with liquid light, and completely relaxed.

Now feel both sides of your body at once and allow this warm, relaxed feeling of soothing liquid light to fill both sides of your body evenly and completely.

Now, focus in on the top of your head. Imagine and feel a slow-moving waterfall of warm, soothing, liquid light flowing from the top of your head, down the back of your head, down the back of your neck, down between your shoulder blades, down through your lower back, down through the base of your spine, and down into the ground. Feel this whole waterfall at once, from the top of your head, down your spine, and down into the ground. Imagine and feels it's relaxing and releasing any tension along your spine and washing it down into the ground.

Now, feel your body as a whole from the inside. Sense the entire space inside your skin. Allow the feeling of warm, soothing, liquid light to fill your whole body evenly and completely. Smile as you enjoy this warm soothing feeling of liquid light filling your whole body.

Become aware of this warm, soothing, liquid light flowing outward in all directions, so it fills the space you're in. Feel this energy flowing beyond this space to all of us gathered together doing this meditation, to those whom you love, to all beings, and the whole planet. Imagine all beings and the whole planet smiling together as we appreciate this feeling of warm, soothing, liquid light.

This Light is our Life, the lifeblood which flows through us all. Imagine this warm, soothing, liquid light flowing outward Infinitely, in all directions, through the whole Universe, across all time.

Imagine and feel you are floating in an Infinite Sea of warm, soothing, liquid light. . . . Imagine and feel you are floating in an Infinite Sea of warm, soothing, liquid light. . . . Imagine and feel you are floating in an Infinite Sea of warm, soothing, liquid light. . . .

Now, feel the entire space inside your skin.

Notice how you feel. If you could sum this up in a word, phrase, or image, what would this be? Record this word, phrase, or image along with this feeling in every cell of your body, so you remember it, bring it with you, and can use it as a landmark to return this state of deep relaxation and warm, soothing, liquid light any time.

Slowly open your eyes and take in the space around you. Feel the warm soothing sensation of liquid light inside and around you, with your eyes open. Feel the top of your head, your hands on your legs, and your feet on the ground.

Reflect on this soothing relaxed feeling of Infinite Light. Imagine what a difference it would make if you approached life with this deep sense of relaxation, knowing you are supported, infused, and surrounded by Infinite Light. How might this change how you relate to others and events in your life? Take a few moments to write down anything you'd like to remember from this meditative experience along with any insights.

Then, stand, stretch, and move in whatever way feels good to you. Well done!

2. Five Gates of Mindfulness

Before you begin, consider your environment as a sanctuary, a sacred place, a mandala, filled with energies and spaciousness that is conducive to this meditation.

Sit comfortably with your hips level with or slightly above your knees.

Ideally, sit upright on the front edge of your seat with the soles of your feet flat on the ground and parallel with each other. Rest your hands, palms cupped, right palm uppermost, resting in the left in your lap, with the tips of your thumbs touching lightly.

Now, lightly, close your eyes.

Notice how you feel right now. . . . Bring your intention from the beginning, the intention to help us all to return home, to align with that feeling.

Now, as you listen to these preliminary instructions, allow your attention and intention to align with the technique and its purpose. The sequence of this meditation begins with cues for posture, relaxation, and positive energy, then moves into calm-happiness-breath awareness to focus attention. After becoming completely absorbed in breathing, we'll shift to the instructions to guide us into deeper and deeper states of mindfulness. We will do this five times, in the traditional nature and practice of mindfulness of breathing.

The purpose is to raise our vibration to embody the frequencies of Peace through mindfulness of breathing, so this becomes established as the baseline state from which we live our lives—and to dissolve limiting tensions of self that interfere with the flow of finer frequencies.

As you follow this meditation, practice mindfulness by paying attention, on purpose, in the present moment, non-judgmentally—like a curious observer. If your attention wanders, practice the 3Rs: recognize what has grabbed your attention, release this, and return

251

to following the guided cues. Do this as often as your attention wanders, as best as you can without self-judgment. Keep in mind that mindfulness is a skill that improves through consistent practice over time.

To begin, focus down into the soles of your feet and feel the sensations of your feet contacting the ground. Allow your feet to soften and relax, imagining that your feet are melting down into the ground.

Focus in on your palms and fingers and feel the sensation of contact with your legs. Allow your palms and fingers to soften and relax, imagining that they are melting down into your legs.

As your hands relax, allow your arms and shoulders to relax down, releasing any tension in your shoulders and neck.

Imagine a string attached to the top of your head, drawing your spine gently upright, giving you a feeling of vertical spaciousness up through the core of your body, up through your spine, through the top of your head.

Tuck your chin in slightly, gently lengthening the back of your neck.

Roll the tip of your tongue up to touch the roof of your mouth.

Smile a subtle smile of appreciation and gratitude for this time to consciously relax, let go, and awaken to mindful awareness.

Allow the feeling of smiling to relax your jaw and your eyes. Release any tension in your eyebrows and forehead.

Allow the feeling of smiling to wash down through your whole body, creating a positive inner environment. Imagine every cell is smiling, opening up, communicating with every other cell, and radiating pure positive energy.

Become aware of the sensations of this present moment, as a curious observer, a witness to what is, right now.

Feel the deep stillness of the body, silence of the speech, spaciousness of the mind and heart.

Look at what you see in your mind.

You cannot find anything.

You can only find the one who is looking at it.

Your mind.

Look at the mind.

Who is it? Where is it?

Look closer, now closer still.

You cannot find that either.

There is only emptiness, spaciousness.

Look closer into emptiness.

It is not just empty.

There is awareness, alert, awake.

Pure Presence.

This pure presence is luminous, pure consciousness is alive.

As you rest here, in the union of awareness and emptiness, a deep sense of joy arises,

And with it the Buddha Smile.

A deep sense of bliss.

The bliss washes through your entire body.

The bliss is right here, right now, in the present moment, free of any other focus.

You are awake, aware, and witnessing.

Your breathing is calm and happy.

This is the First Gate into deeper states of meditation, being a witness, observing with curiosity.

"I am aware of the present moment, letting go the past and future."

Calm and happy.

The Second Gate is silence.

"I am silently aware of the present moment, letting go of commentary, evaluations, and judgments, resting in what is."

Calm, happiness.

The Third Gate is the breath.

"I am silently aware of the breath in the present moment, releasing all other perceptions and thoughts."

Focus down into your lower abdomen and become aware of the sensations of breathing there.

Calm Happiness.

As you inhale, notice the subtle expansion of your abdomen. As you exhale, notice the subtle relaxation inward.

Calm Happiness.

"I am silently aware of the breath in the present moment, releasing all other perceptions and thoughts."

Calm Happiness.

The Fourth Gate is the whole breath in every moment.

"I am silently aware of the ebb and flow of the whole breath, continuously, every moment."

Calm, happiness, equanimity.

See if it's possible to stay present in the whole cycle of your breathing, so you notice the moment you begin to inhale and follow your in-breath until you naturally pause. Then, notice the moment you begin to exhale and follow your out-breath until you naturally pause. . . .

To track your attention, count your breaths each time you exhale, in cycles of ten. If you lose count, begin again at one. If you get to ten, begin again at one. . . . If your attention wanders, it's OK. Recognize what grabbed your attention, release this, and return to counting your out-breaths in cycles of 10.

"I am silently aware of the ebb and flow of the whole breath, continuously, every moment."

Allow your attention to become completely absorbed in the subtle sensations of breathing, as if nothing else matters at this moment. . . .

"I am silently aware of the ebb and flow of the whole breath, continuously, every moment."

As you continue to count your out-breaths, allow your breathing to become subtle, quiet, and soft until the sensation is barely perceptible in your lower abdomen. . . .

The Fifth Gate is awareness of Awareness itself. Become the witness of Awareness itself. Pure consciousness without content. Choiceless Attention. Still, silent, spacious Awareness. Who is aware of this space? The space itself is aware. There is only Awareness. Infinite Spacious Awareness.

Now, become aware of the entire space inside your skin. . . .

Slowly half open your eyes and become aware of the space inside your body within the space around you. Feel the top of your head, your hands in your lap, and your feet on the ground. Notice how you feel. If you could sum this up in a word or phrase, what would this be?

Consider practicing this meditation twice a day, read spiritual texts, surrender to the process, and realize the truth of who you are: a being of still, silent, spacious awareness, part of One Life we all share, One vast spacious Awareness.

Take a moment to write down anything that is important for you to remember from this meditative experience. What were the most poignant moments? Did you face any challenges? What can you take from this experience and apply to your life and your relationships?

Now, bring the Five Gates of Mindfulness with you wherever you go. Well done!

3. Seven Blessings

The Seven Blessings Meditation uses interoception and mindfulness to cultivate postural alignment and subtle energy awareness. We do this by concentrating on the seven spinal energy centers or chakras. What inhibits postural alignment is tension along the spine. This tension relates to issues stored in the seven chakras. So, in this meditation, we bring mindful awareness to the spine and note what arises at each chakra. We then bless the seven chakras by bringing divine light, primordial sound, and the awareness of space to each one.

Sit comfortably, feet on the floor parallel with each other, hands resting cupped in your lap with the tips of your thumbs touching lightly. Lightly close your eyes.

Check in with how you feel. If you could sum this up in a word or a phrase, what would this be?

Let's begin by focusing down into the soles of both feet and feel the sensation of the feet on the floor, allowing them to soften and relax, imagining them melting into the earth.

Now focus in on your palms and your fingers, feel the sensation of contact with your legs, feel them soften and relax, imagining them melting into your legs.

Allow your arms and shoulders to relax, releasing any tension in your neck.

Imagine a string pulling you from the top of your head, giving you a feeling of vertical spaciousness up your spine, up through the top of your head.

Tuck your chin in slightly, lengthen your neck, and place the tip of your tongue on the roof of your mouth just behind your upper teeth.

Smile the smile of the Buddha, of appreciation and gratitude for this present moment, for now. Let go and focus within, into the sensations of gentle peace, soft love and liquid light flowing through our bodies.

The light of your smile washes down your body, creating a positive inner environment for all your cells. Every cell has this divine smile, opening and communicating with every other cell and radiating pure positive energy.

Now, focus in on breathing in the lower dantian. Begin with a breath of gentle peace. You can note the breath and the feeling if you wish by saying "peace" silently within, or simply be aware of the flow of peace riding on the breath. Be mindful when other thoughts or sounds or feelings arise and note them for a moment by being with whatever arises, saying to yourself, "dog barking" or "tight shoulder." You are not pushing it away, but merely noting it before returning to the breath of peace.

Allow the breath of peace to open your awareness.

In this vast space of pure awareness all around you, become aware of the space at the perineum and tip of your tailbone, the base of your spine, **the first chakra.**

Become aware of it.

Resonate with the light in this space.

The center.

Filled with liquid light.

Like a star.

Where did this light come from?

The elements within you were made in the crucible of stars.

Who are you?

A star being.

A light being.

Feel it.

Open up to it.

Bring your attention to it, totally, absolutely.

So that in this present moment, there is nothing else.

This wonder, that is you, is within you, and all around you.

This beauty, we call, "the deeper I", is the universe looking at itself.

Rest your awareness fully in this space of the first chakra, this presence.

And resonate with the sound in this space. OM.

Become aware of the energy of space.

The wonder.

The miracle of you.

That exists as pure awareness around this center.

Now become aware of the space of your sacrum, between your hips, **the second chakra**.

Pure awareness, in space.

Pure consciousness.

Pure bliss.

Tune in to the energy of the sound and light of this center within you and all around you. OM

Feel from the center.

Become one with it.

Allow your awareness to extend out from this center of the second chakra and bless the space around you and beyond you.

Now become aware of the place in your spine directly opposite your navel, in the middle of your lower back, **the third chakra.**

In this vast space of pure awareness all around you,

Become aware of it.

Resonate with the light in this space.

The center.

Filled with liquid light.

Feel it.

Open up to it.

Bring your attention to it, totally, absolutely.

So that in this present moment, there is nothing else.

This wonder, that is you, is within you, and all around you.

This beauty, we call, "the deeper I", is the universe looking at itself.

Rest your awareness fully in this space of the third chakra, this presence.

And resonate with the sound in this space. OM

Become aware of the energy of space.

The wonder.

The miracle of you.

That exists as pure awareness around this center.

Pure awareness, in space.

Pure consciousness.

Pure bliss.

Now become aware of the space behind your heart, **the fourth chakra**.

In this vast space of pure awareness all around you,

Become aware of it.

Resonate with the light in this space.

The center.

Filled with liquid light.

Feel it.

Open up to it.

Bring your attention to it, totally, absolutely.

So that in this present moment, there is nothing else.

This wonder, that is you, is within you, and all around you.

This beauty, we call, "the deeper I", is the universe looking at itself.

Rest your awareness fully in this space, this presence.

And resonate with the sound in this space.

Become aware of the energy of space.

The wonder.

The miracle of you.

That exists as pure awareness around this center.

Around your chest.

Pure awareness, in space.

Pure consciousness.

Pure bliss.

Tune in to the energy of the sound and light of this center within you and all around you. OM.

Receive it, with gratitude.

Feel from the center.

Become one with it.

Allow your awareness to extend out from your heart and bless the space around you and beyond you.

Now become aware of the space in the center of your throat, **the fifth chakra**.

In this vast space of pure awareness all around you,

Become aware of it.

Resonate with the light in this space.

The center.

Filled with liquid light.

Feel it.

Open up to it.

Bring your attention to it, totally, absolutely.

So that in this present moment, there is nothing else.

This wonder, that is you, is within you, and all around you.

This beauty, we call, "the deeper I," is the universe looking at itself.

Rest your awareness fully in this space, this presence.

And resonate with the sound in this space.

Become aware of the energy of space.

The wonder.

The miracle of you.

That exists as pure awareness around this center.

Around your neck.

Pure awareness, in space.

Pure consciousness.

Pure bliss.

Tune in to the energy of the sound and light of this center within you and all around you. OM.

Feel from the center.

Become one with it.

Now feel the alignment of these first five chakras, from the base of your spine to the center of your throat.

Allow your awareness to extend out from all five centers at once and bless the space around you and beyond you.

Now become aware of the space in the center of your brain, the pineal gland, and its connection to the third eye in the center of your forehead, **the sixth chakra**.

In this vast space of pure awareness all around you,

Become aware of it.

Resonate with the light in this space.

The center.

Filled with liquid light.

Feel it.

Open up to it.

Bring your attention to it, totally, absolutely.

So that in this present moment, there is nothing else.

This wonder, that is you, is within you, and all around you.

This beauty, we call, "the deeper I," is the universe looking at itself.

Rest your awareness fully in this space, this presence.

And resonate with the sound in this space.

Become aware of the energy of space.

The wonder.

The miracle of you.

That exists as pure awareness around this center.

Around your head.

Pure awareness, in space.

Pure consciousness.

Pure bliss.

Tune in to the energy of the sound and light of this center within you and all around you. OM.

Feel from the center.

Become one with it.

Feel the power of the primordial sound OM, activating the pineal gland and extending out through the third eye, as if carried by a divine wind OM OM OM OM OM OM

Allow your awareness to extend out from all six chakras and bless the space around you and beyond you.

Now become aware of the space at the top of your head, the crown, **the seventh chakra**.

In this vast space of pure Awareness all around you,

Become aware of it.

Resonate with the light in this space.

The center.

Filled with liquid light.

Like a star.

Where did this light come from?

The elements within you were made in the crucible of stars.

Who are you?

A star being.

A light being.

Feel it.

Open up to it.

Bring your attention to it, totally, absolutely.

So that in this present moment, there is nothing else.

This wonder, that is you, is within you, and all around you.

This beauty, we call, "the deeper I," is the universe looking at itself.

Rest your awareness fully in this space, this presence.

And resonate with the sound in this space. OM

Become aware of the energy of space.

The wonder.

The miracle of you.

That exists as pure awareness around this center.

Around the top of your head.

Pure awareness, in space.

Pure consciousness.

Pure bliss.

Tune in to the energy of the sound and light of this center within you and all around you. OM.

Feel from the center.

Become one with it.

Now become aware of **all seven chakras at once, like a string of pearls from the base of your spine through the top of your head**.

Allow your awareness to extend out from all seven centers at once and bless the space around you and beyond you. OM. Feel the power of the primordial sound all around you.

Keep your attention on your crown at the top of your head.

Allow the light and sound to travel all the way to the heavens above connecting with the light and sound from above.

Hold your attention there at the crown. Surrender to the greater light and sound, the divine light and sound from above and be still.

Be still and know God, Source, divine light and sound, pure consciousness, existence and bliss.

Now, allow this Light and sound to flow down through the top of your head, down your spine, like a waterfall, a roar of liquid light and sound, down through the Central Channel into your heart, where it transforms into the purest Divine Love, the Love of a Divine Mother who embraces you Unconditionally. Feel the warm embrace of Unconditional Love. Allow this Love to expand from your heart through your whole body. . . . Bask in the warmth of Unconditional Love. . . .

Hold your attention here, hold it, hold it, infuse it with love, hold it and now surrender to the greater love, the divine love and be still.

Feel the whole inner spine.

Feel the space inside your body.

Slowly half open your eyes and become aware of the space inside your body within the space around you. Feel the top of your head, your hands in your lap, and your feet on the ground.

Notice how you feel. If you could sum this up in a word or phrase, what would this be?

Take a moment to reflect on this meditation. What were the most poignant moments? Did you notice any moments when your state of consciousness shifted? Was there a moment when you let go and became fully absorbed in the experience? What insights can you take from this experience that will make a difference in your life and relationships? Take a few moments to write down anything you'd like to remember from this meditative experience along with any insights and inspirations.

Consider practicing this meditation twice a day, read spiritual texts, surrender to the process, and realize the truth of who you are: a being of Peace, Love, and Light, part of One Life we all share, One vast spacious Awareness.

Well done!

4. Inner Smiling-Liquid Light Version
(Instructional graphics follow script)

Before you begin, arrange your **environment** so that it's conducive to meditation. Set up a comfortable seat in a quiet private space and turn off the volume on your phone. A good seat height sets your hips level with or slightly above your knees. Consider the lighting, sounds, visual images, and scents, so that you create a sacred space.

In this meditation, we combine the calm happiness of a subtle inner smile with the sensation of warm, soothing, liquid light flowing through the internal organs and spine. The purpose of this meditation is to support the health and healing of your body and a relaxed, positive, inner state of calm happiness. It encourages the smooth flow of vital energy, so that every cell, fiber, and vibration of your being is infused with pure positive energy.

As you follow this meditation, practice **mindfulness** by paying attention, on purpose, in the present moment, non-judgmentally—like a curious observer. If your attention wanders, practice the **3Rs**: recognize what has grabbed your attention, release this, and return to following the guided cues. Do this as often as your attention wanders.

Let's begin by sitting comfortably and upright with the soles of your feet flat on the ground and parallel with each other. If you are able to, sit far enough forward so you feel some weight in your feet, perhaps all the way on the front edge of your seat. Feel the weight of your feet firmly on the ground. If you need back support, you can sit back against a seatback.

Rest your hands, palms cupped, in your lap, with your right hand resting in the left, and the tips of your thumbs touching lightly. Lightly, close your eyes.

Take a moment for a Check-in inside. Notice how you feel right now. If you could sum up this feeling in a word, phrase, or image, what would this be?

Bring to mind your intention for your practice.

Now, focus down into the soles of both feet. Feel the sensations of contact between the soles of your feet and the ground. Allow your feet and toes to soften and relax, as if they are melting down into the ground.

Focus in on the sensations in your hands and fingers. Feel the sensations of contact with your legs. Allow your hands and fingers to soften and relax, as if they are melting down into your legs.

As your hands and fingers relax, allow your arms and shoulders to relax down, releasing any tension in your neck and shoulders.

Imagine a string attached to the top of your head drawing your spine gently upright, giving you a feeling of vertical spaciousness up through the core of your body, up through your spine, and through the top of your head.

Tuck your chin in just slightly, gently lengthening the back of your neck.

Roll the tip of your tongue up to touch the roof of your mouth or touch the tip of your tongue to the gumline behind your upper front teeth, whichever is more comfortable. Soften and relax your tongue here. Smile, a subtle smile of calm happiness.

Allow the feeling of smiling to relax your jaw, relax your eyes, and release any tension from your eyebrows and your forehead.

Now, imagine a radiant spiritual sun shining rays of pure positive energy down on your face. Allow the warming rays of this sun to combine with the feeling of smiling, so your whole face glows with calm happiness.

Allow the warm, smiling energy to wash down your face, like liquid Light, down the front of your throat, and down into your heart. Smile into your heart. In your heart, this warm smiling energy becomes the color ruby red, a radiant ruby red. Smile into your heart.

Allow the warm, smiling, liquid Light to flow out to the left and the right into your lungs. Smile into your lungs. In your lungs, the warm smiling energy becomes pearl white, a pure pearl white. Smile into your lungs.

Allow the warm, smiling, liquid Light to flow downwards on your right side, just beneath your ribs into your liver. Smile into your liver. In your liver, the warm smiling energy becomes emerald green, a glowing emerald green. Smile into your liver.

Allow the warm, smiling, liquid Light to flow around your ribs on the right side to your back, on both sides of your spine, just under your ribs, into your kidneys. Smile into your kidneys. In your kidneys, the warm smiling energy becomes sapphire blue, a shimmering sapphire blue. Smile into your kidneys.

Allow the warm, smiling, liquid Light to flow around your left side, returning to the front of your body, just to the left and behind your stomach, into your spleen and pancreas. Smile into your spleen and pancreas. In your spleen and pancreas, the warm smiling energy becomes solar yellow, a shining solar yellow. Smile into your spleen and pancreas.

Allow the warm, smiling, liquid Light to flow down to your navel and then collect in your lower abdomen, the lower dantian.

Now, return your attention to your face, your forehead, and your eyes. Imagine and feel the spiritual sun shining down on your face. Allow the warm, smiling energy to flow down into your mouth. Take a deep swallow. Imagine and feel the warm, smiling, liquid Light flowing down your throat into your stomach. Smile into your stomach. In your stomach, the warm smiling energy becomes citrus orange, a soothing citrus orange. Smile into your stomach.

270

Allow the warm, smiling, liquid Light to flow from your stomach out to the right, into your small intestine. Follow it as it folds back from right to left across your upper abdomen. Then back from left to right behind your navel. Back from right to left just below your navel. And back from left to right across the lowest part of your abdomen. Follow the warm smiling energy as it turns and flows upward on your right side to just under your liver, and then turns from right to left deep across your upper abdomen, then down your left side and out of your body at your anus.

Feel your whole digestive system as a whole from your mouth, down your throat, to your stomach and through your intestines, filled with warm, smiling, liquid Light.

Now, focus again on your forehead and your eyes and again imagine and feel the spiritual sun shining down on your face. Allow the warm, smiling, liquid Light to flow in through your forehead and your eyes, into the center of your brain, and through to the top of your spine. Allow the warm smiling energy to flow down your spine, down through your neck, down between your shoulder blades, down through your lower back, down through your sacrum, and down into the ground. Feel this whole path at once, from your forehead, through the center of your brain, to the top of your spine, and down your spine into the ground. Allow the flow of warm, smiling, liquid Light to wash any tension down your spine and down into the ground.

Now, feel the warm smiling energy in your spine radiating outward to fill every cell in your whole body. Feel the entire space inside your skin infused with calm happiness.

Become aware of this pure positive energy filling the space around you. . . . Become aware of this energy infusing all of us practicing this meditation together. . . . Become aware of warm, smiling, liquid Light flowing across our whole planet infusing all beings and the whole planet. We are all smiling together. . . . This radiant life energy infuses and surrounds our Planet . . . and extends Infinitely in all

271

directions across all time. . . . We are floating in an Infinite Sea of warm, smiling, liquid Light. Floating in an Infinite Sea of warm, smiling, liquid Light. . . . Floating in an Infinite Sea of warm, smiling, liquid Light. . . .

Now, become aware of the warm smiling energy filling the space inside your skin. Smile and enjoy the sensation of calm happiness in your whole body. Record this sensation in every cell, so you remember it and bring it with you.

Notice how you feel. If you could sum this up in a word, phrase, or image, what would this be? Record the feeling of Inner Smiling with your word, phrase, or image to use as a Landmark to return to this experience any time.

Slowly open your eyes and take in the space around you. Feel the sensation of calm happiness inside your body and in the space around you.

Feel the top of your head, your hands in your lap, and your feet on the ground.

Reflect on your meditative experience. What were the most poignant moments? Did you notice any moments when your state of consciousness shifted? Was there a moment when you let go and became fully absorbed in the experience? What insights can you take from this experience that will make a difference in your life and relationships? Take a few moments to write down anything you'd like to remember from this meditative experience along with any insights and inspirations.

Then, stand, stretch, and move in whatever way feels good to you.

Bring the calm happiness of Inner Smiling into your life and share it wherever you go. Well done!

(On the next page are graphics for the Inner Smiling Meditation.)

Graphics for visualizing the Inner Smiling Meditation:

 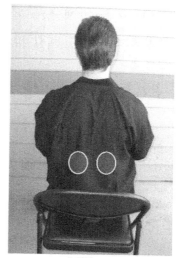

Yin Organ Path: Eyes, Heart, Lungs, Liver ——————→Kidneys
Spleen & Pancreas, ◄——————
Lower Dantian

Digestive System Path:
Forehead & Eyes, Mouth,
Throat, Stomach, Small
Intestine, Large Intestine

Spinal Path: Forehead,
Center of Brain, Spine

273

5. Lower Dantian Breathing

Before you begin, arrange your environment so that it's conducive to meditation. Set up a comfortable seat in a quiet, private space and turn off the volume on your phone. A good seat height sets your hips level with or slightly above your knees. Consider the lighting, sounds, visual images, and scents, so you can create a sacred space.

The purpose of this meditation is to develop Concentration and cultivate Vital Energy in the Lower Dantian by focusing on the sensations of breathing here. By focusing on breathing, you may also have insight into Impermanence, how all things arise, linger for a while, and dissolve. By expanding your felt sense of breathing to include the Universal Breath, you may have insight into the Oneness of All Beings through the One Life Energy we all share.

As you follow this meditation, practice mindfulness by paying attention, on purpose, in the present moment, non-judgmentally—like a curious observer. If your attention wanders, practice the 3Rs: 1) Recognize what has grabbed your attention, 2) Release this, and 3) Return to following the guided cues. Do this as often as your attention wanders.

Let's begin by sitting comfortably upright with the soles of your feet flat on the ground and parallel with each other. If you are able to, sit far enough forward so you feel some weight in your feet, perhaps all the way on the front edge of your seat. Feel the weight of your feet firmly on the ground. If you need back support, you can sit back against a seatback.

Rest your hands, palms cupped, in your lap, with your right hand resting in the left, and the tips of your thumbs touching lightly. Lightly, close your eyes.

Take a moment for a Check-in inside. Notice how you feel right now. If you could sum up this feeling in a word, phrase, or image, what would this be?

Bring to mind your intention for your practice.

Now, focus down into the soles of both feet. Feel the sensations of contact between the soles of your feet and the ground. Allow your feet and toes to soften and relax, as if they are melting down into the ground.

Focus in on the sensations in your hands and fingers. Feel the sensations of contact with your legs. Allow your hands and fingers to soften and relax, as if they are melting down into your legs.

As your hands and fingers relax, allow your arms and shoulders to relax down, releasing any tension in your neck and shoulders.

Imagine a string attached to the top of your head drawing your spine gently upright, giving you a feeling of vertical spaciousness up through the core of your body, up through your spine, and through the top of your head.

Tuck your chin in just slightly, gently lengthening the back of your neck.

Roll the tip of your tongue up to touch the roof of your mouth or touch the tip of your tongue to the gumline behind your upper front teeth, whichever is more comfortable. Soften and relax your tongue here. Smile a subtle smile of calm happiness.

Allow the feeling of smiling to relax your jaw, relax your eyes, and release any tension from your eyebrows and your forehead.

Allow the feeling of smiling to wash down through your whole body, creating a positive, nurturing, inner environment in which all your cells relax, open up, communicate with each other, and radiate pure positive life energy. Calm happiness.

Now, focus in on your lower abdomen and imagine a radiant sphere of energy here, the lower dantian. Imagine and feel this lower dantian sphere is breathing. As you inhale, imagine and feel this sphere fills with energy, expanding from the center outward in all directions. As

275

you exhale, this sphere relaxes inward to the center, concentrating the energy here. . . .

See if you can be present in the whole cycle of breathing, so you notice the moment you begin to inhale and follow your in-breath until you naturally pause. Then, notice the moment you begin to exhale and follow your out-breath until you naturally pause. Allow your mind to become completely absorbed in the sensations of this breathing sphere, so everything else fades to the background and dissolves. Enjoy the gentle rhythm of breathing in, pausing, breathing out, pausing. . . .

If you find your mind wandering to other thoughts, feelings, memories, images, or sensations, gently recognize them, release them, and return to feeling the sensations of lower-dantian breathing. . . .

Imagine your breath is feeding the lower dantian sphere, so it glows warmer and brighter, so it feels alive and full of energy. You are breathing vital Life Force Energy. . . .

Now, we'll shift the breathing pattern to a six-direction sequence: first inhale and feel the lower dantian sphere expand forward; exhale and allow it to relax inward to the center. Next, inhale and allow the lower dantian sphere to expand backward; exhale and allow it to relax inward to the center. Then inhale out to the left and exhale back to center. Inhale out to the right and exhale back to center. Inhale and expand upward and exhale back to center. Inhale and expand downward and exhale back to center. Continue with this cycle of six-direction breathing at whatever pace feels good to you. . . .

As you continue with breathing in six directions, imagine and feel the energy concentrating and growing in the center of the lower dantian each time you exhale. . . .

Now, when you finish the current cycle of six directions, return to feeling the dantian sphere expand outward in all directions as you

276

inhale and relax inward to the center as you exhale. Notice any difference in the felt sense of energy in the lower dantian after doing the six directions. . . .

Now, as you inhale become aware of your whole body filling up with vital energy. As you exhale, your whole body empties out. . . .

Now, become aware of the whole space around you, breathing in and breathing out. . . .

Become aware of all of us practicing this meditation, breathing in and breathing out together. . . .

Become aware of the whole planet and all beings breathing in and breathing out. We are all breathing together. . . .

Become aware of the whole Universe breathing in and breathing out. . . .

Become aware of the Universal Breath. . . . Rest in the gentle rhythm of the Universal Breath. . . .

The Universe is breathing you . . . the Universe is breathing you. . . the Universe is breathing you. . . .

Rest in the Universal Breath. . . . Rest in the Universal Breath. . . . Rest in the Universal Breath. . . .

Now become aware of the entire space inside your skin. Feel the subtle sensations of breathing inside your body, especially in your lower abdomen.

Notice how you feel. If you could sum this up in a word, phrase, or image, what would this be? Record this feeling with your word, phrase, or image in every cell of your body to use as a Landmark to return to this experience any time.

Slowly half open your eyes and take in the space around you.

Feel the top of your head, your hands in your lap, and your feet on the ground.

Reflect on your meditative experience. What were the most poignant moments? Did you notice any moments when your state of consciousness shifted? Was there a moment when you let go and became fully absorbed in the experience? What insights can you take from this experience that will make a difference in your life and relationships? Take a few moments to write down anything you'd like to remember from this meditative experience along with any insights and inspirations.

Then, stand, stretch, and move in whatever way feels good to you. Well done!

6. One Shared Heart

The purpose of this meditation is to develop Concentration into Absorption by embodying Unconditional Love and Compassion through the One Shared Heart.

In this meditation, we direct our attention and our breathing to the heart, where through mindfulness of deep absorption in the breath of love, the energy of our being transforms into, and becomes the purest Unconditional Love. We'll feel this love, like the warm embrace of a Mother's Love in our bodies, then become aware of it extending outward to all beings, the whole Planet, and the entire Universe.

Consider your intention today and apply deep devotion and faith to your intention as we meditate together. If it is to return home, then let that be your most fervent desire for the time we spend together.

I also want you to consider the witnessing presence—watch your breath—who is it that observes? . . . listen to the silence—who is it that listens? . . . feel the energy, the body sensation—who is it that feels? The witnessing presence. Be aware as you meditate of the witnessing presence.

Become aware of your environment, consider it a sanctuary, a sacred place or space that is conducive to meditation.

If it is comfortable for you, sit upright on the front edge of your seat with the soles of your feet flat on the ground and parallel with each other. A good seat height sets your hips level with or slightly above your knees. Rest your hands, palms cupped, right palm uppermost, resting in the left in your lap, with the tips of your thumbs touching lightly. Lightly, close your eyes.

Notice how you feel right now. . . . If you could sum this up in a word, phrase, or image, what would this be?

As you follow this meditation, practice mindfulness by paying attention, on purpose, in the present moment, non-judgmentally— like a curious observer. If your attention wanders, practice the 3Rs: 1) Recognize what has grabbed your attention, 2) Release this, and 3) Return to following the guided cues. Do this as often as your attention wanders.

Now, focus down into the soles of your feet and feel the sensations of your feet contacting the ground. Allow your feet to soften and relax and imagine that your feet are melting down into the ground.

Focus in on your palms and fingers and feel the sensation of contact with your legs. Allow your palms and fingers to soften and relax, and imagine they are melting down into your legs.

As your hands relax, allow your arms and shoulders to relax down, releasing any tension in your shoulders and neck.

Imagine a string attached to the top of your head, drawing your spine gently upright, giving you a feeling of vertical spaciousness up through the core of your body, up through your spine, through the top of your head.

Tuck your chin in slightly, gently lengthening the back of your neck.

Roll the tip of your tongue up to touch the roof of your mouth.

Smile a subtle smile of appreciation and gratitude for this time to consciously relax, let go, and awaken to the finer frequencies of Unconditional Love.

Allow the feeling of smiling to relax your jaw and your eyes. Release any tension in your eyebrows and forehead.

Allow the feeling of smiling to wash down through your whole body, creating a positive inner environment. Imagine every cell is smiling, opening up, communicating with every other cell, and radiating pure positive energy. Calm happiness.

Now, focus down into your lower abdomen and become aware of the sensations of breathing here. As you inhale, notice the subtle expansion of your abdomen. As you exhale, notice the subtle relaxation inward. See if it's possible to stay present in the whole cycle of your breathing, so you notice the moment you begin to inhale and follow your in-breath until you naturally pause. Then, notice the moment you begin to exhale and follow your out-breath until you naturally pause. . . .

To track your attention, count your breaths each time you exhale, in cycles of 10. If you lose count, begin again at one. If you get to ten, begin again at one. . . . If your attention wanders, it's OK. Recognize what grabbed your attention, release this, and return to counting your out-breaths in cycles of 10.

Allow your attention to become completely absorbed in the subtle sensations of breathing, as if nothing else matters at this moment. . . .

As you continue to count your out-breaths, allow your breathing to become subtle, quiet, and soft until the sensation is barely perceptible in your lower abdomen. . . .

Feel the stillness of the body.

Listen to the inner silence.

Become aware of the clear and open space of mind and heart.

With the focus at the heart chakra inhale.

Re-inhale and feel the subtle breath spread throughout the chakra.

Guide the subtle breath into the heart strengthening your life force at the heart chakra.

Hold it—and feel the subtle breath cleansing and bringing bliss to the heart.

Then release the breath slowly through the nose at first, then exhale more sharply, pulling in with your diaphragm.

Imagine the subtle breath releases at your heart chakra, clearing all obscurations as you listen.

Rest with clear attention in the openness of the space of the heart chakra.

Allow the Light of Love to flow into your heart, where it transforms into the purest Divine Love, the Love of a Divine Mother who embraces you Unconditionally. Feel the warm embrace of Unconditional Love.

Breathe Unconditional Love in and out through your heart. . . .

Breathe Unconditional Love in and out through your heart. . . .

Breathe Unconditional Love in and out through your heart. . . .

Allow this Love to expand from your heart through your whole body. . . . Bask in the warmth of Unconditional Love. . . . Become aware of this Love extending outward from your heart to your loved ones . . . to all beings . . . and the whole Planet. . . . Become aware of this Love extending Infinitely in all directions. You now realize this Infinite Love is the energy that brought forth and gave birth to all of Creation. This Love is the energy that connects us All through One Shared Heart. Smile as you feel the warmth of Unconditional Love radiating through the whole Universe, across all time, through the One Shared Heart. . . .

Breathe the Infinite Love of the One Shared Heart through your heart to All. . . .

Breathe the Infinite Love of the One Shared Heart through your heart to All. . . .

Breathe the Infinite Love of the One Shared Heart through your heart to All. . . .

Now, become aware of the entire space inside your skin. . . . Feel Unconditional Love infusing every cell of your body. . . .

Slowly half open your eyes and become aware of the space inside your body within the space around you. Feel the top of your head, your hands in your lap, and your feet on the ground.

Notice how you feel. If you could sum this up in a word or phrase, what would this be?

Now, record the feeling of Unconditional Love in every cell of your body, so you can remember it, bring it with you, and return to it whenever you need.

Take a moment to reflect on this meditative experience. What were the most poignant moments? What would you like to remember and take with you? Write down anything that is important for you to remember from this meditative experience and what it means for your life and your relationships with others.

Then, slowly stretch and move in whatever way feels good to you.

Bring Unconditional Love with you wherever you go. Well done!

7. & 8. Light, Love, and Peace
(LLP Versions One and Two)

Before you begin, arrange your environment so it's conducive to meditation. Set up a comfortable seat in a quiet private space and turn off the volume on your phone. A good seat height sets your hips level with or slightly above your knees. Consider the lighting, sounds, visual images, and scents, so you can create a sacred space.

The purpose of this meditation is to raise our vibration to resonate with the frequencies of Peace, Love, and Light and live in a state of elevated Awareness.

As you follow this meditation, practice mindfulness by paying attention, on purpose, in the present moment, non-judgmentally—like a curious observer. If your attention wanders, practice the 3Rs: 1) Recognize what has grabbed your attention, 2) Release this, and 3) Return to following the guided cues. Do this as often as your attention wanders.

Let's begin by sitting comfortably upright with the soles of your feet flat on the ground and parallel with each other. If you are able to, sit far enough forward so you can feel your perineum resting on the front edge of your seat and you can feel the weight of your feet firmly on the ground. If you need back support, you can sit back against a seatback.

Rest your hands, palms cupped, in your lap, with your right hand resting in the left, and the tips of your thumbs touching lightly. Lightly, close your eyes.

Take a moment for a Check-in inside. Notice how you feel right now. If you could sum up this feeling in a word, phrase, or image, what would this be?

Bring to mind your intention for your practice.

Now, focus down into the soles of both feet. Feel the sensations of contact between the soles of your feet and the ground. Allow your feet and toes to soften and relax, as if they are melting down into the Earth.

Focus in on the sensations in your hands and fingers. Feel the sensations of contact with your legs. Allow your hands and fingers to soften and relax, as if they are melting down into your legs.

As your hands and fingers relax, allow your arms and shoulders to relax down, releasing any tension in your neck and shoulders.

Imagine a string attached to the top of your head drawing your spine gently upright, giving you a feeling of vertical spaciousness up through the core of your body, up through your spine, and through the top of your head.

Tuck your chin in just slightly, gently lengthening the back of your neck.

Roll the tip of your tongue up to touch the roof of your mouth or touch the tip of your tongue to the gumline behind your upper front teeth, whichever is more comfortable. Soften and relax your tongue here. Smile, a subtle smile of calm happiness.

Allow the feeling of smiling to relax your jaw, relax your eyes, and release any tension from your eyebrows and your forehead.

Allow the feeling of smiling to wash down through your whole body, creating a positive, nurturing, inner environment in which all your cells relax, open up, communicate with each other, and radiate pure positive energy. Calm happiness.

Focus down into your lower abdomen, the lower dantian, and become aware of the sensations of breathing here. As you inhale, notice the subtle expansion of your abdomen. As you exhale, notice the subtle relaxation inward.

Allow your attention to become completely absorbed in the subtle sensations of breathing, as if nothing else matters at this moment. . . .

See if it's possible to stay present in the whole cycle of your breathing, so you notice the moment you begin to inhale and follow your in-breath until you naturally pause. Then, notice the moment you begin to exhale and follow your out-breath until you naturally pause. . . .

To track your attention, count your breaths each time you exhale, in cycles of 10. If you lose count, begin again at one. If you get to 10, begin again at one. . . . If your attention wanders, it's OK. Recognize what grabbed your attention, release this, and return to counting your out-breaths in cycles of ten.

As you continue lower-dantian breath counting, imagine and feel your breath is feeding the energy here, so it glows warmer and brighter and feels alive and full of energy.

As you continue to count your out-breaths, allow your breathing to become subtle, quiet, and soft until the sensation is barely perceptible in your lower abdomen. . . . Feel the vital energy, warm and glowing, in the lower dantian, like a holy fire. . . .

Now, allow the energy to gather and collect at the perineum. Imagine and feel it glowing and tingling here. Now become aware of the energy glowing and tingling at the perineum and at the top of your head. See if it's possible to feel both points at once and the path between them.

Now, we'll shift to breathing up through the Central Channel and around in a torus flow down to the perineum again. As you inhale, gently contract your perineum and feel the current of your in-breath drawn upward, from the base of your spine, up through your spine, through the center of your brain, the upper dantian, to the top of your head. Pause and feel the tingling sensations of energy at the top of your head. As you exhale, allow the current of your out-breath to flow up, out, around, and down to the perineum, in a torus flow. Continue breathing up through the Central Channel and around in a torus flow to the perineum. Each time you pause at the top of your head, feel the energy building here. Feel it tingling and pulsing, like an electric current.

See if it's possible to feel the energy up through your whole spine and around the torus flow to the perineum all at once, in a continuous flow.

Now, focus on the top of your head and concentrate on the tingling, pulsing feeling of energy here. Imagine the top of your head opening to a column of Light from above, the guiding Light. Above your head is an energy center, the Soul Star, which contains information about your life purpose and energy to fulfill it. Concentrating here allows inspired information to download into your subconscious where it becomes available as inner guidance about who you are and what you are here to do.

Rest your attention up here in the Soul Star. Breath in, feeling the upward pull into this energy center and breathe out feeling as if you are plugged in to energy from the Source above.

Continue focusing and breathing into the Soul Star. As you inhale, feel the upward pull in the current of your breath into the energy pulsing here. As you exhale, feel as if you are plugged in, infused, and informed by the Light from above.

Now, let go of breathing, and rest your attention in the Light above the crown, in the Soul Star. The high-frequency energy here has a powerful activating and synchronizing effect across your whole brain, which lights up with a tingling, pulsing, electrical charge. Feel the tingling electric current in your whole brain as it's infused with Light from above.

Now, allow this Light to flow down through the top of your head, down through the center of your brain, and down through the Central Channel into your heart, where it transforms into the purest

Divine Love, the Love of a Divine Mother who embraces you Unconditionally.

With your focus at the heart, the middle dantian, breathe into this energy center. Re-inhale and feel the subtle breath spread throughout your heart. Guide the subtle breath into the heart, strengthening your life force at this powerful energy center.

Hold it—and feel the subtle breath cleansing and bringing the bliss of Unconditional Love to your heart.

Then, release the breath slowly through the nose at first, then exhale more sharply, pulling in with your diaphragm. Imagine the subtle breath releases through your heart, clearing all obscurations.

Rest with clear attention in the openness of the space of the heart.

Feel the warm embrace of Unconditional Love in your heart. Breathe this Love through your heart. As you inhale, feel Love flowing into your heart. As you exhale, feel this Love flowing to every cell. Bask in the warm embrace of Unconditional Love. . . .

Become aware of this Love extending from your heart to your loved ones . . . to all of us practicing this meditation together . . . to all beings . . . and the whole Planet. . . . Become aware of this Love extending Infinitely in all directions. You realize this Infinite Love is the energy that brought forth and gave birth to all of Creation. This Love is the energy that connects us All through One Shared Heart. Smile as you feel the warm embrace of Unconditional Love radiating through the whole Universe, across all time, through the One Shared Heart. . . .

Now, breathe this Love of the One Shared Heart through your heart. . . .

As you breathe in, feel this Love of the One Shared Heart flowing through your heart outward in all directions to all beings and the whole universe. As you breathe out, feel this Love flowing back through your heart. . . .

Breathe in, feeling the Love of One Shared Heart flowing through your heart outward in all directions to all beings and the whole universe. Breathe out, feeling this Love flowing back through your heart. . . .

We live as One Body, One Shared Heart, One Love. . . . Breathing this Divine Relationship, this Infinite Love every moment . . . see it and feel it in everyone and everything—everywhere. . . . Bask in the warm embrace of Unconditional Love. . . .

Now, allow the energy to flow from your heart down through the Central Channel to a still point in the perineum. Rest your attention in this still point. If you notice any movement of thought, feeling, body, or attention, let go into stillness. Imagine and feel this still point sinking deep down into the Earth, where it anchors a rock-solid, immutable, peace, in the Earth Star, an energy center in the Earth underneath your feet. Focus deep down into this still point. Let go. . . . Be still. . . . Let go. . . . Be still. . . . Let go. . . . Be still. . . .

Feel the stillness underneath all movement. . . .

Listen to the silence underneath all sound. . . .

Sense the Infinite Space of Awareness. . . .

Rest in the deep Peace of still, silent, spacious Awareness. . . .

Rest in the deep Peace of still, silent, spacious Awareness. . . .

Rest in the deep Peace of still, silent, spacious Awareness. . . .

Light, Love, and Peace (Version 2)

For Version 2, add the section below:

Within this still, silent, spacious Awareness become aware of the Entire Field of Being extending infinitely in all directions across all time. . . . You are a point of awareness within this Infinite Field.

Become aware that the Whole Field is Aware. There is only Awareness. Infinite Spacious Awareness. . . . Infinite Spacious Awareness. . . . Infinite Spacious Awareness. . . .

Listen to, sense, and feel this Infinite Space of Awareness. You may notice it has a signature, a vibration, a subtle hum. You may begin to hear or feel the vibration of this Field, like the hum of the Universe, the OM.

Listen closer to this subtle sound under the silence. Tune in to this subtle vibration. It is the hum of the Infinite Space of Awareness itself. At first, it may feel like nothing at all.

Then, faintly, it is like listening to the wind, a distant ocean in a conch shell, or the gentle purring engine of the Universe. As you listen to, sense, and feel this OM vibration, you realize OM is the home signal, the signal from the Source, sustaining Life, supporting All. It is constant and unwavering. It contains the primary frequencies of Peace, Love, and Light and permeates the Entire Universe with Awareness.

(Chant) OM . . . OM . . . OM . . .

Your body resonates with OM, which integrates, heals, and transforms your entire being—so you become a pure channel of Awareness, expressing the primary frequencies of Peace, Love, and Light.

--- --- ---

(Both versions finish with this section)

Now, feel your body as a whole from the inside. Sense the entire space inside your skin.

Notice how you feel. If you could sum this up in a word, phrase, or image, what would this be? Record this feeling with this word, phrase, or image in every cell of your body to use as a Landmark to return to this experience any time.

290

Slowly half open your eyes and take in the space around you.

Feel the top of your head, your hands in your lap, and your feet on the ground.

Reflect on your meditative experience. What were the most poignant moments? What inner cues were most significant for you? Did you notice any moments when your state of consciousness shifted? Was there a moment when you let go and became fully absorbed in the experience? What insights can you take from this experience to support you in living a more compassionate life? Take a few moments to write down anything you'd like to remember from this meditative experience along with any insights and inspirations.

Then, stand, stretch, and move in whatever way feels good to you.

Share Peace, Love and Light wherever you go. Well done!

--- --- ---

Brainwave Graphics

At the end of the LLP there is a profound coherence of the whole brain:

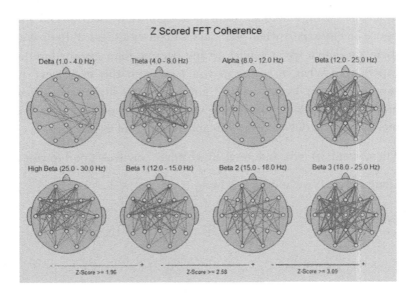

Brainwave Overview: In meditation, **beta** correlates with focused attention; **alpha** correlates with internalizing of attention to relaxed inner states; **theta** correlates with inner stillness and access to intuitive information within the Whole Field; **delta** correlates with empathy and states of healing and regeneration; and **gamma** with high frequency states of elevated and/or expanded energy and focus.

Stephen, Kevin, and their ROV Core Group of practitioners have observed a number of different brainwave pattern signatures in Subtle Energy Meditation. Here are some of the most prominent ones:

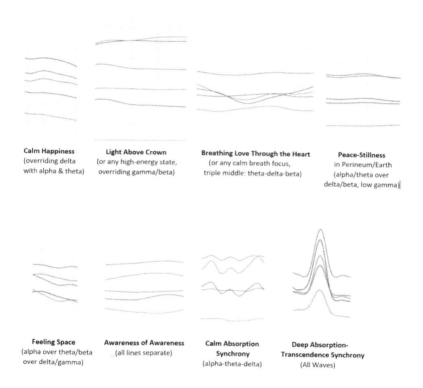

Calm Happiness
(overriding delta
with alpha & theta)

Light Above Crown
(or any high-energy state,
overriding gamma/beta)

Breathing Love Through the Heart
(or any calm breath focus,
triple middle: theta-delta-beta)

Peace-Stillness
in Perineum/Earth
(alpha/theta over
delta/beta, low gamma)

Feeling Space
(alpha over theta/beta
over delta/gamma)

Awareness of Awareness
(all lines separate)

**Calm Absorption
Synchrony**
(alpha-theta-delta)

**Deep Absorption-
Transcendence Synchrony**
(All Waves)

EEG Graphics of The Light, Love, and Peace Meditation

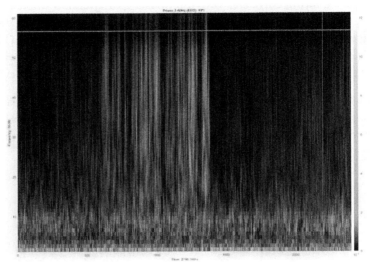

One of Kevin's LLP sessions with elevated gamma frequencies
in the Light section

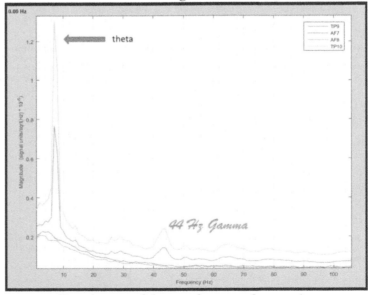

Prominence of theta and gamma frequencies
in one of Stephen's LLP sessions

FOOD & MOOD LOG

Day & Date _____

Length & Quality of Last Night's Sleep: _____

Time (Be specific)	Ate (What & How Much)	Drank (What & How Much)	Mood (Brief Description)	Energy (Brief Description)	Mental Clarity (Brief Description)
_____am					
7:___am					
8:___am					
9:___am					
10:___am					
11:___am					
12:___pm					
1:___pm					
2:___pm					
3:___pm					
4:___pm					
5:___pm					
6:___pm					
7:___pm					
_____pm					

MEDITATION LOG

DATES: _____ to _____

Day of Week & Time	Meditation Practice Name/Style	Inner Cues	Inner Felt Experience	Energy 0-10	Mood 0-10	Mental Clarity 0-10

About the Authors

Kevin Schoeninger is an author and teacher of Mind-Body training. In 1984, he had a profound experience of still, silent, spacious, Nondual Awareness on a backpacking trip through the wilderness that set him on a lifelong quest exploring higher states of consciousness. This quest led him to study T'ai Chi, Qigong, mindfulness, meditation, Centering Prayer, Kriya Yoga, Holy Fire Reiki, and other mind-body training techniques.

Kevin graduated from Villanova University in 1986 with a Master's degree in Philosophy, and is Certified as a Personal Trainer, Life Coach, Qigong Meditation Master Instructor, and Holy Fire Karuna Reiki Master Teacher. He's had the pleasure of writing about and teaching these techniques for over 35 years. Kevin now lives in Colorado with his wife and two sons. Kevin is the author of *Clear Quiet Mind: Four Simple Steps to Deep Inner Peace.*

To learn more about Kevin's work, visit: http://clearquietmind.info

Stephen Skelton (aka Altair) is an author and teacher of Light Body Awakening, including Mindfulness and Meditation. At a very early age, Stephen had a dream of being a monk and experiencing the cosmic sound and light, an experience which fostered his awakening into self-awareness and a curiosity and deep love for all spiritual paths. This curiosity led him to study T'ai Chi, Qigong, meditation, Kriya Yoga, Reiki, and other mind-body training techniques. Stephen graduated from Auckland and Otago University with degrees in Education and Business and was Certified as a Counsellor with the Counsellors and Psychotherapists Association of New South Wales in Australia. He has been writing and teaching meditation techniques for over 30 years. Stephen now lives in Japan with his wife and daughter. Stephen is the author of *Diary of a Yogi: A Book of Awakening*.

To learn more about Stephen's work, visit: www.altairshyam.com

Kevin and Stephen are passionate about the awakening of awareness, uplifting of human consciousness, and care of all beings and our Planet through meditation, compassionate action, and daily practice.

To find out more about Raising Our Vibration, please visit:

https://raisingourvibration.net

Raising Our Vibration Community on Facebook: https://www.facebook.com/groups/2311653182426829/

Notes

[1] David Chalmers, "Facing Up to the Problem of Consciousness," *Journal of Consciousness Studies,* 2, no. 3 (March 1995): 200-219.

[2] As found, for example at https://choosemuse.com.

[3] Jon Kabat-Zinn, *Mindfulness for Beginners: Reclaiming the Present Moment—And Your Life* (Boulder, CO: Sounds True, 2012), 1.

[4] Jerry Alan Johnson, *Chinese Medical Qigong Therapy: A Comprehensive Clinical Guide* (Pacific Grove, CA: The International Institute of Medical Qigong, 2000), 3.

[5] See: https://www.brucelipton.com, https://www.amitgoswami.org, https://www.fredalanwolf.com, https://lynnemctaggart.com, https://noetic.org.

[6] See: https://www.cihs.edu and https://holosuniversity.org.

[7] Found at https://yogananda.org/.

[8] Doc Childre and Howard Martin, *The HeartMath Solution* (New York, NY: HarperCollins, 1999), 33. More information about the HeartMath Institute can be found at https://www.heartmath.org.

[9] Eben Pagan, *Opportunity: How to Win in Business and Create a Life You Love* (Carlsbad, CA and New York, NY: Hay House, 2019).

[10] For more detailed information, visit: https://osher.ucsf.edu/maia.

[11] For more information, visit: http://raisingourvibration.net.

[12] Walpola Rahula, *What the Buddha Taught* (London: Gordon Fraser, 1959), 51.

[13] Jon Kabat-Zinn, *Mindfulness for Beginners: Reclaiming the Present Moment—And Your Life* (Boulder, CO: Sounds True, 2012), 1.

[14] Tim Lomas, Itai Ivtzan, and Cynthia, Fu, "A Systematic Review of the Neurophysiology of Mindfulness on EEG Oscillations," *Neuroscience & Behavioral Reviews,* 57 (October 2015): 401-410. DOI: 10.1016/j.neubiorev.2015.09.018.

[15] Erik Hoffmann, "Mapping the Brain's Activity after Kriya Yoga," https://www.yogameditation.com/reading-room/mapping-the-brains-activity-after-kriya-yoga/.

[16] Dan Mager, "Mindfulness and Emotional Intelligence: Mindfulness Practices Can Significantly Upgrade Your Internal Operating System," *Psychology Today*, March 22, 2019, https://www.psychologytoday.com/gb/blog/some-assembly-required/201903/mindfulness-and-emotional-intelligence.

[17] Erik Hoffmann, "Mapping the Brain's Activity after Kriya Yoga," https://www.yogameditation.com, accessed 2.28.20, https://www.yogameditation.com/reading-room/mapping-the-brains-activity-after-kriya-yoga/.

[18] Kevin Schoeninger originally heard this definition in a talk given by psycho-neuro-immunologist, Dr. Myrin Borysenko at a Wellness Conference in the 1990s.

[19] Hans Selye, "Stress and the General Adaptation Syndrome," in *British Medical Journal* 1, 4667 (June 1950): 1383-1392, DOI 10.1136/bmj.1.4667.1383.

[20] Suzanne Kobasa, Salvatore R. Maddi, Mark Puccetti, and Marc Zola, "Effectiveness of Hardiness, Exercise and Social Support as Resources Against Illness," *Journal of Psychosomatic*

Research, 29, no. 5 (1985): 525–533,
https://doi.org/10.1016/0022-3999(85)90086-8.
[21] Martha Davis, Elizabeth Robbins Eshelman, and Matthew
McKay, *The Relaxation and Stress Reduction Workbook* (Sixth
Edition, Oakland, CA: New Harbinger Publications, 2008),
10.
[22] Herbert Benson and Eileen Stuart, *The Wellness Book: The
Comprehensive Guide to Maintaining Health and Treating Stress-
Related Illness* (New York, NY: Simon & Schuster, A Fireside
Book, 1992).
[23] Bruce Lipton, *The Biology of Belief: Unleashing the Power of
Consciousness, Matter & Miracles* (Carlsbad, CA: Hay House,
20052004/2015).
[24] Naropa, in *Mahāmudrā: The Quintessence of Mind and
Meditation,* Takpo Tashi Namgyal, trans. Lobsang P.
Lhalungpa (Delhi, India: Motilal Banarsidass, 1993/2001),
147.
[25] Keith Holden, "Power of the Mind in Health and Healing,"
Udemy course, https://www.udemy.com/course/power-of-
the-mind-in-health-and-healing/.
[26] Jamie Hale, "The Benefits of Focused Attention,"
PsychCentral, July 8, 2018, https://psychcentral.com/blog/the-
benefits-of-focused-attention/).
[27] Alex Hankey, "Studies of Advanced Stages of Meditation in
the Tibetan Buddhist and Vedic Traditions. I: A Comparison
of General Changes," *Evidence-Based Complementary and
Alternative Medicine,* 3, no. 4 (2006), 513-521,
https://doi.org/10.1093/ecam/nel040.
[28] Paramahansa Yogananda, *Autobiography of a Yogi* (Los
Angeles, CA: Self-Realization Fellowship), 405.
[29] Shinzen Young, *What is Mindfulness* (2016), 15,
https://www.shinzen.org/wp-
content/uploads/2016/08/WhatIsMindfulness_SY_Public_v
er1.5.pdf
[30] Krishnamurti Foundation of America, *Bulletin 53-Special
Issue* (Spring/Summer 1986), 4.

[31] Krishnamurti Foundation of America, *Bulletin 53-Special Issue* (Spring/Summer 1986), 18-19.

[32] Jiddu Krishnamurti, *The Collected Works of J. Krishnamurti: 1962-1963: A Psychological Revolution* (Ojai, CA: The Krishnamurti Foundation of America, 1992), 267.

[33] Jenny Wade, "After Awakening, the Laundry: Is Nonduality a Spiritual Experience?" *International Journal of Transpersonal Studies*, 37, no. 2 (2018), 88-115, http://dx.doi.org/https://doi.org/10.24972/ijts.2018.37.2.88).

[34] Matthew Fox, *Christian Mystics: 365 Readings and Meditations* (Novato, CA: New World Library: 2011), 3.

[35] Marie Kondo, *The Life-Changing Magic of Tidying Up: The Japanese Art of Decluttering and Organizing* (New York: Ten Speed Press, 2015).

[36] Kristin Neff, "Self-Compassion: An Alternative Conceptualization of a Health Attitude Toward Oneself," *Self and Identity*, 2 (2003): 85-101.

[37] Carl Rogers, *A Way of Being* (Boston, MA: Houghton Mifflin, 1980), 116.

Printed in Great Britain
by Amazon

22078091R00189